≪ ALL KNOWN METAL BANDS ≫

compiled and edited by

DAN NELSON

AS OF 2007 C.E.

Through space the universe grasps me up like a speck;
through thought I grasp it.

It is wretched to know that one is wretched,
but there is greatness in knowing one is wretched.

—Blaise Pascal

...Aaaarrghh...
...and Here I Lie
...And Oceans
A Blind Prophecy
A Blood Born
  Pathogen
A Canorous Quintet
A Caress of Twilight
A Cold Reality
A Colour Cold Black
A Dank Season
A Dark Halo
A Dark Performance
A Darkened Sea
A Dawn Serene
A Dawn Within

A Day Once Dead
A Day to Fall
A Dream of Poe
A Fonds Perdu
A Foot in the Grave
A Forest
A Good Day for
  Killing
A Gruesome Find
A Javelin Reign
A Legend Falls
A Life Less Alive
A Life Once Lost
A Losing Season
A Love Ends Suicide
A Lower Deep

A Mind Confused
A Mors et Bello
A New Dawn
A Night to
  Dismember
A Perfect Failure
A Perfect Murder
A Perpetual Dying
  Mirror
A Psychic Opera
A Punto
A Ravens Forest
A Red Dawn
A Retch of Blood
A Shattered Dream
A Sickness Called
  Conscious
A Solemn Death
A Sombre Prospect
A Sorrowful Dream
A Switch Below
A Terrible Night for a
  Curse
A Texas Funeral
A Thousand Times
  Repent
A Thousand Years
  Slavery
A II Z
A Tortured Soul
A Tribute to the
  Plague
A Tu Puta Kara
A Very Sad Story
A Vision Grotesque

A Waking Nightmare
A Winter Within
A((Wake))
A*Teem
A. R. Berdiales
A.B. Spitfire
A.C.O.A.
A.D.N.
A.Death.Experience
A.I.D.S.
A.I.T.H.
A.M.
A.M.E.S.
A.M.P.
A.M.Q.A.
A.N.A.E.L.
A.N.I.M.A.L.
A.O.D.
A.R.G.
A.S.A.P.
A.S.D.
A.T.T.
A.U.X.
A.W.A.S.
AAAAARGH! Bloody
  2-Handed Chainaxe
  Blow
Aaarghh
Aaarghh
Aaarghhh
Aabsinthe
Aaen Anima
Aahas
Aäkon Këëtrëh
Aamonhammer

Aanyl Pane
Aarcon
Aardia
Aardtmann Op
  Vuurtopberg
Aardvarks
Aarmaroth Nathrath
Aarni
Aaron Pearson
Aaronsrod
Aasimon
Aaskereia
Aastyra
Aava
Aavas
Ab:Norm
Abömydögs
Ababil
Ababil
Ababil
ABACABB
Abacinate
Abacinate
Abacinator
Abaddon
Abaddon
Abaddon
Abaddon
Abaddon
Abaddon
Abaddon
Abaddon Incarnate
Abaddon Krist
Abaddons Breed

Abaddyon
Abadia
Abadis
Abadon
Abandon
Abandon
Abandon
Abandon
Abandon Hope
Abandoned Sphinx
Abate Macabro
Abathor
Abatoir
ABBand
Abdicate
Abel Is Dying
Aberrancy
Aberrant Path
Abgator
Abgefuckt
Abhorred Despiser
Abhorrence
  Dementia
Abhorrence
  Of Adramelech
Abigail
Abissal
Abitbollus
Ablaze
Abnegation
Abnormity
Abnormity
Abolition
Abolition
Abominal Mortus

Abomination
Abordazh
Aborior
Aboriorth
Above the Rim
Abramelin
Abrasion
Abrasion
Abrasion
Abrasive
Abraxas
Abraxas
Abraxas
Abrogar
Abrogation
A-Bros
Abruptum
Abs Conditus
Abscess
Abscess
Abscess
Abscess
Abscess
Abscess Plague
Abscesy
Abscience
Abscond
Absemia
Absence
Absence
Absence
Absence
Absence Falling
Absence of Dawn
Absence of Presence
Absence of the Sacred

◀ Absent

Absent Mind	Absolute Zero	Absurd	Abwhore	Abyss	Acaros	Aceldama
Absent Silence	Absolution	Absurd	Abxenta	Abyss Angel	Acarus Sarcopt	Aceldama
Absenta	Absolution	Absurd	Abxtract	Abyss Angel	Accelerate	Aceldama
Absentation	Absolutus	Absurd	Abydos	Abyss Lord	Accelerator	Aceldama
Absenth	Absonant Cadence	Absurd	Abÿfs	Abyss of Darkness	Accept	Acephale
Absentia	Absonus Noctis	Absurd Conception	Abygor	Abyss of Doom	Accept Death	Acephalia
Absentia	Absorb	Absurd Conflict	Aby-Kem	Abyssal	Acceptus Noctifer	Acephalous
Absentia	Absorbcia	Absurd Existence	Abysal	Abyssal	Access Beyond	Acephalus
Absentia Lunae	Absorbed	Absurd Mangler	Abysm	Abyssal Mind	Access Denied	Acephalus
Abside	Absorbed	Absurd?	Abysma	Abyssal Suffering	Access Denied	Acer Fury
Absidia	Absorbed	Absurdeity	Abysmal	Abyssals	Accessory	Acerbitas
Absidia	Absorbed	Absurdity	Abysmal	Abyssaria	Accio Directa	Acerbus
Absinth	Absorbed in Thought	Absurdium	Abysmal	Abyssgale	Accid Reign	Aceria
Absinth	Absorption	Absurdo Culto	Abysmal Darkening	Abyssia	Accident	Acero
Absinthe	Abstinenz	Absurdum	Abysmal Dawn	Abyssian Desolation	Accidental Death	Acero
Absinthe	Abstract	Absurdus	Abysmal Desolation	Abyssic Hate	Accidental Suicide	Acero de Guerra
Absinthebolik	Abstract	Absurter Cryst	Abysmal Fall	Abyssmal Nocturne	Accidentals	Acero Liquido
Absinthium	Abstract	Absyde	Abysmal Fate	Abyssos	Accomplice	Aces of the Spade
Absinthium	Abstract Agony	Absynt	Abysmal Forest	Abyssphere	Accuşer	Acess
Abske Fides	Abstract Butchery	Absynth	Abysmal Gates	Abyssum	Accubitorium	Acetic Voice
Absolom	Abstract Essence	Absynthium	Abysmal God	Abyssus	Accuracy	Aceton
Absolom	Abstract Rapture	Absyntho	Abysmal Grief	Abystic Ritual	Accursed	Acetylene
Absolom	Abstract Satan	Abszess	Abysmal Hate	Abythos	Accursed	Acetylene
Absolut Destruktion	Abstract Shadows	Abuse	Abysmal Solitude	Abyz	Accursed	Achael
Absolute	Abstracta	Abuse	Abysmal Torment	Abyzz	Accursed	Achaemenid
Absolute Defiance	Abstraction	Abuse Ritual	Abyss	Abzintas	Accursed	Acheron
Absolute Defiance	Abstrakt	Abused	Abyss	Abztract Fortune	Accursed	Acheron
Absolute Disgrace	Abstrakt Algebra	Abused Majesty	Abyss	Acabó El Silencio	Accursed	Acheron
Absolute Disorder	Abstrus	Abusiveness	Abyss	Acacia	Accursed Dawn	Acheron
Absolute Grief	Abstruse	Abuso Verbal	Abyss	Acacia	Accurst	Acheron
Absolute Misery	Abstruse	Abusus	Abyss	Acalmy	Accuser	Acheron Gates
Absolute Steel	Absturz	Abutor Ensis	Abyss	Acantha	Ace	Acheronian Dirge
Absolute Zero	Absu	Abutre	Abyss	Acantha	Ace the Raven	Acheront
Absolute Zero	Absurd	Abuzorg	Abyss	Acarien	Acedia	Acherontis
Absolute Zero	Absurd	Abvul Abashy	Abyss	Acaro	Acedio	Acherusia
					Aceium	

Advice

Adviser
Advocate
Advocate
Advocate
Advocatua Diaboli
Advocatus Diaboli
ADX
Adytum
Adytum
AEA
Aeba
Aebsence
Aecron
Aegir
Aegir
Aegirson
Ægre
Aegrimonia
Aegrimonia
Aegrus
Aeiou
Aemerald
Aemeth
Aendria
Aeneas
Aenigma
Ænigma
Aeoga
Aeolian Fire
Aeon
Aeon
Aeon
Aeon
Aeon
Aeon 9

Aeon Dragon
Aeon Ex Cathaedra
Aeon Noctis
Aeon of Death
Aeon of Fear
Aeon Vortex
Aeonic
Aeons
Aeons Confer
Aeons End
Aeons of Eclipse
Aeons of Old
Aeons of Sorrow
Aeons ov Frost
Aequinoctium
Aeracura
Aerik Von Band
Aes
Aes Dana
Aesculetum
Aeshma
Aeshva Daeva
Aesma Daeva
Aesth
Aesthenia
Aesthesia
Aetas
Aetas Obscura
Aeterna
Aeternal
Aeternitas
Aeternitas Nox
Aeternom
Aeternum
Aeternum

Aeternus
Aeternus
Aeternus Obscuritas
Aeternus Odium
Aethenor
Aetheres
Aetheriam
Aetherium
Aetherius
Aetherius
Aetherius Obscuritas
Aetherna
Aethra
Aethyria
Aeturnus
Aeturnus Dominion
Aeverland
Aeveron
Aevlord
Aevum
AF
Afaktor
Afasia
Afflicted
Afflicted Convulsion
Affliction
Affliction
Affliction
Affliction
Affliction
Affliction
Afflitus
Affluent of Styx
Affy Puff
Afgrund

Afgunst
Afraid Of Clowns
Afsprengi Satans
After All
After Dark
After Dark
After Dark
After Death
After Death
After Fall
After Forever
After Genocide
After Life
After Life
After Oblivion
After Omega
After the Dark
After the Eulogy
After the Last Sky
After the Silence
After the Sun
After the Sun
After Therapy
Afterbirth
Afterbirth
Afterbirth
Afterblast
Afterburning
Afterdeath
Afterdeath
Afterglow
Afterglow
Afterglow
Afterimage
Afterlife

Afterlife
Afterlife
Afterlife
Afterlife
Afterlife
Aftermass
Aftermath
Aftermath
Aftermath
Aftermath
Aftermath A.D.
Afternoon at
   the Autopsy
Aftershock
Aftershok
Aftertayst
Afterworld
Agabahan
Agabus
Agadon
Agahareth
Agailiarept
Again
Against
Against
Against All
Against All
Against Death
Against Nature
Against the Flow
Against the Grain
Against the Grain
Agaliarepth
Agalirept
Agalloch

Agamas
Agamemnon
Agamendon
Agankast
Agares
Agares
Agaroth
Agartha
Agartha
Agarthi
Agarthia
Agarwaen
Agarwaen
Agarwean
Agathion
Agathocles
Agathodaemon
Agathodaimon
Agathothodion
Agatta
Agatus
Agaurez
Agazgul
Age of Aggression
Age of Agony
Age of Agony
Age of Carnage
Age of Desolation
Age of Despair
Age of Distrust
Age of Evil
Age of Fury
Age of Heresy
Age of Illusion
Age of Illusion

Age of Madness
Age of Nemesis
Age of Pain
Age of Plague
Age of Rage
Age of Rebellion
Age of Ruin
Age of Silence
Age of Storm
Age of Thor
Age One
Ageless
Ageless
Ageless Kingdoms
Ageless Wisdom
Agenda of Swine
Agent Metal
Agent of the Morai
Agent Omega
Agent Orange
Agent Steel
Agents of Oblivion
Agents of Satan
Ages Gone
Aggelos
Agger
Aggressa
Aggression
Aggression Core
Aggression Overload
Aggressive
Aggressive
Aggressive Agricultor
Aggressive
   Crepitation

Aggressive Disorder

Aggressive Intent	Agnosia	Agonizer	Agresja	Ahriman	Airraid	Akeldama
Aggressive Mind	Agnosia	Agonizer	Agresor	Ahriman	Airspeed	Akeldama
Aggressive Tyrants	Agnosis	Agonizing Terror	Agression	Ahti	Airut	Akelot Tük
Aggressor	Agnosis	Agony	Agressive	Ahumado Granujo	Airwolf	Aker
Aggressor	Agnosys	Agony	Agressor	Ai Muro	Aisling	Aker
Aggressor	Agnus Dei	Agony	Agressor	Aiaibunch	Aisnatorn	Akerbel Kropos
Aggressor	Agnus Dei	Agony	Agressor	Aic Miquina	Aither	Akerbeltz
Aggressor	Agnus Dei	Agony	Agressor	Aichmophoba	Aiumeen Basoa	Akerbeltz
Aggressor	Agnus Negrae	Agony	Agressor	Aida	Aivarim	Akercocke
Aggressor	Agogh	Agony	Agretator	AIDS Infected Corpse	Aiwaiss	Akhenaton
Aggressor	Agommorah	Agony	Agrevyum	Aifur	Aiwass	Akhkharu
Aggressor	Agon	Agony Bag	Agro	Aigro Mucifelam	Aiwass	Akhkharu Noctis
Aggressor	Agon	Agony Column	Agroth	Aikaryu	Aiwass	Akhramort
Aggressor State	Agon	Agony Conscience	Agrypnie	Ailament	Aiwass	Akhtamar
Aggro	Agon Origin	Agony Divine	Agurs Words	Aim Deep	Aiwaz	Akihma
Aghast	Agone	Agony Face	Aguynguerran	Aim for the Head	Ajattara	Akilla
Aghast	Agoni	Agony Lords	Agyptus	Aiming High	Ajdath	Akilles
Aghast	Agonia	Agony of Deceit	Agyvérzés	Aimless	Ajna	Akin
Aghast	Agonia	Agonychild	Ah Dzam	Aimoptysi	AK-47	Akira Takasaki
Aghast Insane	Agonia	Agora	Ahab	Aina	Akael	Akitsa
Aghazagrimmr	Agonia	Agora	Ahasverus	AinMatter	Akal Sari	Akma
Aghiatrias	Agonia	Agoraphobia	Ahat	Ainshval	Akallabeth	Akoma
Aghora	Agonia	Agoraphobia	Ahemait	Aïnsoph	Akallabêth	Akphaezya
Aghorum	Agonía	Agoraphobic	Ahilestyx	Aion	Akaname	Akramen
Agiel	Agonie	Nosebleed	Ahma	Aion	Akanatomb	Akrateia
Aglaomorpha	Agonist	Agorazheim	Ahmasiah	Air Borne	Akantophis	Ákratos
Aglare Light	Agonize	Agorgoth	Ahnenstahl	Air Raid	Akashah	Akriel
Aglarond	Agonize	Agorhy	Ahnkou	Air Sickness Bag	Akashic	Akrival
Agmen	Agonize	Agoria	Ahoora	Airborn	Akbal	Akroma
Agnes Vein	Agonize Death	Agoria	Ahpuch Oztoc	Aird Righ	Ak'Bal	Akromusto
Agnesdei	Agonized	Agorona	Ahrcana	Airdash	Akbru	Akron
Agnivolok	Agonized	Agrath	Ahret Dev	Aireard	Akela	Aktebore
Agnosia	Agonized	Agratz	Ahrihann	Airfax	Akelarre	Akuma
	Agonizer	Agregator	Ahrimah	Airged L'amh	Akeldam	Akumsrazor
	Agonizer	Agresión	Ahriman	Airhead	Akeldama	Akurakus

Al Azif
Al Azred
Al Candello
Al Iblis
Al Na'ir
Al Otro Lado
Al Sirat
Alabama Thunderpussy
Alabarda
Alaghom
Alakran
Alalutu
Alamogordo
Alannah
Alarm
Alarum
Alas
Alas Negras
Alaska
Alaska
Alaska Fire
Alasthor
Alastis
Alastor
Alastor
Alastor
Alastor
Alastor
Alastor Sanguinary Embryo
Alatyr
Alatyr'
Alatyr
Alazif

Alazith
Alban Arthan
Albatrhoz
Albatros
Albatross
Albedrio
Alberzakh
Albion
Albion
Alborde
Alboys
Alcatraz
Alcatrazz
Alcest
Alchemist
Alchemy
Alchemy
Alchemy of Life
Alchemy X
Alchera
Alchil
Alcoholic Mosh
Alcoholic Smashing War
Alcohólica
Alcoholica
Alcoholicoma
Alcoholika La Christo
Alcoholikiller
Alcoholocaust
Alcoolicaos
Alcyon
Aldaaron
Aldaron
Aldebaran

Aldehezt
Aldevia
Aldren Liebe
Alea Jacta
Alea Jacta
Aleación
Aleatory
Alebrije
Alecheon
Alecrate
Alef
Alegory
Aleister
Aleister C.
Aleister Wild
Alejandro Silva Power Cuarteto
Alendalua
Aleph
Aleph
Aleph
Alesys
Aletheia
Aletheia
Aletheia
Alètheia
Aletheian
Alex De Rosso
Alexander Scardavian
Alexandria
Alexandria
Alexandria
Alexandria
Alexey Strike
Alfa

Alfa Eridano Akhernar
Alfajor del Dolor
Alfheim
Algaion
Algeroth
Algesic Massacre
Alghazanth
Algiz
Algiz
Algiz
Algol
Algol
Algol
Algol3
Algophobia
Algor
Algor Mortis
Algorn
Algoz
Alhana
Aliaj
Alianza
Alias
Alias Eye
Alias Mangler
Alibi for a Murder
Alice in Darkland
Alice 'N Thunderland
Alice's Garden
Alidad
Alien
Alien
Alien Boys
Alien Deviant Circus

Alien Dream Hyper Dimensions
Alien Force
Alien Nation
Alien On My Mind
Alien Squad
Alienacja
Alienated
Alienation
Alienation Cold
Alienation Mental
Alienchrist
Aliengates
Alight
Alignak
Alik Granovskiy
Alimine
Alinian
Alioth
Alioth
Alioth
Alioth
Alison
Alison Hell
Alister
Alive in Torment
Aliy Rassvet
Aljahilia
Alkaid
Alkateya
Alkatraz
Alkbottle
Alkehol
Alkemyst
Alkerdeel

Alkhon
Alkonost
Alkonosta Pesn' Pechali Smertnoy
All Blessed
All Dies
All Hallow's Evil
All Hell's Fury
All Hopes Aside
All Immune
All in Vain
All Is Lost
All Is Suffering
All Life Ends
All My Sins
All of a Murder Art
All Out Aggression
All Out War
All Shades of Grey
All Shall Perish
All Souls' Day
All That I Bleed
All That Is Evil
All That Remains
All the Pretty Horses
All Too Human
All Will Fall
All Will Rise
Allatus Adeo
Allegiance
Allegiance
Allegiance
Allegoria
Allegory
Allegory

Allegra Combricca
Allegro
Allen / Lande
Allergo
Allergy
Alleri Ahe
Allerjen
Alleyrat
Allfader
Allfather
Allfather-Odinn
Allhelluja
Alliance
Alliance
Allied Forces
Allied Forces
Allienatyon
Allies
Alligator
Allison Gross
Allochesia
Allow
Alloy Czar
Alltheniko
AllTheSame
Alluciuspustus
Allusion
Allvater
Allvaters Zorn
Allzheimer
Alma de Invierno
Alma Mater
Almacridaem
Almafuerte
AlmaMorta

Amir Hassan
AmisegardauQ
Ammattammen Bas
Ammit
Ammit
Amnesia
Amnesia
Amnesia
Amnèsia
Amnesie
Amnesis
Amnesty
Amnesty
Amnesty
Amnesty
Amnesty
Amnesty
Amnezia
Amnion
Amniorrehexis
Amniotic Count
Amnom
Amnos
Amnos
Amoebe
Amoebic Dysentery
Amok
Amok
Amok
Amok
Ámok
Amok Vedar
Amon
Amon
Amon
Amon

Amon
Amon
Amon Amarth
Amon Din
Amon Goeth
Amon Hen
Amon Hen
Amon Incarnate
Amon Ra
Amon Sul
Among the Atrocities
Among the Betrayed
Among the Decayed
Among the Living
Among the Missing
Among the Mist
Among the Ruins
Amongst the Swarm
Amonicide
Amon-Ra
Amor Committed
    Suicide
Amor e Morte
Amor e Morte
Amora Savant
Amorak
Amoral
Amorbital
Amoreen
Amoricide
Amoris Umbra
Amorpha
Amorphia
Amorphic Form
Amorphis

Amorphous
Amorte
Amortez
Amorticure
Amortis
Amos
Amoteph
Ampast
Ampér
Ampgeezer
Amphiaraus
Amphigory
Amphion
Amphion
Amphitrium
Amphitryon
Amphoteros
Amphytrion
Amplified Heat
Amplifire
Amputated
Amputated Christ
Amputated Genitals
Amputation
Ampütator
Amputist
Amset
Amsvartner
Amsvartnir
Amsvartnit
Amuk
Amulance
Amurg
Amuza
Amyanka

Amygdala
Amylias Circus
Amyris
Amystery
AN
An End to Flesh
An Erotic Funeral
An Unearthly Child
Ana Black
Anaal Nathrakh
Anabantha
Anaboth
Anacephal
Anachorete
Anachronaeon
Anachronia
Anachronic
Anachronoz
Anaconda
Anaconda
Anaconda
Anacreon
Anacrusis
Anacrusis
Anactoria
AnaDies
Anael
Anaemia
Anaemia
Anaemia
Anaemica
Anaflaxia
Anagathon
Anaiash
Anak Tomb

Anaka
Anakron
Anaktorian
Anal Afterbirth
Anal Asthma
Anal Beard
Anal Blasphemy
Anal Blast
Anal Bleeding
Anal Buffet
Anal Collision
Anal Death
Anal Dissected Angel
Anal Dissection
Anal Fissure
Anal Foetus
Anal Harikiri
Anal Nosorog
Anal Penetration
Anal Prolapse
Anal Pus
Anal Putrefaction
Anal Putrefaction
Anal Spewicide
Anal Stench
Anal Thrust
Anal Torture
Anal Turbo Monster
Anal Vaginatör
Anal Vomit
Analgesia
Analgin
Analimal
Analizator
Anally Regurgitated

Analni Karakter
Analog
Analog
Analogy
Analsturm
Analysis
Anamnasia
Anamú
Ananke
Anaon
Anaphalaxie
Anaphilaxy
Anapilis
Anarazel
Anarca
Anarchsphere
Anarchus
Anarchus
Anarchus
Anarchuz
Anarchy Divine
Anarhia
Anarion
Anarkhon
Anarkía
Anarkitan
Anarko
Anartria
Anasarca
Anashi
Anastasis
Anata
Anathema
Anathema
Anathema

Anathema
Anathema
Anathemized
Anathorn
Anatolian Wisdom
Anatomia
Anatomiae Occultii
Anatomical Necropsy
Anatomist
Anatomy
Anatomy
Anatomy
Anatomy of Sadness
Anatriz
Anax
Anaxagazaroth
Anaxim
Ancalagon
Ancalagon
Ancara
Ancelot
Ancepsdea
Ancestor
Ancestor
Ancestor
Ancestor
Ancestor
Ancestors
Ancestors Blood
Ancestral
Ancestral
Ancestral
Ancestral
Ancestral
Ancestral

Ancestral Damnation	Ancient Hatred	And Harmony Dies	Andromeda	Angel	Angel Retard	Angels & Demons
Ancestral Fog	Ancient Malus	And Hell Followed	Andromeda	Angel	Angel Rot	Angels Abortion
Ancestral Goetia	Ancient Misery	And Here I Lie	Andromeda	Angel	Angel Smile	Angel's Blood
Ancestral Legacy	Ancient Moonlight	and oceans	Andromeda	Angel Accelerator	Angel Tears	Angels Decay
Ancestral Majesty	Ancient Moonrise	And Seven Escape	Andromeda	Death	Angel Trumpet	Angel's Decay
Ancestral Malediction	Ancient Mystery	And Summer Dies	Androphagous	Angel Beast	Angel War	Angel's Decay
Ancestral Myth	Ancient Myth	And the Hero Fails	Androphin	Angel Blake	Angel Witch	Angel's Diary
Ancestral Prophecy	Ancient Necropsy	And the Sky Went	Andros	Angel Blanco	Angel X	Angels Fall
Ancestral Stigmata	Ancient Oath	Red	Andy Reisert &	Angel Butcher	Angelblood	Angels Fate
Ancestral Terror	Ancient Poetry	And Then There	Natural Disaster	Angel Corpse	Angelcide	Angels Grace
Ancestral Volkhves	Ancient Prophecy	Were None	Anekdoten	Angel Crash	Angelcoma	Angels in Black
Ancestros	Ancient Reign	And They Will Meet	Anemonia	Angel de Metal	Angelcorpse	Angels in Exile
Ancesttral	Ancient Rites	God	Anemosity	Angel Death	Angelcrypt	Angel's Last Breath
Ancêtres	Ancient Rune	And Utero Dominae	Anencephalus	Angel Dissection	AngelDeath	Angels of
Anchor	Ancient Sadness	Andabata	Anestesia	Angel Dust	Angeles del Infierno	Armageddon
Anchoreth	Ancient Season	Andaja	Anestesia	Angel Dust	Angelfire	Angels of Deception
Ancient	Ancient Season	Andark	Anestesia	Angel Dust	Angelgoat	Angels of Fall
Ancient	Ancient Sign Glorify	Andarta	Anestesic	Angel Easy	Angelgoat	Angels Torment
Ancient Art	Ancient Skin	Andeathion	Anestezia	Angel Fallen	Angeli di Pietra	Angels With Dirty
Ancient Ascendant	Ancient Slumber	Andeavor	Anestezija	Angel Grinder	Angelic Damnation	Faces
Ancient Ceremony	Ancient Souls	Andem	Anesthesia	Angel Guts	Angelic Force	Angelus
Ancient Creation	Ancient Summoning	Anderę	Anesthesia	Angel Hammer	Angelic Requiem	Angelus
Ancient Cross	Ancient Supremacy	Andhrimnir	Anesthesia	Angel Martum	Angelica	Angelus
Ancient Cult of	Ancient Tale	Andhrímnir	Anesthesia	Angel Negro	Angelize	Angelus
Pandemonium	Ancient War Spirit	Andi Deris	Anesthesia	Angel Nocturno	AngelKill	Angelus Apatrida
Ancient Curse	Ancient Wargod	Andlát	Anesthesy	Angel Nocturno	Angelknight	Angelus Diaboli
Ancient Curse	Ancient Winds	Andover	Anethetic	Angel of Blasphemy	Angelkunt	Angelus Infernus
Ancient Darkness	Ancient Wisdom	Andra	Anetia Insignis	Angel of Damnation	Angellic Rage	Angelus Mortis
Ancient Dawn	Ancient Wound	Andralls	Aneurysm	Angel of Disease	Angelot	Angeluz
Ancient Death	Ancient Wyrm	Andramelech	Anfall	Angel of Light	Angelrage	Anger
Ancient Dome	Ancientblood	Andrarakh	Angantyr	Angel of Mercy	Angelrape	Anger
Ancient Drive	Ancienterror	Andras	Angantyr	Angel of Pain	Angelreich	Anger
Ancient Existence	Ancienthorn	Andrasta	Angava	Angel Powder	AngelRuin	Anger
Ancient Goat	Ancillae	André Andersen	Angband	Angel Power	Angelrust	Anger
Ancient Gods	Ancor	Andrea Torretta	Angband	Angel Reaper	Angels	Anger Management

Anger Within	Angry Angels	Anima	Animosity	Annihilation	Anonymous Souls	Ansur
Angerfix	Angry Demon	Anima Adversa	Animosity	Annihilation	Anonymus	Ansur
Angerise	Angryon	Anima Damnata	Animus	Annihilation	Anopheles	Ansuz
Angerstorm	Angst	Anima Inmortalis	Animus	Annihilation Text	Anopheles	Antacid
Angerstrike	Angst	Anima Naive	Animus	Annihilator	Anopheles	Antaeus
Angertea	Angst	Anima Poetae	Animus	Annihilatus	Anopsy	Antagaroth
Angerwound	Angstridden	Ánima Sola	Animus Barathrum	Annihilism	Anora Dimentia	Antagon
Angher	Angtoria	Anima Vilis	Animus Herilis	Annihilus	Anorexia	Antagonism
Angiha	Anguis Aeturnus	Anima Vilis	Animus Mortis	Anno Daemonicus	Anorexia	Antagonist
Angis	Anguish	Animal	Animus Necandi	Anno Domini	Anorexia Nervosa	Antagonist
Angizia	Anguish	Animal Alpha	Anit-Ben	Anno Domini	Anorexic Cannibals	Antagonist
Angkor	Anguish·	Animal Foreskin	AnJ	Anno Domini Mortus	Anorma	Antagonist Mortiis
Angkor	Anguish	Animal Hate	Anjos de Salém	Anno Zero	Anorrectal	Antagony
Angkor Bat	Anguish	Animal Soul	Ankara	Annon Vin	Protuberance	Antagony
Angkor Vat	Anguish	Animalfarm	Anken	Annotations of	Another	Antagony
Angkor Vat	Anguish	Animalize	Ankh	an Autopsy	Another	Antaios
Angkor Wat	Anguish Force	Animals Grace	Ankhagram	Annoy	Another Day	Antar
Anglachel	Anguish in Exile	Animals Killing	Ankhara	Annoying Life	Another Dying	Antarctica
Anglachel	Anguish Sublime	People	Ankhelgloknar	Annthennath	Democracy	Antarctis
Anglagard	Angurvadel	Animam Trahere	Ankle Deep in Blood	Annulation	Another Left Behind	Antares
Angmar	Angus	Animas	Ankor	Annunaki	Another Life	Antares
Angmar	Angus McDeth	Animas	Ankorjed	Annwn	Another Messiah	Antares
Angor	Anhedonia	Animas Belli	Ankrismah	Annwn	Another Sad	Antares
Angor	Anhedonia	Animas Herejes	Anksddronenn	Anodize	Another Sick Tribe	Antarhes
Angora	Anhedonia	Animas Negras	Anksunamon	Anomalia	Another Side	Antarktis Utopia
Angra	Anhelitus	Animate Death	Anlace	Anomally	Anoxia	Antarktyk
Angra Mainyu	Anhkrehg	Animated Dead	Annalist	Anomalous	Anoxia	Antaro
Angra Mainyu	Anhoxia	Animestesia	Annatar	Anomaly	Anoxia	Antártica
Angrbada	Anhthrone	Animetal	Annathema	Anomaly	Anoxie	Antartide
Angrboda	Anialator	Animi Vultus	Anneksia	Anomaly	Anpher	Ante Cryst
Angrenost	Anic	Animos	Annex	Anomaly in Effigy	Anphisbenah	Ante Lucem
Angrenost	Anigma	Animos Nocti	Annihilate	Anomalya	Anschluss	Antechristus
Angriff	Anihilated	Animosity	Annihilate	Anomy	Anshar	Antedeum
Angrist	Anima	Animosity	Annihilate the Hero	Anonima Disastri	Ansia	Antediluvian
Angrist	Anima	Animosity	Annihilation	Anonyma	Ânsia de Vômito	Antediluvian

Anterior	Anthropomancy	Antídoto	Antithese	Anubiz	Aosoth	Aphrodisiac
Anteros	Anthropophagical	Antifreeze	Antithesis	Anublar Cetro	Apartheide	Aphses
Antesser	Warfare	Antigama	Antithesis	Anubyss	Apartment 213	Apis
Antestor	Anthropophagus	Antiglare	Antithesis	Anus	Apathemy	Apnea
Antevirus	Anthropophagus	Antigonë	Antitox	Anus Brigade	Apathetic Discharge	Apoc Death
Anthagonist	Anthropophagus	Antihuman	Antix	Anus de Satanus	Apathy	Apocalips
Anthares	Anthropophagy	Antikriist	Anton	Anus Praeter	Apathy	Apocalipsis
Anthares	Anthropophagy	Antileben	Antonamasia	Anus Tumor	Apathy	Apocalipsis
Antharès	Anthropophobe	Antim Grahan	Antracit	Anus Tumor	Apathy	Apocalypse
Antharos	Anti	Antimatter	Antraks	Anusgore	Apator	Apocalypse
Anthea	Anti	Antimon	Antraks	Anuus Altaar	Ape	Apocalypse
Anthelion	Anti Doctrine	Antinomus	Antro	Anvil	Ape	Apocalypse
Anthelion	Anti-Ben	Antiparasitär	Antrochaotic	Anvil Bitch	Apeiron	Apocalypse
Anthem	Antibody	Antipathy	Antropofagus	Anvil Chorus	Apeiron	Apocalypse
Anthem	Antichrisis	Antiphrasis	Antropoid	Anvil of Doom	Apeiron	Apocalypse
Anthem	Antichrist	Antípoda	Antropomorfia	Anwariad	Aperient	Apocalypse
Anthem	Antichrist	Antipope	Antropomorphia	Anwech	Apex Null	Apocalypse
Anthemon	Antichrist	Antiqua	Antropophobia	Anweld	Aphaeresis	Apocalypse
Anthems of	Antichrist	Antiquarium	Antrum	Anwyl	Aphangak	Apocalypse
Gomorrah	Antichrist	Antique	Antrum	Anwynn	Aphasia	Command
Anthenora	Antichrist Terrorist	Antiquus	Antrum Mortis	Anxiety	Aphasia	Apocalypse Now
Antheom	Antichristi Miles	Antiquus	Antubel	Anxiety	Aphelion	Apocalypse Survivors
Anthesteria	Anti-Christian	Antiquus Scriptum	Anu	Anxiety	Aphelion	Apocalypse Theatre
Antheus	Assault	Antira	Anubi	Anxiety	Aphelion	Apocalypse Warhead
Anthony	Anticipate	Anti-Régimen	Anubis	Anxious Death	Aphelion	Apocalypse Woman
Anthracite	Anticipation	Antisacrum	Anubis	Anxius	Aphelion	ApocalypseHead
Anthracite	Anticipation	Antisect	Anubis	Any Last Words	Aphelion	Apocalypsis
Anthrax	Anticlimax	Antisemitex	Anubis	Anzeray	Aphelion	Apocalypta
Anthriel	Anticristo	Antisilence	Anubis	AOC	Aphelion Aphrodites	Apocalyptic
Anthrocite	Antidemon	Antisistema	Anubis	Aonikenk	Aphelon	Apocalyptic
Anthrofuge	Anti-Depressive	Antisma	Anubis	Aoora	Apherial	Apocalyptic
Anthropia	Delivery	Antisocial	Anübis	Aorta	Aphis	Apocalyptic
Anthropicide	Antidogma	Anti-Systematic	Anubis Gate	Aorta	Aphob	Apocalyptic Agony
Anthropolatri	Antidogmatic	Antítese	Anubis Gates	Aórta	Aphoom Zhah	Apocalyptic Christ
Anthropomancy	Antidote	Antitheos	Anubis Rising	Aorta	Aphornon	Apocalyptic Clash
					Aphotic	Apocalyptic Fear

Apocalyptic Visions
Apocalyptica
Apocrafyx
Apócrifus
Apocryph
Apocryph
Apocrypha
Apocrypha
Apócrypha
Apocryphal
Apocryphal
Apocryphal
Apocryphal Death
Apocryphal Voice
Apocryphos
Apofigeus
Apogheum
Apokalipsa
Apokalipszis Árnyék
Apokalyptic Raids
Apokalyptic Warlust
Apokatastasia
Apokatastasis
Apokefale
Apokrifos
Apokrypha
Apokryphos
Apokryphus
Apoleon
Apolion
Apolion's Genocide
Apollgon
Apollo Ra
Apollyon
Apollyon

Apollyon
Apollyon Sun
Apologist
Apolokia
Apolokia
Apolyom
Apophenia
Apopheniac
Apophis
Apoplex
Apoplexy
Apoplexy
Apoplexy
Apoplexy
Apoplexy
Apoplexy
Apoplexy
Aposento
Aposento
Apost
Apostasia
Apostasia
Apostasia
Apostasy
Apostasy
Apostasy
Apostasy
Apostasy
Apostasy
Apostasy
Apostasy
Apostate
Apostate
Apostate
Aposthate

Apostisy
Apostle
Apostle
Apostle of Dementia
Apostle of Perversion
Apostle of Solitude
Apostles of
    Perversion
Apostolum
Apotasy
Apotheosis
Apotheosis
Apotheosis
Apotheosys
Apothys
Appalling Spawn
Apparition
Apparition
Appearance
    of Nothing
Appendix
Applehead
Appomattox
Appomattox
Apprentice Bards
Approached by a God
Approaching Zero
Approx
Apraxia
Aprezeus
Apriaca
April Ethereal
April Morning
Apriori
Aproctous

Aprosopy
Apshait
Aptakhar
Aptorian Demon
Apud Inferos
Apud Inferos
Aquam Igni
Aquamorta
Aquanet
Aquaria
Aquarian
Aquaritia
Aquelarre
Aquelarre
Aquer
Aqueronte
Aqueronte
Aqueronte
Aquila
Aquila
Aquilhonia
Aquillion
Aquilon
Aquilus
Aquilus
Aquincum
AR
Ara
Arabesque
Arachnaphilia
Arachnes
Arachnica
Arachnid
Arachnid
Arachnotaur

Arachnovore
Arachos
Arachula
Aracner
Aracranios
Aradia
Aradin Azun
Arafel
Aragathor
Aragon
Aragon
Aragon
Aragon
Aragorn
Aragorn
Aragorn
Arai
Arakacian
Arakain
Ara'kus
Arallu
Aramathea
Aramazd
Aran Elda
Arandor
Araneum
Aranrùth
Arantaxia
AraPacis
Aras
Aras
Arastral
Arathorn
Arathyr
Aratron

Arawen
Arawn
Arawn
Araxa
Arbach
Arbiter
Arbiter of Conceit
Arbitrary Element
Arbitrater
Arbitrator
Arbitrator
Arbitrium
Arbor Ira
Arbor Vitae
Arborea
Arboris Mortuus
Arbour
ARC
Arç Blanc
Arc Fatalis
Arcadia
Arcadia
Arcadia
Arcadia
Arcadian Nocturne
Arcaica
Arcan
Arcana
Arcana Coelestia
Arcana Difamia
Arcana Major
Arcana XIII
Arcana XXII
Arcanae Legioniis
Arcanar

Arcane
Arcane
Arcane
Arcane
Arcane
Arcane
Arcane Aeon
Arcane Church
Arcane Dimension
Arcane Grail
Arcane Legion
Arcane Necrosis
Arcane Shadows
Arcane Sun
Arcane Visions
Arcane Wisdom
Arcangel
Arcángel
Arcania
Arcania
Arcania
Arcanjos
Arcano
Arcanu Anima
Arcanum
Arcanum
Arcanum XIII
Arcanus
Arcanus Nox
Arcanvm Woods
Arcatharis
ArCease
Arceye
Arch Angel
Arch Demon Choir

Arch Nemesis	Archean Demon	Arctic Circle	Ares Wrath	Argus	Arisse	Arkenstone
Arch of Hell	Archegonus	Arctic Fields	Aresz	Argus	Aristaeus	Arkenstone
Arch of Thorns	Archemeday	Arctic Flame	Árész	Argus	Aristaeus	Arkeronn
Arch Rival	Archemenia	Arctic Frost	Arganath	Argus Megere	Aristide	Arkha Sva
Arch Rival	Archenar	Arctic Light	Argar	Argyrian	Arius	Arkh'aam
Arch Vile	Archenemy	Arctic Symphony	Argath	Arhont	Arize	Arkham
Archa	Archenterum	Arctic Thunder	Argathron	Ari Koivunen	Arizen	Arkham
Archaea	Archenum	Arctifall	Arge	Aria	Ark	Arkham
Archaean Harmony	Archeon	Arctum	Argen	Aria	Ark of Sin	Arkham
Archaemenio	Archer	Arcturon	Argenraza	Ariadna Project	Ark Storm	Arkham Asylum
Archaeon	Archer	Arcturus	Argent	Arian Vaejah	Arkadia	Arkhamian
Archaeus	Archestry	Arcturus	Argento	Arianrhod	Arkadia	Arkhan
Archagathus	Archetype	Arda	Argento	Arianrhod	Arkaik	Arkhanhell
Archai	Archevil	Ardent Flames	Argentum	Arida Vortex	Arkaim	Arkhasis
Archaic	Archfiend	Ardisia	Argharus	Ariel n' Caliban	Arkaim	Arkhaytulmayt
Archaic	Archgoat	Arditi	Argharus	Arijskij Sturm	Arkaina	Arkhe
Archaic Argot	Archie Bunker	Ardkore	Arghon	Arimā	Arkan	Arkhè
Archaic Cessation	Archistra	Ardual	Arghoslent	Arima Sutan	Arkana	Arkhesia
Archaic Guilt	Architect of Seth	Ardulph Ardebahr	Argile	Ariman	Arkandur	Arkheth
Archaic Horror	Architect of the Most	Wald	Argir	Arimonium Rex	Arkane	Arkhon
Archaic Icon	Terrible Dreams	Are You God?	Argon	Arioch	Arkanen	Arkhon Infaustus
Archaic Mass	Architecture	Area	Argonath	Arion	Arkangel	Arkhón Tôn
Archaic Torse	of Aggression	Area 51	Argonath	Arisah	Arkangel	Daimoniôn
Archaic Winter	Archmages	Area 54	Argonath	Arischer Krieg	Arkania	Arkillery
Archaicus	Archon	Area Disaster	Argonath Warriors	Arise	Arkanos	Arkngthand
Archain	Archons	Arena	Argonautica	Arise	Arkanot	Arkona
Archaios	Archontes	Arena Age	Argor	Arise	Arkanum	Arkona
Archaios Ophios	Archotype	Arenah	Argos	Arise	Arkanus	Arkona
Archaios Ophis	Arckan Obscura	ArenariS	Argos	Arise	Arkanus	Arkona
Archandrja	Arckanum	Ares	Argos	A-Rise	Arkanus	Arkonen
Archangel	Arckham Hearse	Ares	Argoth	Arise and Ruin	Arkanus	Arkonian
Archangel	ArcLite	Ares	Arguel	Arise Eternal	Arkanus	Arkthos
Archangellus	Arconova	Ares	Argument Soul	Arise From Oblivion	Arkanus Ad Noctum	Arkus
Archanger	Arcorais	Ares Kingdom	Argus	Arise From Thorns	Arkavus	Arloch
Archantia	Arcosoulium	Ares Letum	Argus	Arisk Priest	Arkenemy	Armada

Aryon
Aryos
Arysk
As a River
As Blood Runs Black
As Cities Burn
As Creation Falls...
As Divine Grace
As Dramatic Homage
As Dusk Unfolds
As Eden Burns
As Fate Burns
As Hollow
As Hope Dies
As I Die
As I Fall
As I Lay Dying
As I Lay Dying
As It Burns
As Light Dies
As Light Fades
As Long As I Breathe
As Long as People Die
As My Victims Bleed
As Prophecies
As Sahar
As Sanity Fades
As Serenity Fades
As She Screams
As Stormclouds Gather
As The Blade Falls
As the Leaves Fall in a Crimson Autumn

As the Oceans Dream Eternal
As the Sea Parts
As the Shadows Fall
As the Sky Bleeds
As the Sun Sets
As the Tide Consumes
As Tomorrow Dies
As Vampiric Shades and Belial Winds
As We Destroy
As We Fight
As You in Agony Cry
As4del
ASA
Asa Foetida
Asafated
Asag
Asaian
Asakku
Asaradel
Asarhadon
Asaru
Asathor
Asathor
Asatru
Ásatrú
Asbath Oculta
Asbeel
Asbel
Asbest
Asbest
Asbestos Playground
Asbestosdeath

Asbreaker
Ascaria
Ascaris
Ascaris
Ascaroth
Ascendancy
Ascendancy
Ascendancy
Ascendancy
Ascendant
Ascendant
Ascending Ashes
Ascension
Ascension
Ascension of the Watchers
Ascension Theory
Ascent
Ascent
Ascent
Asche
Asche des Lebens
Aschefall
Aschenglas
Aschmicrosa
Ascraeus
Asebia
Aseidad
AseraphymN
Ases
Asesino
Asesino Violeta
A-Set
AsEyeAm
Asfault

Asfixia
Asfyx
Asgaard
Asgaia
Asgard
Asgard
Asgard
Asgard
Asgard
Asgard
Asgard
Asgard
Asgard Legionnaires
Asgard Warriors
Asgaroth
Asgarth
Asgaut
Asgeirr
Asguard
Ash
Ash & Elm
Ash Devili
Ash Inheritance
Ash Lee Blade
Ash Nazg
Ash Pool
Ash to Ashs
Ashbrain
Ashbury
Ashdautas
Ashen
Ashen Dawns
Ashen Epitaph
Ashen Images
Ashen Light

Ashen Mortality
Ashent
Asher
Ashes
Ashes
Ashes
Ashes
Ashes Against Oblivion
Ashes and Dust
Ashes of Babylon
Ashes of Destiny
Ashes of Eden
Ashes of Icons
Ashes of Lord
Ashes of Remembrance
Ashes of Utopia
Ashes on Your Grave
Ashes Reburnt
Ashes to Ashes
Ashes To Ashes
Ashes You Leave
Ashkark
Ashlan
Ashmedai
Ashmolean
Ashore of Decadence
Ashra
Ashtar
Ashtorath
Ashtureth
Ashura
Ashville
Asian Black

Asiana
Asinesia
Asiz
Aska
Aska
Askalon
Askalon
Askaris
Askariz
Aske
Aske
Askedal
Askehorde
Askes
Askesis
Askuror
Aslan
Aslan
Asleep
Ásmegin
Asmodæo
Asmoday
Asmodee
Asmodée
Asmodée
Asmodem
Asmodeu
Asmodeus
Asmodeus
Asmodeus
Asmodi
Asmodia
Asmodina

Asmodina
Asmodis
Asmon
Asmorod
Asmyraii
Asofy
Asomvel
ASP
Aspect
Aspect
Asper
Aspergillosis
Aspergillus Flavus
Asperity
Asphalt
Asphalte
Asphodel
Asphodemus
Asphyx
Asphyx
Asphyxia
Asphyxia
Asphyxia
Asphyxia
Asphyxia
Asphyxia
Asphyxiate
Asphyxiate
Asphyxiate
Asphyxiated
Asphyxiation
Asphyxiation
Asphyxiation
Asphyxiation
Asphyxiation

Asphyxiator	Assassination	Astarium	Astomatous	Astromancer	At Nightfall	Atavism
Asphyxihate	Assassination	Astarot	Astoroth	Astronomy	At No End	Atavism
Aspid	Assassins	Astarot	Astoryas	Astroqueen	At Odds With God	Atavist
Aspid	Assault	Astaroth	Astövidatüs	Astrum	At One With Chaos	Atavix
Aspid	Assault	Astaroth	Astra	Astrum Aurora	At Radogost's Gates	Ataxia
Aspiration	Assault Attack	Astaroth	Astra	Astur Ignis	At the Carcass of God	Ataxia
Aspiration	Assaulter	Astaroth	Astra Khan	Asunder	At the Gates	ATC
Aspiration	Assaulter	Astaroth	Astraeus	Asura	At the Lake	Ate
Aspire	Asschapel	Astaroth	Astraeus	Asura	At the Mercy of	A-Team
Asrafil	Assedio	Astaroth	Astrahan	Asura	Inspiration	Atem
Asrai	Assedium	Astaroth	Astral	Asva	At the Sky	Atemno
Ass	Asseedio	Astaroth	Astral	Asvaran	At the Throne	Atemtor
Ass Ache	Assemblent	Astaroth	Astral	Asvynn	of Judgment	Aten
Ass Flavour	Assertiveness	Astaroth	Astral Aeon	Asxvell	At Vance	Atenas
Assacre	Assesor	Astaroth	Astral Carneval	Asylium	At War	Atenoux
Assacrentis	Asshole	Astarott	Astral Demise	Asylum	At War With Gods	Ater
Assail	Assholeparade	Astarte	Astral Division	Asylum	At War with Self	Ater
Assail	Assholes on	Astarte Syriaca	Astral Doors	Asylum	At Winter's End	Ater
Assailant	Distortion	Astartehorns	Astral Flames	Asylum	Ata D'arc	Ater Fatum
Assailant	Assignment	Astarus	Astral Forest	Asylum	Atacama	Ater Letum
Assailant	Assigns	Astathica	Astral Gate	Asylum Phenomena	Atahan	Ater Tenebrae
Assailant	Assisting Sorrow	Asteden	Astral Gates	Asyndess	A'tak	Aterial
Assailant	Asskicker	Astenias	Astral Kingdom	Asynja	Atake del Dragon	Aterius
Assailant	Assorted Heap	Asteria	Astral Rising	Asystole	Atakhama	ATG
Assailant	Assorted Nails	Asterius	Astral Sleep	At All Cost	Atakor	Athalay
Assalant	Assoult	Asterlot	Astral Symphony	At Arms	Atalaya	Athame
Assamalla	Asspera	Asteroid	Astrath	At Daggers Drawn	Atalja	Athame
Assassin	Asspounder	Asteroidea	Astray	At Dawn	Atanab	Athanator
Assassin	Asstellyte	AsteroidicA	Astrayed	At Dawn They Sleep	Atanatos	Athanor
Assassin	Assück	Asthar	Astre Macabre	At Domine	Ataraxie	Athanor
Assassin	Assumption of Might	Astharoth	Astreas Domains	At Dusk	Atargatis	Athanor
Assassin	Assur	Astharoth	Astriaal	At First Light	Ataria	Athanor
Assassin	Assur	Astheria	Astrodust	At Gunpoint	Atavi	Athanor
Assassin	Assyria	Asthma	Astrofaes	At Life's End	Atávica	Athanorr
Assassin	Astaarth	Astimi	Astrogence	At My Funeral	Atavism	Athar Doilleir

Axiom
Axiomhorde
Axis
Axis
Axis
Axis
Axis
Axis of Advance
Axis of Evil
Axis Of Perdition
Axis Powers
Axite
Axle
Ax'n Sex
Axom
Axon
Axt
Axter
Axthara
Axtion
Axton
Axton Pryte
Axtura
Axudual Imdurzaam
Axus Bliss
Axuss
Axxis
Axya
Ayahuaira
Ayasiin Salkhi
Ayat
Ayax
Aydra
Ayerdall
Aygghon

Ayperos
Ayreon
Aysenlur
Aytnachr
Az Axel
AZA
Azael
Azael
Azael
Azagatel
Azaghal
Azagthoth
Azag-Thoth
Azahel's Fortress
Azalon
Azamoth
Azanth
Azar
Azarath
Azariath
Azarius
Azarok
Azaroth
Azaroth
Azathor
Azathot
Azathoth
Azathoth
Azathoth
Azathoth
Azathoth
Azatoth
Azaxul
Azazel
Azazel

Azazel
Azazel
Azazel
Azazel
Azazel
Azazel
Azazello
Azazil
Azbuk
Aze
Azeazeron
Azel
Azer
Azerlath
Azeroth
Azeroth
Azeroth
Azeta
Azeuf
Azgar
Azgeroth
Azgeroth
Azhubham Haani
Azif
Azimuth
Azimuth
Azken Garrasia
Azlan
Azmael
Azmaveth
Azmodan
Azog
Azoikum
Azoth
Azoth

Azoth
Azotic Reign
Azotobacter
Azotth
Azra-el
Azrael
Azrael
Azrael
Azrael
Azrael
Azrael
Azrael
Azrael
Azrael Rising
Azrael's Bane
Azrael's Seed
Aztec
Aztec Jade
Azterion
Aztra
Azul Limão
Azure
Azure
Azure
Azure Emote
Azurewrath
Azurnfard
Azuth
Azuzena
Azziard
Azzip

B and R
B.A.R.F.
B.B.P.
B.D.A.
B.D.Ö.
B.E.N.T.
B.G.T.
B.H.P.
B.O.B.
B.O.R.N.
B.S.D.
B.T.R.
B.X.M.S.
Baal
Baal
Baal

Baal
Baal
Baal
Baal Berit
Baal Gadrial
Baal Hamon
Baal Rebirth
Baal Sebul
Baal Therocles
Baal Therocles
Baal Zabub
Baal Zebuth
Baalberith
Baalberith
Baalberith
Baalberith

Baalberith
Baalberith
Baalphegor
Baalstrom
Baalzephon
Baba Yaga
Babel
Babi Liar
Baboon Rising
Baby Stab Horror
Baby Woodrose
Babygrinder
Babylon
Babylon
Babylon A.D.
Babylon Fading
Babylon Mystery
  Orchestra
Babylon Sad
Babylon Whores
Bacchia Neraida
Bacchus
Bacchus
Bacchus
Bachus
Back to Death
Back When
Backbone
Backdraft
Backfire
Backlash
Backlash
Backlash
Backlash
Backmask

Backslash
Backslider
Backstabbing Bastard
BackWardness
Backwater
Backwoods Payback
Backyard Babies
Backyard Burial
Backyard Mortuary
Baco
Bacteria
Bacterial Vaginosis
Bactherion
Bactotavaiy
Bad Acid Trip
Bad Ambition
Bad Blood
Bad Boat
Bad Bone
Bad Comedy
Bad Erection
Bad Face
Bäd Influence
Bad January
Bad Joke
Bad Lizard
Bad Mean Tone
Bad Medicine
Bad News
Bad Steve
Bad Taste
Bad Taste
Bad to the Bone
Bad Yodelers
Badana

Badge
Badger
Badluck
Badoc
Badragath
BadTrippe
Baekdoosan
Bael
Bael
Bael
Bael Occultus
Baerenzorn
Bag of Humans
Baghead
Bagheera
Bagless
Bagronk
Bagronk
Bahal
Bahamut
Bahimiron
Baigaliin Haranhui
Bajen Death Cult
Bajo Tierra
Bajo Zero
BajoMundo
Bajonet
Bak De Syv Fjell
Bakbakwalanooksi-
  wae
Baked Bomb
Bakom
Bakxeios
Bal Sagoth
Balaam

Balam
Balam Acab
Balance Interruption
Balance of Power
Balance of Power
Balance of Silence
Balatonizer
Balberith
Balbulus
Bäld Imperium
Balder
Balder Dead
Balero
Balest
Balezn
Balfare
Balflare
Balfor
Balfor
Baliset
Balistic
Balistik Kick
Balkandji
Ball Gag
Ballantinez
Ballistic
Ballistic Whiplash
Balmog
Balmung
Balmung
Balor
Balor
Balothron
Balrog
Balrog

Balrog
Balrog
Balrog
Bal-Sagoth
Balseraph
Baltak
Balvaz
Bandanos
Bandoso
Bane
Bane
Bane and Illusion
Bane of Existence
Bane of Isildur
Banefull
Banewort
Bang Doll
Bangadrian
Bangin' Moon
Bangkai
Bangsat
Bang-Utot
Banish the Demons
Banished
Banished
Banished Force
Banished Reality
Banished Spirits
Banisher
Banishment
Bann
Banner of Wrath
Bannerwar
Banshee
Banshee

 Banshee

Beyond Terror	Biastema	Bilskirnir	Birkenau	Bizarre Embalming	Black Autumn	Black Comedy
Beyond Grace	Bible Belt Byproduct	Bind	Birkenau	Bizarre of Brutality	Black Autumn	Black Countess
Beyond the Buried	Bible Black	Bind.Torture.Kill	Birkenmoor	Bizarrekult	Black Autumn	Black Crescent
Beyond the Dark	Bible Black	Bio Christ	Birth of Tragedy	Bizarro	Black Axe	Black Cross
Beyond the Dream	Bible of Hatred	BioChrist	Birthdecline	Bizzare Ordinary	Black Babylon	Black Cross
Beyond the Embrace	Bible of the Devil	Biocide	Birthmark	Bizzarre Kings	Black Baptism	Black Cross
Beyond the End	Biblical Infamy	Bioeraser	Birushanah	Bjergtrold	Black Beast	Black Crucifixion
Beyond the Flesh	Biderben	Biogenesis	Biscaya	BK 49	Black Betty	Black Crusader
Beyond the Grave	Bidool	Biolence	Bisclavret	Blaac Abour	Black Bible	Black Cult
Beyond the Labyrinth	Biest	Biolich	Bishop of Hexen	Blaakyum	Black Bile	Black Dama
Beyond the Ninth	Biff Steel	Biologic Enemy	Bishop Steel	Blabbermouth	Black Bile	Black Darkness
Wave	Bifrost	Biological Monstrosity	Bismillah	Black	Black Bitch	Black Dawn
Beyond the	Bifrost	Biomech Race	Bisól	Black & Dark	Black Bleeding	Black Dawn
Northwinds	Bifrost	Biomechanical	Biss	Black Abomination	Black Blood	Black Death
Beyond the Rage	Bifrost	Biomenace	Bitch	Black Abyss	Black Blood	Black Death
Beyond the Realm	Bifröst	Biomorph	Bitch	Black Achemoth	Black Boned Angel	Black Death
Beyond the Sanity	Big Baby Satan	Biophobia	Bitch Infection	Black AD	Black Boned Angel	Black Death
Beyond the Sixth Seal	Big Business	Biopsy	Bitch Rider	Black Adder	Black Book Members	Black Death
Beyond the	Big Daisy	Biopsycunt	Bitch Splitter	Black Affliction	Black Box Pilot	Black Death
Torchlight	Big Heat	Biorhythm	Bitchery	Black Alice	Black Buffalo	Black Death Ritual
Beyond the Wall	Big History	Biosong	Bitches Sin	Black Allegiance	Black Bullet	Black Debbath
of Sleep	Big Iron	Biotech	Bitchslicer	Black Alliance	Black Burn	Black Dementia
Beyond Twilight	Bigos Eaters	Biotech	Bitchslicer	Black Altar	Black Candle	Black Despondency
Beyond Vision	Bigotry	Biotech	Bitchsplitter	Black Angel	Black Candles	Black Destiny
Beyond Within	Bihor Massif	Biotech	Bitter End	Black Angel	Black Candles	Black Dethe
Beyon-D-Lusion	Bila Vezha	Bioterror	Bitter Frost	Black Angels	Black Candles	Black Devil
Bezerker	Bile	Bioterror	Bitter Hærvest	Black Arrow	Black Candle's Mist	Black Diamond
Bezukry	Bile	Biovore	Bitter Legacy	Black Arrows of	Black Chapeaux	Black Diamond
BFH	Bile Nephrosis	Bird Brains	Bitter Orange	Filth & Impurity	Black Chapel	Black Diamond
Bhaobhan Sidhe	Bilharze	Bird of Prey	Bitter Piece	Black Art	Black Chariot	Black Diamond
Bhayanak Maut	Bilharzia	Bird of Prey	Bitterdusk	Black Arts	Black Christ	Black Diamonds
Bhelliom	Bill Ward	Birdflesh	Bitterness	Black Astrology	Black Circle	Black Dimension
Bhoidhos	Billy Knuckles	Birds of Prey	Bitterness	Black Asylum	Black Circle	Black Dove
Biartz	Bilocate	Birdthrone	Bivouac	Black Atom	Black Cobra	Black Draugwath
Bias Authority	Bilox	Birkabein	Bizarr	Black Aurora	Black Coffee	Black Dust

Black Eden
Black Empire
Black Empire
Black Energy
Black Estora Ass
Black Eternity
Black Evil
Black Eye
Black Eye Riot
Black Fabula
Black Face of Evil
Black Faith
Black Fate
Black Fate
Black Fever
Black Fire
Black Flame
Black Flame (Of
  Satan)
Black Flower
Black Fog
Black Forest
Black Forest
Black Forest
Black Fortress
Black Friday
Black From the Pit
Black Frost
Black Fucking Doom
Black Funebre
Black Funeral
Black Funeral
Black Fury
Black Ghost
Black Ghost

Black Goat
Black Goat
Black Goat Attack
Black Goatsemen
Black Grave
Black Harlequin
Black Harmony
Black Harvest
Black Hawk
Black Haze
Black Head
Black Heaven
Black Heaven
Black Hell
Black Hill
Black Hole
Black Hole Generator
Black Hole Theory
Black Holiday
Black Holocaust
Black Horizon
Black Horizons
Black Horizons
Black Horsemen
Black Howling
Black Ice
Black Ice
Black Infinity
Black Invocation
Black Ivory
Black Jack
Black Jack Co
Black Jade
Black Jehovah
Black Jester

Black Katharsis
Black Knight
Black Knight
Black Kreek
Black Label Society
Black Ladies
Black Landscapes
Black League
Black Leaves
Black Legion
Black Lightning
Black Like Vengeance
Black Lodge
Black Lodge
Black Lotus
Black Magick
Black Majesty
Black Majesty
Black Majik Jesus
Black Manta
Black Market Fetus
Black Marsh
Black Masquerade
Black Mass
Black Mass
Black Mass
Black Mass of Absu
Black Mass
  Perversion
Black Mass Pervertor
Black Massacre
Black May
Black Messiah
Black Metal
Black Misanthropy

Black Moon
Black Moon
Black Moon Rising
Black Moon Rising
Black Moor
Black Moria
Black Mourners Veil
Black Mouton
Black Murder
Black Nazareth
Black Nebula
Black Night
Black Nocturnal
  Darkness
Black Nova
Black Obelisk
Black Obsession
Black Obsidian
Black Omen
Black Onyx
Black Orbit
Black Orchid
Black Order
Black Ozone
Black Palace
  Symphony
Black Paladin
Black Panther
Black Pathology
Black Patrons
Black Pearl
Black Pentagram
Black Pentecost
Black Plague
Black Prophecies

Black Prophecy
Black Prophets
Black Putrescence
Black Queen
Black Rain
Black Rain
Black Rain
Black Rain
Black Raven
Black Raven
Black Raven
Black Realm
Black Realm
Black Reign
Black Reign
Black Reign
Black Reign
  for the Ages
Black Riders
Black Rites
Black Ritual
Black River
Black River Project
Black Rose
Black Rose
Black Rose
Black Sabah
Black Sabbath
Black Sand
Black Sapphyre
Black Scrap Metal
Black Seas of Infinity
Black September
Black September
Black Shadow

Black Shape of Nexus
Black Sheep
Black Sheep
Black Shepherd
Black Shining Death
Black Silence
Black Silver
Black Simphony
Black Sin
Black Sister
Black Skies Burn
Black Solitude
Black Soul
Black Soul
Black Space
Black Spiral
Black Spiral
Black Steel
Black Stench
Black Stone Ritual
Black Storm Division
Black Subway
Black Succubi
Black Sugar
Black Sun
Black Sun
Black Sun
Black Sun
Black Sun
Black Sun
Black Sun City
Black Sunrise
Black Swan
Black Swan
Black Swan

Black Swords
Black Syfilis
Black Symphony
Black Syndrome
Black Task
Black Tear
Black Tears
Black Tears
Black Teeth
Black Terror
Black Terror
Black Thirteen
Black Thorn
Black Thorns
Black Thorns Lodge
Black Tiger
Black Tooth Grin
Black Torment
Black Torment
Black Torment
Black Torture
Black Tower
Black Treasure
Black Triangle
Black Tribe
Black Trinity
Black Trinity
Black Trip
Black Tusk
Black Twilight
Black Tyrant
Black Unicorn
Black Vein Prophecy
Black Velvet
Black Vengeance

Blaylök	Bleed in Vain	Blefergoth	Blind Horizon	Blindmann	Blo.Torch	Blood Cult
Blaze	Bleed of Hate	Bleich.	Blind Hostility	Blindness	Bloated	Blood Divine, The
Blaze	Bleed Someone Dry	Blended Sky	Blind Illusion	Blindraft	Bloated Carcass	Blood Drenched
Blaze Bailey	Bleed the Son	Bless The Fallen	Blind Jesus	BlindSeven	Blob	Blood Dries Black
Blaze Inside	Bleed the Tyrant	Bless the Silence	Blind Justice	Blindside	Blockade Runner	Blood Drive
Blaze of Passion	Bleeder	Blessed	Blind Justice	Blindsite Theory	Blockheads	Blood Duster
Blaze of Torment	Bleedfort	Blessed	Blind Legion	Blindspot A.D.	Blockheads	Blood Eagle
Blazemth	Bleedience	Blessed	Blind Man Kills	Blindways	Blod Besvimelse	Blood Emanation
Blazfemur	Bleeding	Blessed Agony	Blind Mirror	Bliss	Blodarv	Blood Emperor
Blazing Corpse	Bleeding	Blessed Are The Sick	Blind Mirror	Bliss of Flesh	Bloden-Wedd	Blood Farmers
Blazing Eternity	Bleeding	Blessed Death	Blind Obsession	Blistered Earth	Blodfest	Blood Feast
Blazing Guns	Bleeding	Blessed in Fire	Blind Petition	Blistered Palms	Blodfrost	Blood For Blood
Blazing Harp	Bleeding Art	Blessed in Sin	Blind Reality	Blitzenhamer	Blodhemn	Blood For Glory
Blazing Skies	Bleeding Aura	Blessed Realm	Blind Roller	Blitzer	Blodkarsk	Blood For The Breed
Blazing Thunder	Bleeding Black	Blessed Sickness	Blind Sight	Blitzkrieg	Blodshunger	Blood Freak
Blazing War Machine	Bleeding Corpse	Blessed Slaughter	Blind Sight	Blitzkrieg	Blodsoffer	Blood From Above
Blaznagar	Bleeding Display	Blessed Suicide	Blind Slime	Blitzkrieg	Blodsrit	Blood from the Breed
Blazon	Bleeding Eyes	Blessedbethyname	Blind Spite	Blitzkrieg	Blodtjern	Blood from the Soul
Blazpheme	Bleeding Faith	Blessing	Blind Stare	Blitzspeer	Blodulv	Blood Gnome
Bleak	Bleeding Fist	Blessing the Hogs	Blind Surgeon	Blitzz	Bloedakker	Blood Haven
Bleak Crowd	Bleeding Harmony	Blessings of Ruin	Blind Tempest	Blizard	Bloedklontering	Blood Hunt
Bleak Destiny	Bleeding Hate	Blessmon	Blind Truth	Blizkrig	Blohole	Blood Island Raiders
Bleak Forest	Bleeding Heart	Bletz	Blind Vengeance	Blizkrig	Bloke	Blood IV
Bleak House	Bleeding Heart	Blight	Blind Vision	Blizzard	Blokke	Blood Kharma
Bleak Shadows	Bleeding Horizon	Blighted Touch	Blind Witness	Blizzard	Blood	Foundation
Bleak Solitude	Bleeding in Black	Blind	Blindead	Blizzard	Blood & Time	Blood Legacy
Bleak Vision	Bleeding Mirror	Blind	Blinded	Blizzard	Blood Angel	Blood Lust
Bleakwail	Bleeding Organs	Blind Assassin	Blinded by Darkness	Blizzard	Blood Asylum	Blood Magic
Bleb Margo	Bleeding Sky	Blind Crusade	Blinded by Faith	Blizzard	Blood Circuit	Blood Mason
Bled	Bleeding Sky	Blind Demon	Blinded by Fear	Blizzard	Blood Clot	Blood Money
Bled Awake	Bleeding Sword	Blind Dog	Blinded Colony	Blizzard	Blood Conquest	Blood 'O Mary
Bleed	Bleeding Thorn	Blind Fury	Blinded Rain	Blizzard	Blood Count Zero	Blood Oath
Bleed	Bleeding Through	Blind Guardian	Blinder	Blizzard	Blood Coven	Blood Obsession
Bleed for Me	Bleeding Tide	Blind Hate	Blinding Fear	Blizzard	Blood Covenant	Blood of Cain
Bleed From Within	Bleeding Visions	Blind Hatred	Blindman	Blizzard Winter	Blood Covered	Blood Of Christ

Blood of Kings	Blood Tears	Bloodcurse	Bloodlust	Bloodshed	Bloodstained Coffin	Bloodwurm
Blood of Kingu	Blood Thirsty Death	Blooddawn	Bloodlust	Bloodshed	Bloodstained Dusk	Bloody
Blood of the Black Owl	Blood Thirsty Demons	Blooddawn	Bloodlust	Bloodshed	Bloodstained Memories	Bloody Altar
Blood Pool	Blood Tribe	Bloodfalls	Bloodlust	Bloodshed	Bloodstar	Bloody Anal Yeast Infection
Blood Quest	Blood Tsunami	Bloodfart	Bloodlust	Bloodshed	Bloodstone	Bloody Axes
Blood Quest	Blood Upon the Altar	Bloodfeast	Bloodlyne	Bloodshed Divine	Bloodstone	Bloody Blasphemy
Blood Rain	Blood Vengeance	Bloodfeast	BloodMist	Bloodshed Nihil	Bloodstone	Bloody Blossom
Blood Rainbow	Blood Victory	Bloodfeast	Bloodmoon	Blood-shedd	Bloodstone	Bloody Butcher
Blood Reaping	Blood Vigil	Bloodfeast A.D.	Bloodmoon	Bloodshedd	Bloodstone	Bloody Clerks
Blood Red Angel	Blood Vomit	Bloodflowers	Blood'n'Fire	Bloodshield	Bloodstorm	Bloody Climax
Blood Red Fog	Blood Warrior	Bloodflowerz	Bloodoline	Bloodshot Eyes	BloodStream	Bloody Creaze
Blood Red Sky	Blood Weeps	Bloodforge	Bloodpack	Bloodshot/BXL	Bloodstrength	Bloody Cross
Blood Red Throne	Blood Windy	BloodForge	Bloodpaint	Bloodshoteye	Bloodstruck	Bloody Cross
Blood Retch	Bloodandpus-fromtheudders	Bloodgasm	Bloodparade	Bloodshrine	Bloodsucker	Bloody Diarrhoea
Blood Ritual		Bloodgin	Bloodpath	Bloodsick	Bloodtaste	Bloody Gore
Blood Sessions	Bloodawn	Bloodgore	Bloodphemy	Bloodsin	Bloodtears	Bloody Hands
Blood Shed	Bloodaxe	Bloodhag	Bloodportal	Bloodsoaked	Bloodthirst	Bloody Harvest
Blood Shot Eye	Bloodbastard	Bloodhammer	Bloodrain	Bloodsoaked	Bloodthirst	Bloody Hell
Blood Shot Eye	Bloodbath	Bloodharvest	Bloodrain	Bloodsoaked	Bloodthirst	Bloody Herald
Blood Simple	Bloodbath	Bloodhorde	Bloodraised	Bloodsoaked	Bloodthirst	Bloody Maria
Blood Soaked Horror	Bloodbath	Bloodhorse	Bloodrealm	Bloodsoaked Glory	Bloodthirsty	Bloody Mary
Blood Spill	Bloodbath	Bloodian	Bloodred Eclipse	Bloodsöffer	Bloodthirsty Massacre	Bloody Mary
Blood Spitting	Bloodbath S.A.F.	Bloodland	Bloodred Hourglass	Bloodsoil		Bloody Panda
Blood Stain Child	Bloodboil	Bloodless	Bloodride	Bloodsoul	Bloodthorn	Bloody Passion
Blood Stained	Bloodbound	Bloodless	Bloodride	Bloodspattered Embrace	Bloodthrone	Bloody Phoenix
Blood Stained Dusk	Bloodbourne	Bloodlet	Bloodroot		Bloodtide XV	Bloody Pickaxe
Blood Stained Host	Bloodchurn	Bloodletting	Bloodrose	Bloodspell	Bloodwake	Bloody Psycho
Blood Star Halo	Bloodcifery	Bloodline	Bloodsaw Baphomet	Bloodsplattered Sledgehammer	Bloodwish	Bloody Revenge
Blood Star Oblivion	Bloodcow	Bloodline	Bloodseal		Bloodwolf	Bloody Ritual
Blood Storm	Bloodcraving	Bloodline to Zero	Bloodshed	Bloodsport	Bloodwoods	Bloody Ritual
Blood Streams	Bloodcum	Bloodlined Calligraphy	Bloodshed	Bloodstain	Bloodwork	Bloody Satisfaction
Blood Sucker	Bloodcum	Bloodlord	Bloodshed	Bloodstain	Bloodwraith	Bloody Scream
Blood Sundae	Bloodcurdling Blandishments	Bloodloss	Bloodshed	Bloodstained	Bloodwritten	Bloody Sign
Blood Sunday		Bloodlust	Bloodshed	Bloodstained	Bloodwritten	Bloody Six
			Bloodshed	Blood-Stained		

Bosque Pagão
Boss
Boss Tweed
Bosse de Nage
Bossk
Botch
Both Guns Blazing
Bothers
Bothildir
Botnia
Bottled
Bottom
Bottom Line
Botulism
Botulistum
Boulder
Boulevard
Bound
Bound and Gagged
Bound by Blasphemy
Bound by Entrails
Bound By Flesh
Bound For Glory
Bound For Tomb
Bound in Entrails
Bound in
   Human Flesh
Boundless Cruelty
Bourbon
Bow Wow
Bowel
Bowel Fetus
Bowel Rupture
Bowel Smasher
Bowel Stew

Bowelism
Bowelmouth
Bowelrot
Bowels of Hell
Bowels Out
Bowelz Out
Bowles
Bowlscraper
Bowtome
Boxer
Bozzio Levin Stevens
Brabazon
Braced For Nails
Brahama
Brahma
Brain
Brain Damage
Brain Damaged Kids
Brain Dead
Brain Dead
Brain Dead
Brain Death
Brain Decay
Brain Drill
Brain Forest Rytual
Brain Gauge
Brain Implosion
Brain in a Cage
Brain Melting
Brain Murder
Brain Police
Brain Police
Brain Sodomy
Brain Storming
Brain Surgeons

Brainamputated
Brainbleed
Brainblood
Braincasket
Brainchild
Brainchoke
Braindamage
Braindance
Braindead
Braindead
BrainDead
Braindead
Braindead
Braindeadz
Braindeath
Braindeath
Brainfade
Brainfever
Brainicide
Brainless
Brainless
Brainoil
Brainpeaches
Brainsane
Brainshake
Brainsic
Brainsic
Brainstorm
Brainstorm
Brainstorm
Brainstorm
Brainstorm
Brainstorm
Brainstormy

Braintoy
Braintrust
Braintrust
Brainwalk
Brainwash
Brainwash
Brainwashed
Brainwashed
Brainwashing
Brainwave
Bralalalala
Bran Barr
Brand New Page
Brand New Sin
Brand X Savior
Branded
Branded Skin
Brandhaard
Branding
Brandpest
Branikald
Branstock
Brant
Braquemard
Brasil Papaya
Brat
Brats
Brave
Brave
Brave Bomber
Braveheart
Braveride
Bravery
Bravus
Braxator

Brayndance
Brazen
Brazen
Brazen
Brazzil
Breach of Ethics
Breadwinner
Break Faith
Break Point
Break the Ice
Break the Silence
Break Your Fist
Breakage Rising
Breakdown
Breakdown
Breakdown
Breakdust
Breaker
Breaker
Breaker
Breaker
Breaker
Breaking Beads
Breaking Silence
Breaking the
   Fourth Wall
Breakneck
Breakout
Breakpoint
Breath of Beherith
Breath of Chaos
Breath of Life
Breath of Sorrows
Breath of the Dying
Breath Stealer

Breathe One's Last
Breather Resist
BreathingViolenceIN
Breathless
Breathless
Breathless
Breathstealer
Brecha
Bredor
Breed
Breed
Breed
Breed Machine
Breed of Darkness
Breed of War
Breeding Chamber
Breeding Fear
Breeding Fear
Breeze Least
Bregma
Breizh Occult
Brejn Dedd
Brenoritvrezorkre
Brent Av Frost
Breschdleng
Breslau
Brethren
Brett Pit
Bretwaldas of
   Heathen Doom
Brewed & Canned
Brewmaster
Brian
Brian
Briar

Briargh
Brick
Brick Bath
Brick Mistress
Bride
Bride Adorned
Bride of the Monster
Bridge of Tears
Bridge to Solace
Brief Respite
Brietal
Brigada Slam
Bright Blade
Bright Ophidia
Brightlights
Brightness
Brilien
Brilliant Coldness
Brimstone
Brimstone
Bring Me the Horizon
Bring Out Your Dead
Bring Your
   Own Knife
Briselas
Brisen
Britannia
Britney
Britny Fox
Britton
Brix
Broadmoor
Broadside
Brob
Broca's Aphasia

C Average	C.O.E.
C of E	C.O.S.
C.A.I.N.	C.O.T.L.O.D.
C.A.R.N.E.	C.P.R.
C.A.S.H.	C.R.Y.
C.C.C.	C.S.S.O.
C.C.S.	C.V.I.
C.D.D.	Caacrinolas
C.I.A.	Caamos
C.L.G.	Caarcrinolas
C.M.P.	Cabal
C.O.A.	Cabal
C.O.D.	Cabal
C.O.D.	Cabal
C.O.D.	Cabal
C.O.D.E.	Cabal

Cabal
Cabal a.d.
Cabala
Cabalistic
Cabaret for Bereaved
Cabeza de Martillo
Cabrero
Caccamon
Cachorro Grande
Cachtice
Cacodaemon
Cacophony
Cacotopia
Cacumen
Cad
Cadaber Incubador
Cadacross
Cadafalso
Cadalso
Cadaver
Cadaver Corpse
Cadaver Ecogenics
Cadaver Inc
Cadaver Incubador
Cadaver Mutilator
Cadavera
Cadavere de Tortugas
Cadaveria
Cadaveric
Cadaveric
    Crematorium
Cadaveric
    Engorgement
Cadaveric Hunter
Cadaveric Incest

Cadaveric Incubator
Cadaveric Stench
Cadavericmutilator
Cadaverment
Cadaverous
Cadaverous
Cadaverous
    Condition
Cadaverous
    Dilaceration
Cadaverous Incarnate
Cadaverous
    Putrescence
Cadaverous Quartet
Cadaveryne
Cadavrosity
Cadavrul
Cade
Cadena Perpétua
Caducity
Caed Dhu
Caedeath
Caedere
Caedere
Caedes
Caedes
Caedes
Caedes
Caedes
Caedes Vocum
Caelum Adustum
Caelvm
Caer Gwydyon
Caer Ibormeith
Caerimonium

Caesarean
Caesarean Section
Cafagiem
Cage
Cage of Serenity
Caibalion
Caid Deceit
Caifaz
Caillech
Caiman
Cain
Cain
Caina
Cain's Alibi
Cair Rigor
Caithness
Caitiff
Caje
Cakewet
Caladbolg
Calamine
Calb O'Roth
Caldera
Calderone
Caldwell
Caledonian
Caledonian
Cales
Cales
Calhoun Conquer
Caliban
Caliban
Calibern
Calibos
Calibra

Calibre 38
Calico
Calico System
California Smile
Caliga
Caliginosity
Caliginosus Obscurus
Caliginous
Caligula
Caligula
Caligulae Crucis
Caligvla
Call ov Unearthly
Call to Arms
Call Us What You Will
Callahan
Callejero
Callenish Circle
Callicles
Calligery
Callisto
Calloused
Calm
Calm
Calm
Calm Hatchery
Calmsite
Calslagen
Calth
Calvaire
Calvaria
Calvaria
Calvário
Calvarium
Calvarium

Calvarium
Calvarium Funestus
Calvary
Calvary
Calvary
Calvary Death
Calvin Korpse
Camargue
Camarosmith
Cambian Dawn
Cambodian
    Powercunt
Camel of Doom
Camelot
Camelot
Camembert
Cameron Vegas
Camilla Rhodes
Camlann
Cammelot
Camorra
Camorra
Camorristas
Camos
Camos
Camp Loco
Campo de Mayo
Camulos
Camulus
Can Abyss
Canaan
Cancelled
Cancer
Cancer Source
Cancerbero

Cancrena
Cancrena
Candela
Candela
Candelabra
Candelabro
Candelora
Candescence
Candiria
Candiru
Candle Serenade
CandleLight
Candlemass
Candy Striper
  Death Orgy
Cangren
Cangrena
Canibale
Canifraz
Caninus
Canis Luna
Canis Lupus
Canker
Canker
Canker Bit Jesus
Cankered Corpse
Cannabis Corpse
Cannabis Sativa
Cannabus of Mourn
Cannabyss
Cannibal Corpse
Cannon
Cannon Vengeance
Canonis
Canopic Jar

Canopy
Canora
Cans
Canserberia
Cant
Cantar
Cantar
Cantára
Cantas Ad Mortuos
Cantata Sangui
Cantens Mortem
Cantus Bestiae
Cantus Infame
Canvas Solaris
Canvasion
Canvasser
Canyon Creep
Caos
Caos
Caos
Caos Dementia
Cap de Craniu
Capacity
Capazo
Capdetrons
Capela das Almas
Capellan
Capharnaum
Capharnaum
Capitalist War
  Machine
CapitisDamnare
Capitollium
Cappanera
Capra Hircus

Capri Sancti
Capricorn
Capricorn
Capricorn
Capricorn
Capricorns
Capricornus
Captain Cleanoff
Captain Flint
Captain Gutted
Captain Trips
Captivity
Captivus Diaboli
Captor
Captor
Captura
Captured Dreams
Carach Angren
Caramba Bella
Carat
Caravela
Caravellus
Carbide
Carbon
Carbon Cage
Carbon Deposit
Carbonized
Carbonized
Carbonized 16 Year
  Old Victim
Carbure
Carcan
Carcariass
Carcaroht
Carcase Inc.

Carcass
Carcass Lyrics
  Dictionary
Carcassinova
Carcava
Carcava
Carceri
Carcharodon
Carcharoth
Carcharoth
Carcharoth
Carcinogen
Carcinogen
Carcinogenic
Carcinoma
Carcinosi
Carcrash
Cardamon
Cardania
Cardavercus
Cardiac
Cardiac Arrest
Cardiac Arrest
Cardiac Cease
Cardiac Compression
Cardiac Necropsy
Cardiak
Cardiant
Cardinal
Cardinal
Cardinal Sin
Cardinal Sin
Cardinale
Cardiovascular
  Sub-Hypothermia

Care of Souls
Caress
Caress
Caress
Cargo
Caricature
Carillon
Carina Alfie
Carisma
Carking Massacre
Carl August
  Tidemann
Carl Turns Fifty
Carmegfal
Carmilla Morte
Carmina
Carmina Noctis
Carnacain
Carnage
Carnage
Carnage
Carnage
Carnage
Carnage
Carnage
Carnage
Carnage
Carnage
Carnage
Carnage
Carnage Valley
Carnage666
Carnal
Carnal
Carnal Apostle
Carnal Creation

Carnal Decay
Carnal Decimate
Carnal Delusion
Carnal Diafragma
Carnal Dissection
Carnal Feelings
Carnal Forge
Carnal Grief
Carnal Leftovers
Carnal Lust
Carnal Rapture
Carnal Redemption
Carnal Rites
Carnal Sickness
Carnal Tomb
Carnalfeast
Carnality
Carnality
Carnapple
Carnarium
Carnaticum
Carnavage
Carneous
Carneus
Carniburo
Carniça
Carniceira
Carnifex
Carnifex
Carnifex
Carnifex
Carnification
Carnificina
Carnified
Carnival Creation

Carnival in Coal
Carnival of Carnage
Carnival Of Souls
Carnivean
Carnivora
Carnivore
Carnivore Diprosopus
Carnivore Horde
Carnivore Mind
Carnivorous
Carnivorous
Carnivorous Cadaver
Carnivorous Vagina
Carnun
Carnun Rising
Caro Maledicta
Caroline Blue
Caronte
Caronthe
Carpadium
Carpathia
Carpathia
Carpathia
Carpathian
Carpathian Dream
Carpathian Forest
Carpathian Full Moon
Carpathian Gate
Carpathian Lords
Carpatia
Carpatus
Carpe Diem
Carpe Diem
Carpe Diem Envy
Carpe Mortem

Carpe Noctem	Carved in Stone	Castigation	Catacomb	Cataria	Catharsis	Caustic
Carpe Noctum	Casablanca	Castigation	Catacombs	Catarnet	Catharsis	Caustic
Carpe Tenebrum	Casbah	Castillion	Catacombs of Sodomy	Catarot	Catharsis	Caustic
Carpediem	Cascabel	Castillos de Cristal	Catacumba	Catarrh	Catharsis Nocturna	Caustic
Carpocrade	Cascade	CastInStone	Catafalc	Catarrh	Cathedral	Caustic Anal Vomit
Carpticon	Cased	Castle	Catafalque	Catarrhal	Cathedral Canceria	Caustic Celebratum
Carrasco	Casket	Castle	Catafalque	Catarsis	Catherine La Voisin	Caustic Novena
Carrie	Casket	Castle Blood	Catafalque	Catasexual Urge	Catherines Cathedral	Caustic Strike
Carried the Weight	Casket	Castle in the Air	Cataglyphis	Motivation	Catheter	Caustic Thought
Carrier Flux	Casket Garden	Castle of Pain	Catagramma Lepta	Catashaná	Catheter	Caustic Velocity
Carrion	Casket of Dreams	Castle of Thorns	Catal Höyük	Catastrophe	Catholicon	Cauterized
Carrion	Casket Slumber	Castle Party	Catalepsia	Catastrophe	Catrabbits	Cauterizer
Carrion	Casketgarden	Castle Ruins	Catalepsy	Catastrophe	Catrabbits	Cauteror
Carrion	Casper Openface	Castle Well	Catalepsy	Catastrophic	Cattle Decapitation	Cautivo
Carrion	Cassandra	Castlevania	Catalepsy	Catastrophy	Catwitch	Cavalar
Carrion	Cassandra	Castration	Catalepsy	Catatonic	Catyph	Cavalince
Carrion Carnage	Cassiopeia	Castrator	Catalepsy	Schizophrenia	Cauchemar	Cavaticus
Carrion Crawler	Cassiopeia	Castrofate	Catalepsy	Catch 22	Cauda Draconis	Cave In
Carrion Ghost	Cassiopeia	Castrum	Catalepsy	Catch Rag	Cauldran	Caveat
Carrion Lord	Cassis	Castrum	Catalepsy	Catchfire	Cauldron	Cavefish
Carrion	Cassle	Castrum	Catalepsy	Catedral	Cauldron	Caveman
Necrophagous	Cast Asunder	Castrum	Catalepsy	Catenas	Cauldron	Cavernicolas
Carrion of Torrent	Cast Away	Casual Silence	Cataleptic	Catenatam Lucem	Cauldron	Cavernoma
Carrion of Vigrid	Cast From Eden	Casually Mephitic	Cataleptic	CatEye	Cauldron	Cavevomit
Carrioned	Cast in Silence	Casuist	Catalexie	Cathacomb	Cauldron Black Ram	Cavillator
Carslay	Cast in Stone	Casus Belli	Catalyst	Cathalepsy	Cauldron Born	Cavity
Carthago	Cast of Shadows	Casus Belli	Catalyst	Cathanion	Cauldron of Puke	Cavum
Carthago	Cast the Stone	Cat of Nine Tails	Catamenia	Cathar	Cause and Effect	Cayne
Carthasis	Castaway	Catabasis	Catamenia Oulu	Catharcyst	Cause For Effect	Cea Serin
Carthaun	Castaway	Catabolignes	Catamount	Catharsis	Cause of Death	Cease of Breeding
Cartilage	Castigador	Cataclysm	Cataphract	Catharsis	Cause of Death:	Cease to Exist
Cartilage	Castigate	Cataclysm	Cataplexy	Catharsis	Suicide	Ceasefire
Carve	Castigate	Cataclysmic Avatar	Catapuration	Catharsis	Cause of Divorce	Cebren-Khal
Carved Fetus	Castigate	Catacomb	Cataract	Catharsis	Causemos	Cedamus
Carved in Flesh	Castigation	Catacomb	Cataracta	Catharsis	Causing Chaos	Cegador

Cities of Sleep
Citizen Dick
Citron
City of God
City Weezle
Civil Carnage
Civil Defiance
Civil Disobedience
Civil Ruin
Civilization One
Civitas Inferni
CJSS
Clad In Darkness
Clagg
Clair de Lune Morte
Clair Obscur
Clairvoya
Clairvoyant
Clamath
Clamatorius
Clamor
Clampdown
Clamus
Clan of Chaos
Clandestine
Clandestine Blaze
Clangforge
Clangor
Clanraven
Clanrock
Clanrock
Clapatria
Claptrap
Clarity
Clashing Blade

Classic Rage
Classica
Classmate
Claude Zircle
Claudio Marciello
Claustro
Claustrofobia
Claustrophobia
Claustrophobia
Claustrophobia
Claustrophobia
Clauz
Clavion
Claw
Clawfinger
Clawn
Clayforge
Clayman
Claymords
Claymore
Claymore
Claymore
Claymore
Claymore
Claymore
Clean Flesh
Clear as Mud
Clemency
Clenched Fist
Cleopatra
Clientelle
Clifton
Climate
Climax
Cline's Mind

Clinging to the Trees
    of a Forest Fire
Clinic
Clinic Carnage
Clinical
Clinicamente Morti
Clip
Clit Ripper
Cliteater
Cliteater
Clitorture
Cloacal Kiss
Cloakwheel
Clockwork
Clonaeon
Clone the Fragile
Clonecircle
Cloon d.C.
Closed Casket
Closed Eye Visions
Closed Eye Visuals
Closer
Closer Than Kin
Closing
Clot
Cloth Tape
Clotted Symmetric
    Sexual Organ
Cloud Forest
Cloud Nine
Cloudburst
Clouds Disperse
Clouds Turned Black
Cloudscape
Cloven Hoof

Clover
Clover Haze
Clown Alley
Club Hell
Clubber Lang
Clusterfux
Clusterhead
Clutch Mental
    Hospital
Clyson
CM
CMKY
Co:ßmik
Coagulated Blood
Coagulation
Coaie Pe Zacusca
Coal Chamber
Coal Mine Canary
Coalesce
Coalition
Coan Teen
Coarse
Coathanger Abortion
Cobalt
Cobalto
Cobi's Death
Cobolt 60
Cobra
Cobra
Cobra
Cobra
Cobra Verde
Cocaine Cowboys
Cock and Ball Torture
Cock-Knocker 666

Cocklips
Cockney Rejects
Cockroach
Cockroachs
Cocobat
Cocytus
Coda
Code
Code Black
Code Black
Code of Honour
Code of Perfection
Code of Silence
Code of Silence
Code of the Zodiac
Code Red
Code Red
Code Red
Codename:Wingless
Codeon
Codex Gigas
Coding Sequence
Codru
Coercion
Coercive
Coffee Grinders
Coffin
Coffin
Coffin
Coffin Birth
Coffin Birth
Coffin Born
Coffin Dancer
Coffin Fodder
Coffin for Mary

Coffin Frost
Coffin Fuck
Coffin Grinder
Coffin of Lament
Coffin Syrup
Coffin Texts
Coffinfeeder
Coffins
Cofradía
Cogency
Cogneedle
    Funhouse
Coherent
    Liquid Form
Cohol
Cohort
Cohort
Coilback
Coine
Coitus
Coitus Interruptus
Colapso
Colcothar
Cold
Cold Blasphemy
Cold Blood
Cold Blood
Cold Blood
Cold Colours
Cold Corrosion
Cold Cowshed
Cold Embrace
Cold Empire
Cold Empty Hall
Cold Eternity

Cold Evocation
Cold Existence
Cold Fire
Cold Fullmoon
Cold Grey Dawn
Cold Grows
    the Season
Cold Hands
    of Autumn
Cold Insanity
Cold Meat
Cold Moon
Cold Moon
Cold Mourning
Cold Northern
    Vengeance
Cold Passion
Cold Reality
Cold Steel
Cold Void
Cold Void
Cold War Survivor
Coldblood
Coldblooded
Coldblooded
Colder Than Moon
Colder thy Kiss
Coldhand
Coldness
Coldseed
Coldwar
Coldway
Coldworker
ColdWorld
Colemesis

Corrigenda
Corroded
Corroosion
Corrosão
Corrosão Caótica
Corrose
Corrosif
Corrosion
Corrosion
Corrosion of
   Conformity
Corrosive
Corrosive
Corrosive
Corrosive
Corrosive
Corrupt
Corrupt Soul
Corrupt the
   Righteous
Corrupted
Corrupted
Corrupted
Corrupted
Corrupted Grave
Corrupted Innocence
Corrupted Melody
Corrupted Mutation
Corrupted Reputation
Corruption
Corruption
Corruption
Corruption
Corruption
Corruption
Corruption Inc.

Corruption of Virtue
Corruptor
Corrupture
Corruptus
Corsa Noshtra
Corsario
Corsário
Corsario Negro
Cortege
Cortege
Cortège Funèbre
Cortez
Cortina de Ferro
Cortisol
Corum
Corvo
Corvus
Corvus
Corvus Corax
Corvus Morti(s)
Corwen
Cosmic Church
Cosmic Death
Cosmic Haze
Cosmic Heresy
Cosmic Invaders
Cosmic Spell
Cosmic Sphere
Cosmic
   Transmigration
Cosmical Aura
Cosmicsphere
Cosmo Awen
Cosmosquad
Cospectu Mortis

Costra
Côte d'Aver
Cothurnus
Cough
Could Be Worse
Couldron
Council of the Fallen
Count De Nocte
Count My Fears
Count Nosferatu
Count Nosferatu
   Kommando
Count Raven
Count Sinister
Count Von Count
Countdown
Countdown Zero
Counter World
   Experience
Counterblast
Counterbore
CounterClockwise
CounterParts
CounterShaft
Countess
Countess Bathory
County Medical
   Examiners
County Morgue
Coup De Grace
Coup de Grace
Courage
Courageous
Couragous
Course Death

Course of Anger
Course of Empire
Course of Fate
Court Jester
Court of Azomor
Coúrthouse
Courtyard
Cova
Cova Rasa
Covariance
Coven
Coven
Coven
Coven Curse
Coven of the Worm
Covenance
Covenant
Covenant
Covenant
Covenant
Covens
Covenslayer
Coventide
Coverage
Coverage
Covered in Ashes
Covet the Knife
Coward
Cowhandler
Coz
CP24
CR
Crab Phobia
Cracen
Crack

Crack Addict
Crack Buster
Crack Down
Crack Jaw
Crack Up
Crackdown
Crackdust
Cracked Mirror
Crackerjack Tattoo
Crackwhore
Cradle of Filth
Cradle to Grave
Craft
Craft Diner
Crag
Craig Goldy's Ritual
Craine
Cráneo
Crang
Cranial
Cranial Devourment
Cranial Dust
Cranial Incisored
Cranial Nectar
Cranial Rectosis
Cranial Torment
Cranial Torment
Cranioclast
Craniology
Craniosacral
Craniotomy
Cranitripsy
Cranium
Cranium
Cranium

Cranium
Cranthorpe
Crapulas
Crapulence
Crapulence
Crapulence
Crash
Crash
Crash
Crash And Burn
Crash Noise
Crash Test
Crashdaf
Crashdiet
Crashed
Crater
Craterface
Craven Idol
Craving
Craving Angel
Craving for Valusia
Craving Gore
Crawcell
Crawl
Crawl
Crawl "420"
Crawler
Crawler
Crawline
Crawling Death
Crawling Due
Crawling Through
   Infinity
Crawlspace
Crawlspace

Crawlspace
Crawlspace
Crawlspace
Craydawn
Crazer
Crazy About Silence
Crazy Band
Crazy Cabuxa
Crazy Lazy
Creamface
Creamstar
Created to Kill
Creation
Creation D.
Creation is
   Crucifixion
Creation of Death
Creation of
   Destruction
Creations Demise
Creation's Ode
Creations Tears
Creative Urge
Creative Waste
Creature
Creature
Creature
Creature
Creature of Habit
Creatures of Dawn
Crebain
Credence
Credic
Credo
Credo

Creed	Cremation	Crescendo of Pain	Crimson	Crimson Steel	Cristeros	Cromlech
Creed	Cremator	Crescent	Crimson Altar	Crimson Steel	Cristian Rigon	Cromlech
Creedless Minds	Cremator	Crescent	Crimson Black	Crimson Sun	Criteria	Cromlech
Creep	Cremator	Crescent Shadow	Crimson Blade	Crimson Sunset	Criteria	Cromlech
Creep Colony	Crematorial Death	Crescent Shield	Crimson Bloodthorns	Crimson Tears	Criterion	Cromlech
Creep Colony	Crematorian	Cresdence	Crimson Chaos	Crimson Tears	Criterios	Cromlech
CreeperDeath	Crematorio	Cresent	Crimson Dawn	Crimson Tears	Criterivm	Cromlech
Creepfog	Crematorio	Crest of Darkness	Crimson Dawn	Crimson Thorn	Critical Assault	Cromlech
Creepin' Death	Crematório	Crestfallen	Project	Crimson Winds	Critical Damage	Cromm Cruac
Creeping	Crematorium	Crestfallen	Crimson Death	CrimsonSkull	Critical Death	Cromm Cruaich
Creeping Death	Crematorium	Crestfallen	Crimson Death	Criogenia	Critical Error	Cromok
Creeping Devastation	Crematorium	Cretin	Crimson Evenfall	Crionic	Critical Mass	Cromonic
Creeping Maid	Crematorium	Cretin	Crimson Fall	Crionic	Critical Mass	Cromwell
Creeping Vengeance	Crematorium	Cretinous Breed	Crimson Falls	Crionics	Critical Point	Cromwell
Creepmime	Crematory	Cretoria	Crimson Fire	Crionics	Critical State	Cromwell
Creepozoid	Crematory	Crevasse	Crimson Garden	Cripper	Criva	Crone
Creepshow	Crematory	Criba	Crimson Glory	Cripple	Criven	Cronian
Crefetus	Crematory	Crienium	Crimson Jimson	Cripple Bastards	Crize	Cronic
Crehate	Crematory	Cries on Blood	Crimson Lotus	Cripple Christ	Crna Udovica	Cronic Disorder
Cremador	Crematory	Crifotoure Satanarda	Crimson Massacre	Cripple Crew	Crnobog	Cronium Mare
Cremain	Creófago	Crikey	Crimson Messiah	Cripta Oculta	Croam	Cronos
Cremains	Creon	Crillson	Crimson Midwinter	Crisalida	Croatan	Cronos
Cremaster	Creophagous	Crime	Crimson Moon	Crisandemia	Croatan	Cronos
Cremate	Creozoth	Crime Academy	Crimson Moonlight	Crises	Crocell	Cronos
Cremated	Crepar	Crimen	Crimson Nightfall	Crisis	Crodonium	Cronos
Cremated	Creperum	Crimen Exceptum	Crimson Orchid	Crisis	Crodor	Cronos Titan
Cremated Souls	Crepitation	Criminal	Crimson Red	Crisis	Crom	Cronus
Cremation	Crepitus	Criminal Christ	Crimson Relic	Crisis	Crom	Croon
Cremation	Creptum	Criminal Element	Crimson Roots	Crisis de Fe	Crom	Cropment
Cremation	Crepuscular	Criminal Hate	Crimson Scythe	Crisis Never Ends	Crom	Croque-Mort
Cremation	Decadence	Criminal Judge	Crimson Shadows	Cristal	Crom Cruach	Croskill
Cremation	Crepuscularia	Criminal Justice	Crimson Shroud	Cristal y Acero	Crom Dubh	Cross
Cremation	Crepuscule	Criminal Vagina	Crimson Sky	Cristalys	Cromb	Cross
Cremation	Crepuscule	Criminally Insane	Crimson Sky	Cristandade	Cromkruach	Cross Bones
Cremation	Crépuscule Hivernal	Crimson	Crimson Sleep	em Chamas	Cromlech	Cross Borns
Cremation	Crepusculum					

◄ Cwn Annwn

◁ Cyaegha

Cyan
Cyan Bloodbane
Cyanid
Cyanid
Cyanide
Cyanide
Cyanide Baptism
Cyanide Breed
Cyanide Soul
Cyanodium
Cyanosis
Cyanotic
Cyanure
Cybele
Cyber Angel
Cyber Baphomet
Cyberchrist
Cybergrind
Cyberhed
Cyberya
Cyborg
Cycle Sluts From Hell
Cycles
Cyclic Creation
Cyclone
Cyclone P.
Cyclone Temple
Cyclope
Cyclophenia
Cyclopia
Cyclops
Cyclops
Cyclosis
Cyco Miko
Cycorax

Cydhie Genoside
Cydne Raven
Cydonia
Cydonia
Cydonian
Cygnet of
    Darkness
Cygnus Loop
Cygnus Rift
Cyhiriaeth
Cyhyreath
Cyklon
Cyklon-B
Cylidian
Cymbiotic
Cymophane
Cyndustry
Cynerys
Cyness
Cynge
Cynic
Cynic
Cynical Bastard
Cynical Limit
Cynicism
Cynicon
Cyperus
Cypher
Cypher Seer
Cyphoria
Cyphosis
Cyprian
Cypruss
Cyrcle IX
Cyrish

Cyrka
Cyrograph
Cyrus Zain
Cyruss
Cyst
Cyst
Cysted
Cystic Dysentery
Cysticerosis
Cystifelleus
    Introspection
CYT
Cythadel
Cytheran Theory
Cythraul
Cythraul
Cythraul
Cythrawl
Cythrawl
Cyttorak
Czakan
Czar
Czarci Œwit
Czernoknizhnik
Czort

◈

D. Tendency	D.I.Y.
D.A.D.	D.M.C.
D.A.M.	D.N.O.
D.A.M.N.	D.N.R.
D.A.R.	D.O.C.
D.A.V.	D.O.D. 333
D.B.C.	D.O.M.
D.C. Lacroix	D.O.T.A.C.
D.C.M.	D.R.E.P.
D.D.T.	D.R.I.
D.D.T.	D.R.Y.
D.F.C.	D.S.K.
D.H.	D.T. Seizure
D.H.N.	D.T.W.
D.I.E.	D.V.C.
D.I.V.	Da Capo

Da Vang
Daargesin
Daath
Dachnavar
Dadarioth
Daedalion
Daedalous
Daedalus
Daedalus
Daedeloth
Daedeloth
Daedeloth
Dæmentia
Dæmentia
Dæmentia
Daemogorgon
Daemon
Daemon
Daemon
Daemon Est Deus Inversus
Daemonarch
Daemonbrahms
Dæmones Imperium
Daemongrinder
Daemonheim
Daemonhorn
Daemonia Nymphe
Daemoniaca
Daemonic Alchemy
Daemonic Possessions
Daemonicide
Daemonicium
Daemonicus

Daemonicus
Daemoniis
Daemonium
Daemonium
Daemonius
Daemonlord
Daemonolatreia
Daemonolatria
Daemonolith
Daemons Embrace
Daemonum
Daemonus
Daemora
Daemos
Daemusinem
Daeonia
Daevas
Daff
Dafne
Dag Mora
Daga
Dagalur
Dagas
Dagger
Dagger
Dagger
Dagger of the Mind
Daggerfalls
DaggerSpawn
Daghda
Dagnes
Dagoba
Dagon
Dagon
Dagon

Dagon
Dagon
Dagor
Dagor
Dagor Dagorath
Dagorath
Dagorlad
Dagorlad
Dagorquest
Dagoth
Dagoth Ur
Dahlia's Tear
Dahmer
Dahmer
Dahmer
Dahmerized
DAI
Daigoro
Daij
Daily Reign
Daily Terroristen
Daimon
Daimon
Daimones
Daimonion
Daimonion
Daimonion
Daimoth
Daisy Cutter
Daisy Mayhem
Daitya
Dakon
Dakria
Dakrua
Dakrya

Dakryon
Dakryon
Daksha
Daksinroy
Daktal
Dale Blazing
Dali's Dilemma
Dalkhu
Dalmerot's Kingdom
Dalriada
Dam
Dãm
Dama Blanca
Dama Feudal
Dama Negra
Damaar
Damacles
DAMAD
Damaen
Damage
Damage
Damage
Damage
Damage
Damage
Damage
Damage
Damage Case
Damage Done
Damage Done
Damage Done
Damage Factor
Damage Factory
Damage Inc.
Damage OverDose

Damaged
Damaged
Damaged Dreams
Damaged Justice
Damaged Skull
Damageplan
Damager
Damarill
Damascus
Damascus
Damascus Steel
Damask
Damballa
Damcyan
Dame en Noir
Damien
Damien
Damien
Damien
Damien
Damien
Damien
Damien Black
Damien Breed
Damien Kross
Damien Lee Thorr
Damien Steele
Damien Storm
Damien Thorne
Daminor
Dammaj
Dammercide
Dammerung
Damn Nation
Damn Nation

◀ Damn Shark

Dark Insurrection
Dark Intentions
Dark Inversion
Dark Knight
Dark Knight
Dark Knights
Dark Label
Dark Land
Dark Lay Still
Dark Legion
Dark Legion
Dark Legion
Dark Legion
Dark Legions
Dark Liaison
Dark Light
Dark Liturgy
Dark Lord
Dark Lunacy
Dark Lunacy
Dark Lust
Dark Majesty
Dark Man Shadow
Dark Manthra
Dark Martyr
Dark Mass
Dark Master
Dark Matter
Dark Messiah
Dark Mighty Thought
Dark Millennium
Dark Minion
Dark Mirror
Dark Mirror
  ov Tragedy
Dark Mission

Dark Mist
Dark Monarch
Dark Monarchy
Dark Moor
Dark Morbid Death
Dark Mordor
Dark Mutation
Dark Mystery
Dark Mythology
Dark Nightmare
Dark Nights Behest
Dark Nimbus
Dark Noise
Dark North
Dark North
Dark Nova
Dark O Malex
Dark Oasis
Dark Obscenity
Dark Obsession
Dark Omen
Dark Opera
Dark Opera
Dark Opera
Dark Opus
Dark Order
Dark Overlord
Dark Paradise
Dark Paramount
Dark Path
Dark Period
Dark Pestilence
Dark Philosophy
Dark Phoenix
Dark Poetry

Dark Preacher
Dark Predestination
Dark Premonition
Dark Princess
Dark Procession
Dark Prodigy
Dark Prophecies
Dark Prophecy
Dark Prophecy
Dark Prophecy
Dark Psychosis
Dark Quarterer
Dark Rain
Dark Ravage
Dark Reality
Dark Realm
Dark Rebellion
Dark Reflections
Dark Region
Dark Reign
Dark Reign
Dark Reign
Dark Reign
Dark Remains
Dark Requiem
Dark Requiem
Dark Rhapsody
Dark Rise
Dark Ritual
Dark Ritual
Dark Ritual
Dark Rivers Flow
Dark Ruins
Dark Salad
Dark Sanctuaire

Dark Sanctuary
Dark Satan
Dark Savior
Dark Season
Dark Season
Dark Season
Dark Seasons
Dark Secret
Dark Seduction
Dark Sendon
Dark Sensation
Dark Seraf
Dark Serenity
Dark Serpent
Dark Shades
Dark Shadow
Dark Shift
Dark Side
Dark Side
Dark Sign
Dark Silence
Dark Slaughter
Dark Society
Dark Sorcery
Dark Soul
Dark Soul Project
Dark Spirits
Dark Star
Dark Star Kill
Dark Storm
Dark Story
Dark Story
Dark Suffering
Dark Suns
Dark Supremacy

Dark Symphonies
Dark Tales
Dark Tales
Dark Templar
Dark Templar
Dark the Suns
Dark Thunder
Dark Tomorrow
Dark Towers
Dark Tranquillity
Dark Transfixion
Dark Tribe
Dark Trinity
Dark Truth
Dark Tyrant
Dark Union
Dark Veil
Dark Vein
Dark Views
Dark Virgin
Dark Vision
Dark War
Dark White
Dark Wing
Dark Winter
Dark Wire
Dark Wisdom
Dark Wizard
Dark Woodoo
DarkAge
Darkager
Darkager
Darkaltar
Darkane
Darkani

Darkanimal
Darkart
DarkBlack
Darkcide
Darkcide
Darkcide
Darkcreed
Darkcrowned
DarkCrucifix
Darkdayrising
Darkemist
Darkempire
DarkEmpire
Darken
Darken
Darken
Darken
Darken
Darken My Grief
Darken Solis
Darkend Fate
Darkendome
Darkened
Darkened
Darkened Empire
Darkened Fate
Darkened Nocturn
  Slaughtercult
Darkened Skies
Darkened Times
Darkening
Darkening UK
Darkenlight
Darkenwood
Darkenz

Darker Half
Darker Shores
Darkest
DaRkEst DaY
Darkest Day
  of Horror
Darkest Grove
Darkest Hate
Darkest Hate
  Warfront
Darkest Hour
Darkest Insania
Darkest Oath
Darkestrah
Darkfall
Darkfaring
Darkfeast
Darkfire
Darkflight
Darkhat
Darkhole
Darkified
Darkim
Darkkirchensteuer
Darkland
Darkland
Darklands
Darklight
Darklight
Darklight
Darklight
Darklin Reach
Darkling
Darklord
Darklyss

De Occulta Philosophia
De Profundis
De Profvndis Clamavi
De Toi
De Tveksamma
De Vermis Mysteriis
De Vermis Mysteriis
De.mented
De/Test
DEA
Deaconess
Dead
Dead
Dead & Bloated
Dead 2 Rights
Dead Alone
Dead and Forgotten
Dead Astray
Dead Awaken
Dead Axe
Dead Baby
Dead Ballerinas
Dead Beauty
Dead Beyond Buried
Dead Blue Sky
Dead Broke
Dead But Alive
Dead by Dawn
Dead by Dawn
Dead by Dawn
Dead by Dawn
Dead by Dawn
Dead By Nine
Dead Calm

Dead Centre
Dead Child
Dead Christ
Dead Christ Cult
Dead Congregation
Dead Conspiracy
Dead Element
Dead Elizabeth
Dead Emotions
Dead End
Dead End
Dead End
Dead End Future
Dead Eternity
Dead Evil
Dead Eyed Sleeper
Dead Eyed Spider
Dead Eyes Divide
Dead Eyes Under
Dead Fetus
Dead Flesh
Dead Flowers
Dead for Days
Dead for Seven Weeks
Dead for Ten Weeks
Dead Future
Dead Generation
Dead Goat
Dead God in Me
Dead Grey
Dead Haven
Dead Head
Dead Head
Dead Heart Bleeding

Dead Horse
Dead Human Body
Dead Ideas
Dead in Christ
Dead in the Face
Dead in the Water
Dead Infection
Dead Inside
Dead Jesus
Dead Joker
Dead Letter Opener
Dead Light
Dead Mans Fun
Dead Man's Grip
Dead Man's Hand
Dead Man's Root
Dead Meat
Dead Meat
Dead Memories
Dead Men Dream
Dead Messiah
Dead Monuments
Dead Mountain
Dead Nature
Dead November
Dead October
Dead of Night
Dead of Night
Dead of Winter
Dead of Winter
Dead On
Dead on Arrival
Dead On Fourth
Dead Orchestra
Dead Poetry

Dead Poets
Dead Poets Society
Dead Raven Choir
Dead Remains
Dead Reptile Shrine
Dead Revolution
Dead River
Dead Root
Dead Samaritan
Dead Schizo
Dead Sea
Dead Season
Dead Serenade
Dead Serios
Dead Serious
Dead Shape Figure
Dead Silence
Dead Silence
Dead Silence
Dead Silent Slumber
Dead Skin
Dead Skin Mask
Dead Society
Dead Soul
Dead Soul Tribe
Dead Speak
Dead Straight
Dead Summer
Dead Svan Dark
Dead Syndicate
Dead Syndicate
Dead Threshold
Dead to Earth
Dead to Fall
Dead to Rights

Dead to this World
Dead Trees Sway
Dead Trench
Dead Trooper
Dead Twilight
Dead Whore River
Dead Winds
Dead Wish
Dead Within
Dead World
Dead Zone
Deadbird
Deadblood
Deadbodieseverywhere
Deadbolt
Deadborn
DeadByDay
DeadClaw
Deadechoes
Deaden
Deadeyedstare
Deadfall
Deadflash
Deadflesh
Deadflesh
Deadfuck
Deadfuck
Deadgrim Goreblood
Deadhead
Deadhole
Deadhope
Deadicated
Deadication
DeadImage

Deadites
Deadland
Deadlift
Deadlight
Deadline
Deadline
Deadliness
Deadlock
Deadlock
Deadlock
Deadlock
Deadlock
Deadlock
Deadly Blessing
Deadly Carnage
Deadly Creation
Deadly Dark
Deadly Dislocated
Deadly Fate
Deadly Intentions
Deadly Legacy
Deadly Maids
Deadly Manover
Deadly Mass
Deadly Night Shade
Deadly Nightshade
Deadly Pale
Deadly Shadows
Deadly Sin
Deadly Sin
Deadly Sins
Deadly Spawn
Deadly Strike
Deadly Tide
Deadly Vision

Deadman's Tale
Deadmarsh
DeadMinds
DeadMoon
Deadmoon Rising
Deadness
Deadnight
Deadnight
Deadnight Warrior
Deadpoint
Deadpool
Deadpool
Deadringer
Deadringer
Dead's Dawn
DeadSlave
Deadsoil
Deadsoul
Deadsoul Tribe
Deadspawn
Deadspawn
Deadspeak
DeadSpeak
Deadspot
Deadstar Assembly
Deadstream
Deadswitch
Deadwait
Deadwater Drowning
Deadwood Murder
Deaf & Dumb
Deaf Auditorium
Deaf Dealer
Deaf Indians
Deaf Revival

Deafen
Deafening Loneliness
Deafening Silence
Deafening Silence
Deafness
Dealer
Deamon
Deamonition
Dear Black Diary
Dear Demon
Dearly Beheaded
Dearly Beheaded
Death
Death Addict
Death After Life
Death Afterlife
Death Agony
Death Altar
Death
   Amphetamine
Death and Glory.
Death Angel
Death Army
Death Attack
Death Aura
Death Awaits
Death Axe
Death Beast
Death Becomes Me
Death Breath
Death Bringer
Death by Dawn
Death by Design
Death by Design
Death by Dreaming

Death by Hate
Death by Names
Death by Stereo
Death Camp
Death Certificate
Death Chant
Death Con 1
Death Constitution
Death Corps
Death Corpse
Death Corpse
Death Courier
Death Cross
Death Dealer
Death Delirium
Death Destruction
Death Device
Death Dies
Death du Jour
Death Embrace
Death Enthroned
Death Eternal
Death Fiend
Death File
Death Force
Death Force
Death From Above
Death From Above
Death From
   Down Under
Death Fuck
Death Gardens
Death Glory
Death Grader
Death Harmonic

Death Heaven
Death Hymen
Death Ignites
Death in Action
Death in Blood
Death in Embrace
Death in Sight
Death Instincts
Death is Certain
Death Is Eternal
Death Kvlt
Death Legion
Death Line
Death List
Death Living
Death Machine
Death Mask
Death Mask
Death Mechanism
Death Militia
Death Mission
Death Mortor
Death Mosh
Death Oath
Death of Folk
Death of Millions
Death or Glory
Death Penalty
Death Poems
Death Power
Death Project
Death Rape
Death Rate
Death Rattle
Death Rattle

Death Reality
Death Requisite
Death Riders
Death Ritual
Death Room
Death Row
Death Row Earth
Death Scythe
Death Scythes
Death Sea
Death Sentence
Death Sick
Death Silence
Death Skull
Death Slam
Death Slave
Death Smell
Death Squad
Death Squad
Death Squad
Death Squad
Death Squad
Death Squadron
Death SS
Death Strike
Death Thrashers
   Kuopio
Death to Calm
Death to Honor
Death Toll
Death Toll 80k
Death Toll Rising
Death Tower
Death Tripper
Death Triumphant

Death Vomit
Death Vomit
Death Vomit
Death Warrant
Death Warrant
Death Without
   Weeping
Death Wrong
Death Yell
Deathamin
Deathamphetamine
Deatharium
DeathBlack
Deathblow
Deathbound
Deathbringer
Deathcamp Project
Deathchain
Deathchamber
Deathchurch
DeathClaw
Deathcode of
   the Abyss
Deathcon
Deathcore
Deathcorp
Deathcraft
Deathcrush
Deathcrush
Deathcult
Deathcult
Deathcult
Deathdemona
Deathead
Deathector

Deatheory
Deather
Deathert
Deathevocation
Deathevokation
Deathfall
Deathfare
Deathfrost
Deathfrost
Deathgate Arkanum
Deathguy
Deathhammer
Deathinitely
DeathKids
Deathkross
Deathkrush
Deathland
Deathless
Deathless
Deathless
Deathless
Deathless
Deathless
Deathless Anguish
Deathlike Silence
Deathlike Silence
Deathlock
Deathmantra
Deathmarch
Deathmarch
Deathmare
Deathmoon
Deathning
Deathnoise
Deatholation

Deathonator
Deathpeed
Deathpils
Deathrage
Deathrage
Deathraiser
Deathrash
Deathrasher
Deathrider
Deathrider
Deathronation
Deathrow
Deathrune
Death's Angels
Death's Boundaries
Death's Bride
Death's Embrace
Death's Hammer
Deaths Head
Deaths Overture
Deathsaint
Deathscythe
Deathshine
Deathslayer
Deathspawned
Deathspawned
   Destroyer
Deathspell
Deathspell Omega
Deathsquad
Deathsquadron
Deathstars
Deathstrike
Deathstrokardia
Deathterror

Deathtrap	Decade	Decay	Deceiver	Dechrist	Decomposed	Decubitus
Deathtrap	Decade of Death	Decay	Deceiver	Dechristianize	Decomposed	Decyphen
Deathtrap	Decadence	Decay	Deceiver	Decide	Decomposed	Ded Engine
Deathtruction	Decadence	Decay	Decem Maleficium	Decieverion	Decomposed	Ded Leppard
Deathvalley Driver	Decadence	Decay	December	Decimate	Decomposed	DedBeat
DeathWielder	Decadence	Decay	December Aeternalis	Decimate Inc.	Decomposed Cranium	Dedicated for Life
Deathwing	Decadence	Decay Lust	December Child	Decimated	Decomposed Cunt	Dedication
Deathwish	Decadence	Decay of Days	December Dawn	Decimation	Decomposed God	Dedicted
Deathwish	Decadence	Decay of Light	December Fog	Decimation	Decomposing Serenity	Dedkor
Deathwitch	Decadence	Decay of Mankind	December Moon	Decimation	Decon	Dedom Vash
Deathwork	Decadence Death	Decay of Salvation	December Wolves	Decimation	Deconformity	Dedringer
DeathWYSH	Decadence Profound	Decay of Society	Decemberance	Decimation	Decontrolled	Deeds
Debakel	Decadence Within	Decay the Astral Self	December's Cold Winter	Decimation	Decorporate	Deeds of Flesh
DeBartoli's NightWing	Decadenze	Decayed	December's Fire	Decimator	Decortication	Deef
Debase	Decameron	Decayed Divinity	December's Silence	Decimator	Decoryah	Deep
Debauchery	Decapitação Angelical	Decayed Faith	Decembrance	Decision	Decoy Paris	Deep Fear
Debauchery	Decapitado	Decayed Forest	Decended	Decision D	Decreation	Deep in Hate
Debauchery	Decapitados	Decayed Remains	Decent	Decision to Hate	Decrepidemic	Deep Inside Myself
Debauchery	Decapitate	Decayed Soul	Deceptio Visus	Decisive Intrusion	Decrepify	Deep Machine
Debauchery	Decapitated	Decayin'	Deception	Declamatory	Decrepit	Deep Odium
Debauchery	Decapitated	Decaying Corpse	Deception	Declaration of Dependence	Decrepit	Deep Purple
Debauchery	Decapitation	Decaying Form	Deception	Decline	Decrepit	Deep Red
Debauchery Limb	Decapitation	Decayor	Deception	Decline	Decrepit	Deep Red
Debellum	Decapitation	Decay's Delight	Deception	Decline of Humanity	Decrepit Birth	Deep Sense
Debodified	Decapitation	Deccal	Deception Path	Decoherence	Decrepit Cadaver	Deep Silence
Deboning Method	Decapitation Done by Helicopter	Decease	Deceptive	Decolate	Decrepit Cauldron	Deep Sorrow
Déborah	Decapity	Deceased	Deceptive Creation	Decollation	Decrepit Mind	Deep Switch
Debowy Krag	Decaptation	Deceit	Deceptive Silence	Decomposed	Decrepitaph	Deep Throat
Debris	Decaptor	Deceit	Deceptor	Decomposed	Decrepitated	Deep Under Dirt
Debris	Decay	Deceived	Deceptor	Decomposed	Decrepity	Deep Vein
Debris Inc.	Decay	Deceivedgod	Deceptor	Decomposed	Decresens	Deep Well of Horror
Debt of Honor	Decay	Deceiver	Decerebration	Decomposed	Decreto K	Deepain
Debustrol	Decay	Deceiver	Dechained	Decomposed	Decrial	Deepcut
Decadawn	Decay	Deceiver	Déchéance	Decomposed	Decrypt	Deepen Depht
		Deceiver				Deeper Than That

Deep-pression	Defectdead	Definition Sane	Degeneracy	Deimos	Del Buio	Delirium Tremens
Deer Creek	Defection	Definition Unknown	Degenerate	Deimos	Delain	Delirium Tremens
Def Leppard	Defective	Definitive	Degenerated	Deimos	Delayed Action Bomb	Delirium X Tremens
Def-7	Defective Brain	Definitive	Degenerhate	Deimos	Delenda Arcana	Delirium's Dawn
Deface	Defector	Deflagration	Degial	Deimos	Delete	Deliver
Defaced Creation	Defekator	Deflected Sense	Degial of Embos	Deimos	Delete Yourself	Deliver Us
Defacement	Defekt Effekt	Defleshed	Degollacion	Deimos Dream	Deleterius Viator	Deliverance
Defacer	Defence Force	Defleshuary	Degorrot	Deimoth	Deletion	Deliverance
Defacer	Defender	Deflorace	Degradation	Deinonychus	Deletus	Deliverance
Defacing	Defender	Defloration	Degradation	Deinos Mastema	Delhi Download	Deliverance
Defacto Opression	Defender	Deflore	Degrade	Deiphago	Deliah's Prophecy	Deliverance
Défaillance	Defender	Deflower Mind	Degrade	Deiphobus	Delian League	Deliverence
Defamatory	Defender	Deforge	Degrade	Deiseal	Delicate News	Dellamorte
Defamatory	Defender	Deformachine	Degradeath	Deities	Delicta Carnis	dElohim
Defame	Defender KFS	Deforme	Degree Absolute	Deitiphobia	Delictum	Delorean
Defame	Defending the Faith	Deformed	Dehester	Deity	Delictum Initiale	Delphi
Defamer	Defiance	Deformed	Dehiscence	Deity of Carnification	Delight	Delphian
Default	Defiance	Deformed	Dehonest	Deity Undead	Delight Lost	Delpht
Defcon	Defiance	Deformed	Dehorn	Deity's Flesh	Delinquentes Infernae	Delta
Defcon	Defiant	Deforming Mirrors	Dehumanation	Deivos	Delios	Delta 666
Defcon	Defiant Manner	Deformity	Dehumanised	Deivourgue	Deliriä	Delta Force 2
Defcon	Deficit	Deformity	Dehumanized	Deja Vu	Delirio	Delta Operator
Defcon	Defied	Deformity	Dehumanizer	Deja-Vu	Delirion	Deluge
Defcon 2	Defier	Deformity	Dehydrated	Deja-Vu	Delirious	Deluge
Defcon 666	Defilade	Deformity of Society	Dehydrated	Deject	Delirious	Deluge
Defcon One	Defile	Defueld	Dehydrated	Dejecta	Delirium	Deluge
Defeat	Defile	Defunct	Deianeira	Dejected	Delirium	Deluge Master
Defeated Sanity	Defiled	Defunctis	Deiception	Dejkhim	Delirium	Deluge of Djinn
Defeatist	Defiled	Defunctorium	Deicide	Dejmor	Delirium	Delusion
Defecated Abortion	Defiled Dreams	Defuntos	Deidath	Dekadenz	Delirium	Delusion
Defecated Corpse	Defiled Pantheon	Defuze	Deifecation	Dekapitator	Delirium	Delusion
Defecation	Defilement	Defy	Deification	Dekapited	Delirium Endeavor	Delusion
Defect	Defiler	Defy	Deification	Dekar	Delirium Tremance	Delusion
Defect	Defiler	Defyance	Deilegium	Dekrepix	Delirium Tremens	Delusion
	Defilor	Degeneracy	Deimos	Dekrowned	Delirium Tremens	Delusive
						Delusive Dawn

Deus Inversus	Devastator	Devil in Love	Devilyn	Devoured Carnage	Diablerie	Diabolical North
Deus Inversus	Devastator	Devil in the Details	Devine Essence	Devoured	Diableriktus	Klanum
Deus Irae	Devastator	Devil in the Kitchen	Devious	Decapitation	Diablo	Diabolical Principles
Deus Irae	Devastator	Devil Inside	Devious Disharmony	Devourer	Diablo	Diabolical Storm
Deus Otiosus	Devastator	Devil Lee Rot	Deviser	Devourer	Diablo	Diabolical Sword
Deus Pacis	Devastator	D'Evil Leech Project	Devisor	Devourer	Diablo Red	Diabolical Torture
Deus Vult	Devastator	Devil May Cry	Devital	Devourer	Diablo Swing	Diabolicum
Deuterium	Devaste	Devil on Earth	Devlin	Devourgasm	Orchestra	Diabolicus
Deuteron	Devaster	Devil' Smile	Devoid	Devourment	Diaboli	Diabolikal Holokaust
Deuteronomium	Devaster	Devil Sold His Soul	Devoid	Devout	Diabolic	Diabolikös
Deva	Devenir	Devil to Pay	Devoid	Devoyd	Diabolic Force	Diabolique
Deva Yena	Devenustatus	DevilDriver	Devoid of Fate	Devyatiy Val	Diabolic Intent	Diabolique
Devane	Devestate	DevilDriver	Devols Mortem	Dew Fall	Diabolic Lust	Diabolisis
Devanic	Deviance in	Devilhorn	Devolution	Dew of Nothing	Diabolic Possession	Diabolism
Devast	the Mirror	Devilish	Devolution	Dewian	Diabolic Possession	Diabolix
Devastación	Deviant	Devilish	Devolution	Dewok	Diabolic Throne	Diabolo
Devastate	Deviant	Devilish Dance	Devolved	Dew-Scented	Diabolic Voices	Diabolos
Devastate	Deviant	Devilish Distance	Devonian	Dezakrate	Diabolic Vomit	Diabolos Rising
Devastated	Deviant	Devilish Era	Devora	Dezember	Diabolic Witchcraft	Diabolous
Devastated	Deviant	Devilish Impressions	Devoration	Deztroyer	Diabolic Wood	Diabolus Ex Machina
Devastathor	Deviant	Devilium	DeVore	D-Fense	Diabolical	Diabolus Infame
Devastating	Deviant	Devillish	Devotam	DFP	Diabolical	Diabolus Vobiscum
Supremacy	Deviant Creation	Devilmakesthree	Devoted to Hate	DGM	Diabolical	Diachronia
Devastation	Deviant Surgeons	Devil-May-Care	Devotee	Dhak	Diabolical	Diadem
Devastation	Deviant-Tactics	Devilmind	Devotee	Dhark Death	Diabolical Breed	Diadem
Devastation	Deviate Ladies	Devilry	Devotion	Dharma	Diabolical Darkness	Diadem
Devastation	Deviated Instinct	Devils & His Spells	Devotus Regnum	Dharohg	Dissemination	Diadema
Devastation	Deviated Presence	Devil's Champion	Devour	Dhaubgurz	Diabolical	Diadema
Devastation	Deviated Tomb	Devil's Claws	Devour	Dhemonic	Dismemberment	Diadema
Devastation	DeviaThor	Devil's Code	Devoured	Dhornath	Diabolical	Diadema Tristis
Devastation	Device	Devil's Fate	Devoured	Dhraug	Domination	Diademegon
Devastation	Devil Ate My Son	Devil's Island	Devoured	Dhuend	Diabolical Imperium	Diafragma
Devastation	Devil Childe	Devil's Pie	Devoured	Diableria	Diabolical	Diagnose
Devastation Inside	Devil Doll	Devil's Soldiers	Devoured by Hate	Diablerie	Masquerade	Diagnose:
Devastation Run	Devil Host	Devil's Whorehouse	Devoured by Sinners	Diablerie	Diabolical Messiah	Lebensgefahr

DIS
Dis Pater
Disabled
Disablust
Disabuse
Disabused
Disaffected
Disagio
Disagree
Disapathic
Disappearer
Disarm
Disarm
Disarm Goliath
Disarmed Universe
Disarmonia Mundi
Disarray
Disarray
Disassembled
Disassociate
Disaster
Disaster
Disaster
Disaster
Disaster
Disaster Area
Disaster Area
Disaster Area
Disaster Complex
Disaster KFW
Disasters
Disastrous Murmur
Disattack
Disavowed
Disbelief

Disbeliever
Disbeliever
Disbrainer
Discanto
Discard
Discarnate
Discarnate
Discarnated
Discern
Discharge
Dischord
Discidium
Disciple
Disciple
Disciple
Disciple
Disciples of Belial
Disciples of
 Berkowitz
Disciples of Chaos
Disciples of Daath
Disciples of Hate
Disciples of Mockery
Disciples of Power
Discomposed
Discomposure
Disconcert
Disconformity
Disconsolate
Discord
Discordance Axis
Discordant
Discorde
Discordey
Discordia

Discordia
Discreate
Discreation
Discreation
Discrepancy
Discrucior
Disdain
Disdain
Disdained
Disdainer
Disease
Disease
Disease
Disease
Diseased
Diseased
Disembalm
Disembarkation
Disembodead
Disembodied
Disembodied
Disembodied
Disembodied
Disembodied
Disembowel
Disembowel
Disembowel
Disembowel
Disembowel
Disemboweled
Disemboweled
 Corpse
Disembowelled
Disembowelment
Disemburied

Disenchant
Disenchant
Disencumbrance
Disenterment
Disentropy
Disfear
Disfigure
Disfigured
Disfigured
Disfigured
Disfigured
Disfigured Corpse
Disfigured Human
 Mind
Disfigured Victims
Disfigurement
Disfigurement
Disflesh
Disforme
Disforterror
Disgod
Disgore
Disgorge
Disgorge
Disgorge
Disgorge
Disgorge
Disgorge
Disgorged
Disgorged
Disgorged Foetus
Disgorgement of
 Intestinal Lym-
 phatic Suppuration

Disgrace
Disgrace
Disgrace
Disgrace
Disgrace
Disgrace
Disgrace
Disgrace and Terror
Disgraced
Disgraced
Disgracelator
Disguise
Disgust
Disgust
Disgust
Disgust
Disgust
Disgust
Disguster
Disgusting
Disgusting
Disgusting
Disharmonic
Disharmonic Fields
Disharmonic
 Orchestra
Disharmonical
 Tempest
Disharmony
Disharmony
Disharmony
Disharmony
Disharmony
Disharmony
Disharmony's Den

Dished
Disidente Agresor
Disillusion
Disillusion
Disillusioned
Disincarnate
Disincarnated
Disinfect
Disinfected
Disinfected
Disinfection
Disinfest
Disintegration
Disinter
Disinter
Disinter
Disinter
Disinter
Disinter
Disinter Dead
Disinterment
Disinterment
Disinterment
Disiplin
Disjecta
Disjecta Membra
Disjecta Membra
Disjecta Membra
Disjonktation
Diskord
Diskrasic Experiment
Diskreet
Diskriminator
Dislepsia
Dislessy

Dislike Blast
Dislimb
Dislocated Cerebrum
Dislocation
Dislocation
Dis-Lord
Disloyal
Disloyal
Dismaed
Dismal
Dismal
Dismal
Dismal
Dismal
Dismal
Dismal
Dismal Divinity
Dismal Euphony
Dismal Foresight
Dismal Gale
Dismal Gale
Dismal Insanity
Dismal Kingdom
Dismal Past
Dismal Prospects
Dismay
Dismember
Dismembered August
Dismembered Fetus
Dismemberment
Dismhal
Dismorlech
Dismortal
Disobedience
Disobedience

Disorder	Dissectomy	Dissolved	Distortion of	Disturbing Shit Minds	Divine	Divine Syndrome
Disorder	Dissector	Dissolving of	Perception	Disumana Res	Divine	Divine Temptation
Disorder	Dissector	Prodigy	Distortion Skulls	Disyph'r	Divine	Divine Torment
Disorder	Dissector	Dissonance	Distorttion	Disznótor	Burning Angels	Divine Tragedy
Disorder	Disseized	Dissonance	Distortum	Disztraktor	Divine Death	Divine Tragedy
Disorder Infection	Dissembill	Dissonance	Distorze	Dite	Divine Decay	Divine Weep
Disordered	Disseminate	Dissonant	Distorzija Uma	Ditesco Mori	Divine Desecration	Divine X
Disorge	Dissension	Dissonant	Distorzion	Dither	Divine Dynasty	Divine:Zero
Disown	Dissenter	Dissonath	Distract Reality	Dithyrambs	Divine Element	DivineFire
Disown to Alive	Dissenter	Dissouled	Distractions of My	Dittohead	Divine Embrace	Divinis Invocat
Disowned	Dissenters	Dissouled	Psychosis	Diva	Divine Empire	Divinity
Disparaged	Disseverment	Dissymmetry	Distrainers	Diva Destruction	Divine Enslavement	Divinity
Dispatched	Dissidence	Distalis	Distraught	Diva Noctua Entropia	Divine Eve	Divinity Destroyed
Dispelled	Dissidens	Distant	Distraught	Divanity	Divine Fury	Divinus
Dispersia	Dissident	Distant Light	Distream	Divaricate	Divine Genocide	Divinus
Dispersion	Dissident	Distant Past	Distress	Dive in Minds	Divine Heresy	Division
Dispirited	Dissident	Distant Thunder	Distress	Divercia	Divine Insanity	Division 19
Dispondency	Dissident Aggressor	Distarnish	Distress	Diverge	Divine Intervention	Division by Zero
Dispulse	Dissident Aggressor	Distaste	Distress	Diverica	Divine Intuition	Division Hagal
Disrepute	Dissident Aggressor	Distaste	Distress	Diversia	Divine Lust	Division of the Spoils
Disromance	Dissident View	Distilled Spirits	Distrot	Diversia	Divine Massacre	Division S
Disrupt	Dissideo	Distillery	Distrust	Divertigo	Divine Misery	Division X
Disrupted	Dissimulation	Distimia	Distrust	Divide et Impera	Divine Nightmare	Divisione Totenkopf
Disruption	Dissipate	Distorium	Distrust	Dividebyzero	Divine Noise Attack	Divizion S-187
Disruptor	Dissociation	Distorment	Distrust	Divided Multitude	Divine Profanity	Divlje Jagode
Dissatisfaction	Dissociation	Distorted	Distrust	Divider	Divine Pustulence	Divulsion
Dissect	Dissolute	Distorted	Distrust	Dividing Horizons	Divine Rapture	Dizabled
Dissect	Dissolute Paradise	Distorted	Distruzione	Dividing Light	Divine Regale	Dizaster
Dissected	Dissolution	Distorted	Distruzione di Massa	Dividing Line	Divine Rite	Dizkord
Dissected Life	Dissolution	Impalement	Disturbance	Divina Enema	Divine Ruins	Dizorderz
Dissection	Dissolution	Distorted Mind	Disturbed	Divina Inferis	Divine Silence	Djabah
Dissection	Dissolution	Distorted Minds	Disturbed Kaos	Divina Tragedia	Divine Sin	Djeena's Circus
Dissection	Dissolution	Distorted Picture	Society	Divination	Divine Souls	Djëvel
Dissection	Dissolution	Distorted Reality	Disturbed Souls	Divination	Divine Symphony	Djinn
Dissection	Dissolve	Distorted View		Divination	Divine Symphony	Djinn
Dissection Corpse	Dissolve Being	Distortion				

Dormant	Dove	Downscarred	Dr. Steel	Dragon Tears	Dragster	Drama & Delirio
Dormant Misery	Dove	Downshift	Dr. Unknown	Dragon Warrior	Dragula	Dramafall
Dormant Ordeal	Dover Trench	Downsize	Dr.Salazar	Dragonauta	Drahcir	Dramatic Irony
Dormantgod	Down	Downsoul	Draagnacht	Dragonfire	Drahcko	Dramatvm
Dormanth	Down Below	Downspell	Dracena	Dragon-Fly	Drain	DrammaGothica
Dormitorium	Down Factor	Downstar	Drachenord	Dragonfly	Drain of Impurity	Drangsalymir
Dormitory	Down for Go(o)d	Downstroke	Drackma	Dragonfly	Drain S.T.H.	Drastic
Dormitory	Down From the	Downstroy	Dracko	Dragonfly	Drainage X	Drastique
Dormitory Effect	Wound	Downthesun	Dracma	Dragonfly	Draind of Empathy	Drastus
Dormonokt	Down in a Hole	Downthroat	Draco Aerius	DragonForce	Draist Avagnon	Drat
Dorn	Down In Shades	Downtime	Draco Hypnalis	Dragongrass	Drakar	Draug
Dornenreich	Down Syndrome	Downtofail	Dracodacikus	Dragonhammer	Drakar	Draugar
Dornfall	Down the Drain	Downtown	Dracon	Dragonheart	Drake	Draugar
Doro	Down the Well	Downward Spiral	Draconaeon	DragonHeart	Drakher	Draugen
Dorotha	Down Till Dawn	Doxology	Draconi	Dragonia	Drakkar	Drauggard
Dorsal Atlântica	Down Under	Doxomedon	Draconia	Dragonlance	Drakkar	Draugluin
Dorso	Downbreak	Doykod	Draconian	Dragonland	Drakkar	Draugluin
Dórwish	Downcast	Dozd'	Draconian	Dragonlord	Drakkar	Draugnim
Dose Lethal	Downcast	Dozer	Draconian	Dragonlords	Drakkar	Draugr
Dosenhof	Downdriven	Dr. Acula	Draconian	Dragonne	Drakkar Snekkja	Draugsang
dot(.)	Downer	Dr. Braindead	Draconian Order	Dragon's Eye	Drakkard	Draugurz
Double Action	Downfade	Dr. Butcher	Draconian Winter	Dragon's Lair	Drakkath	Draugwath
Double Dealer	Downfall	Dr. Chunk	Draconic	Dragon's Lord	Drakko	Draumvakzeph
Double Devil	Downfall	Dr. Death	Draconis	Dragonsfire	Drakkon	Draupnir
Double Diamond	Downfall	Dr. Doolittle	Draconis Sanguis	Dragonship	Drakma	Drautran
Double Dragon	Downfall	Dr. Faust	Dracul	DragonSlayer	Drakon	Draw the Curtains
Double Edge	DownFall	Dr. Faust	Dracula	Dragonslayer	Drakonhail	Drawback
Double Square	Downfall	Dr. Jekyll	Draemoontias	Dragonslayer	Drakonian Age	Drawline
Doubleblack	Downfall	Dr. Know	Drafted	Dragonspoon	Draksen	Drawn
Doubledrive	Downfall A.D.	Dr. Mastermind	Drag-In	Dragonwind	Drakul	Drawn and Quartered
Doubt	Downhell	Dr. Pretorious	Dragobrath	Dragonwyck	Drakul	Drawned in Tears
Douce Morphine	DownHell	Dr. Satan	Dragon	Dragoons	Dralion	Draxsen
Doug Stapp	Downlord	Dr. Shrinker	Dragón de Hierro	Dragora	Drallion	D-Ray
Douglas	Downright Malice	Dr. Sin	Dragon Lance	Dragosariz	Drama	Drayvarg
Doulos	Downscape	Dr. Skull	Dragon Lord	Dragster	Drama	Dread

Dub Buk	Dungeon	Dusk	DVPLO	Dying Awkward	Dying Victims	Dysgusted
Dub War	Dungeon of Wizard	Dusk	Dwarf's	Angel	Dying Wish	Dyskrasia
Dubh	Dungeon Rage	Dusk	Rebellion	Dying Balance	Dying Wish	Dyslesia
Dubinin - Holstinin	Dungeonbat	Dusk	Dwarka	Dying Behind the	Dykeslayer	Dysmenore
Dubl-1	Dunghill	Dusk	Dwarr	Ghosts of Angels	Dylath-Leen	Dysmorfic
Dublin Death Patrol	Dungortheb	Dusk Chapel	Dweller	Dying Breed	Dyluvian	Dysmorphia
Duch Lasu	Dunkel	Dusk Delight	Dwelling	Dying Christ	Dymaxion	Dysorder
Düel	Dunkel	Dusk Eternal	Dwelling Madness	Dying Clarity	Dynahead	Dysperium
Duel of Fate	Dunkel	Dusk of Eternity	Dwelling Souls	Dying Corpse	Dynamic	Dysphasia
Duelbarrel	Dunkel	Dusk Ov Shadows	Dweorgesblod	Dying Creed	Dynamic	Dysphoria
Dug Pinnick	Dunkel Nacht	Dusk Ritual	Dwergamal	Dying Days	Dynamic Front	Dysphoria
Duh Predaka	Dunkel:heit	Dusken	Dwimmerlaik	Dying Disciple	Dynamic Lights	Dysphoria
Dühkitörés	Dunkelfront	Duskfall	Dwimor	Dying Embers	Dynamo	Dysphory
Duister Maanlicht	Dunkelgrafen	Duskmachine	Dyannand	Dying Embrace	Dynamo	Dysplasia
Duisternis	Dunkelheim	Dust	Dyanna's Infidi	Dying Embrace	Dynamon Dark	Dysposium
Duke	Dunkelheit	Dust	Dybbuk	Dying Embrace	DynamoWar	Dyspraxia
Dukes of Nothing	Dunkelheit	Dust	Dybbuk	Dying Faith	Dynasty	Dysrhythmia
Dulcamara	Dunkelheit	Dust	Dydome	Dying Fetus	Dyngyr	Dyster
Dulcerth	Dunkelheit	Dust	Dyecast	Dying Fields	Dyoxen	Dysterhet
Dum Dum Bullet	Dunkelherzilich	Dust Components	Dyecrest	Dying Fire	Dypherim	Dysterwald
Duma Xesbet	Dunkelkrist	Dust Devil	Dyed in the Wool	Dying Fullmoon	Dypressive	Dysthanasia
Dumah	Dunkell Reiter	Dust Devils	Dyer	Dying Harmony	Dyrnath	Dysthymia
Dump	Dunkelnacht	Dust from Misery	Dyer Dawn	Dying Humanity	Dyroxium	Dystopia
Dumper	Dunkelschreck	Dust To Rise	Dyers Eve	Dying in Your	Dysanchely	Dystopia
Dumpyourload	Dunkelstorm	Düsterwald	Dyers Eve	Beauty Sleep	Dysangelium	Dystopia
Dun Moloch	Dunwich	Dustland	Dyers Eve	Dying Message	Dyscarnate	Dystopia
Dunamys	Dunwich	Dutchess	Dyessence	Dying Passion	Dyscord	Dystopia
Dunce	Duobetic	Dux Herpes	Dygitals	Dying Regret	Dyscrasia	Dystopya
Dunces	Homunkulus	Dvana Pasa	Dying	Dying Rose	Dysenterie	Dystortion Fx
Dune	DuraMadre	Dvergir	Dying	Dying Shadows	Dysentery	Dystrophy
Dunedain	Durin's Bane	D-Vice	Dying	Dying Spirit	Dysentery	Dysuria
Dünedain	Durjana	Dvina	Dying Age	Dying Sun	Dysentery	Dyve
Dungeon	Durst	Dvnaèbkre	Dying Angel	Dying Tears	Dysfigure	DZ Project
Dungeon	Durthang	Dvolvd	Dying Angel	Dying Tribe	Dysfunction	Dzelzs Vilks
Dungeon	Dusk	Dvorhead	Dying Angel	Dying Urge	Dysfunction	Dzlvarv

	Earth A.D.	Ebola	Eciton	Economist	Eden's Fall
	Earth Crisis	Ebola	Eclectic Spawn	Ecryptus	Eden's Onslaught
	Earth Dies Screaming	Ebola	Eclectika	Ecstasy	Edenshade
	Earth Flight	Ebola	Eclectogrinder	Ecstatic Fear	Edenslave
	Earthbound	Ebola Beach Party	Eclips	Ecthalion	Edenyzed
	Earthbound	Ebolical	Eclipse	Ectomia	Edera
	Smoke Ghost	Ebolie	Eclipse	Ectoparasite	Ederia
	Earthburner	Ebolie	Eclipse	Ectopia	Edge
	Earthcorpse	Ebonmortis	Eclipse	Ectopia	Edge of Chaos
	Earthcubed	Ebonsight	Eclipse	Ectoplasm	Edge of Forever
	Earthlord	Ebony Ark	Eclipse	Ectospazz	Edge of Sanity
	Earthmover	Ebony Eyes	Eclipse	Eczema	Edge of Spirit
	Earthquake	Ebony Sorrow	Eclipse	Eczema	Edge of Thorns
	Earthride	Ebony Tears	Eclipse	Ed Gein	Edge of Time
	Earthshaker	Ebonylake	Eclipse	Ed Zeppelin	Edge.of.Thorns
	Earthstream	Eborsisk	Eclipse	Eddie Ojeda	Edgecrusher
	Earthtone9	Ébredés	Eclipse	Eddy Antonini	Edgecrusher
	East	Ebullition	Eclipse	Edelweiss	Edgend
	East Trading Wang	Ebwa	Eclipse	Edelweyss	Edguy

E'Trite Moira	Ea Taesse	East-Area	Écclésia	Eclipse	Edema	Edicius
E!E	Eadwulf	Eastern Orbit	Ecclesia Satani	Eclipse Eternal	Eden	Edicius
E.A.K.	Eagleheart	Easterner	Echidna	Eclipse Hunter	Edén	Edicius
E.C.H. IX	Eagles Preach	Eastgoth	Echidna	Eclipse of the Sun	Eden A.D.	Edip's Cup
E.C.T.	Eald	Easy Feelin	Echo Hollow	Eclipsis	Eden in Ruins	Edison
E.D.I.E.H.	Ear Danger	Easy Rider	Echo Inside	Ecliptic	Eden Obscured	Editor
E.F. Band	Eardelete	Eat My Fuk	Echo of Dalriada	Ecliptic Sunset	Eden weint im Grab	Edmund Welles
E.H.E.	Earection	Eat the Fetus	Echoes of Eternity	Ecliptica	Edenbeast	Edone
E.I.W.D.	Earendil	Eat the Living	Echoes of Fear	Ecliptica	Edenbeast	Ed's Attic
E.K.U.	Earl Shilton	Eat Your Dead	Echoes of Sanity	Ecliptica	Edenbeast	Edu Falaschi
E.N.D.	Early Man	Eaten Alive	Echoes of Silence	Ecliptyka	Edenbridge	Educated Scum
E.N.G.E.L.	Early Warning	Eaten Bones	Echoes of the	Eclosión	Edenfall	Edwin Dare
E.S.T.	Ear-Shot	Eavral	Fallen Messiah	Eclypse	Edenfire	Eerie
E.V. Loud	Earth	Ebanath	Echoriath	Eclypse	Edenhial	Eeriness
E-605	Earth	Ebitalium	Echosilence	Ecnephias	Edenrot	Eezee
Ea	Earth A.D.	Eblis	Echovirus	Econoline Crush	Eden's Demise	EF Band

◆ Espada Negra

Espectrarum	Estigma Purpura	Eternal Blaze	Eternal Dust	Eternal Malediction	Eternal Sin	Eternity
Espectro	EstremArte	Eternal Bleeding	Eternal Elysium	Eternal Mind	Eternal Sleep	Eternity
EspectrosQuasar	Estridencia	Eternal Blood	Eternal End	Eternal Mist	Eternal Solitude	Eternity
Espejo Retrovisor	Estropia	Eternal Breath	Eternal Evil	Eternal Mourning	Eternal Solstice	Eternity
Espials von Lethe	Estrum	Eternal Burden	Eternal Faith	Eternal Mourning	Eternal Sorrow	Eternity
Espinoza	Estrus	Eternal Burden	Eternal Fall	Eternal Mystery	Eternal Suffering	Eternity Black
Espíritu de Hierro	Estuary	Eternal Chaos	Eternal Fall	Eternal Nemesis	Eternal Suffering	Eternity Burning
Espiritual	Estuary of Calamity	Eternal Chaos	Eternal Fear	Eternal Night	Eternal Sunset	Eternity Denied
Espiritualia	Estuprando o	Eternal Combustion	Eternal Flame	Eternal Nightmare	Eternal Tear	Eternity of Darkness
Esqarial	Nazareno	Eternal Conspiracy	Eternal Flight	Eternal Oath	Eternal Tears	Eternity Rage
Esqueleto	Esturion	Eternal Cry	Eternal Fog	Eternal Oath	of Sorrow	Eternity Void
Essatic	Et Verbi Sathanus	Eternal Damnation	Eternal Forest	Eternal Oblivion	Eternal Throne	Eternity Within
Essence	Etagord	Eternal Dark	Eternal Frost	Eternal Oblivion	Eternal Torment	Eternity X
Essence	Etánisis	Eternal Dark	Eternal Frost	Eternal Orchid	Eternal Torture	Eternium Sinfonic
Essence of Existence	Etched in Stone	Eternal Darkness	Eternal Frost	Eternal Order	Eternal Tragedy	Eterno
Essence of Sorrow	Etelantulet	Eternal Darkness	Eternal Frost	Eternal Pain	Eternal Trash	Eternum
Essential Genre	Eterea	Eternal Darkness	Eternal Frost	Eternal Passion	Eternal Twilight	Eternus
Obsession	Etereum	Eternal Darkness	Eternal Funeral	Eternal Past	Eternal Unborn	Eternya
Essenza	Eterflames	Eternal Darkness	Eternal Funeral	Eternal Peace	Eternal War	Ethan
Essex	Eterna	Eternal Darkness	Eternal Gate	Eternal Pestilence	Eternal War	Etharen
Essoupi	Eterna	Eternal Darkness	Eternal Gloom	Eternal Purgatory	Eternal War	Ethel the Frog
Estaca	Eterna Oscuridad	Eternal Darkness	Eternal Glory	Eternal Rage	Eternal Warfare	Ethelyn
Estatic Fear	Eternae	DCLXVI	Eternal Grave	Eternal Reign	Eternal Winter	Ether
Estebun	Eternal	Eternal Death	Eternal Gray	Eternal Rest	Eternal Winter	Ether Breather
Ester	Eternal	Eternal Decision	Eternal Grieve	Eternal Ruin	Eternal Wrath	Ether Shift Theory
Estertor	Eternal	Eternal Deformity	Eternal Hate	Eternal Ruin	EternalBlackMetal	Etherea
Estertor	Eternal	Eternal Delirium	Eternal Hatred	Eternal Ryte	Eternally Devoured	Ethereal
Esthesia	Eternal	Eternal Dementia	Eternal Krieg	Eternal Sacrifice	Eternam	Ethereal
Estigia	Eternal	Eternal Demise	Eternal Lament	Eternal Sadness	Eterne	Ethereal
Estigia	Eternal Aggression	Eternal Desolation	Eternal Legacy	Eternal Saviour	Eternia	Ethereal
Estigia	Eternal Agony	Eternal Devastation	Eternal Lies	Eternal Serenity	Eternia	Ethereal
Estigia	Eternal Agony	Eternal Dirge	Eternal Lord	Eternal Sick	Eternia	Ethereal
Estigma	Eternal Agony	Eternal Doom	Eternal Madness	Eternal Silence	Eternight	E-thereal
Estigma	Eternal Autumn	Eternal Drak	Eternal Madness	Eternal Silence	Eternity	Ethereal Blue
Estigma	Eternal Black	Eternal Dusk	Eternal Majesty	Eternal Silence	Eternity	Ethereal Collapse

◆ Ethereal Omen

Ethereal
   Pandemonium
Ethereal Scourge
Ethereal Sin
Ethereal Spawn
Ethereal Tragedy
Ethereal Travel
Ethereal Woods
Ethereality
Etheria
Etherial Dawn
Etherial Grief
Etherial Winds
Etheric Soul
Etheric Void
Etherized
Etherkall
Ethernal
Ethernal
Ethernia
Ethernity
Etherune
Etherya
Ethnocide
Ethodius
Ethos
Etnocidio
EtonéDicius
Etreum
Etreum
Etrom
Etrusgrave
Etsicroxe
Eturintama
Etymon

Eucharist
Eucrasia
Eudaimonia
Eudine Seythe
Eudoxis
Eufobia
Eugenik
Eulafaye
Eulogium
Eulogy
Eulogy
Euphonic
Euphoria
Euphoric
   Evisceration
Euphrosyne
Eure Erben
Euroforce
Euronymous
Europe
Eurynome
Eusophobia
Eutanasia
Eutanasia
Eutanazia
Eutanos
Euterpia
Euthanasia
Euthanasia
Euthanasia
Euthanasia
Euthanasia
Euthanausea
Eutonazia Kordax
Eva O.

Evade
Evadne
Evanesce
Evanescence
Evanescent Soul
Evangeli
Evangelist
Evangelium
Evasive
Evassion
Eve of Mourning
Eve of Mourning
Eve To Adam
Evelin
Evelyn
Evelyn
Evemaster
Even Song
Even Vast
Evenfall
Evenfall
Evening
Evening Star
Evenlost
Evenrain
ÉvenSong
Evenstorm
Event
Event Horizon
Event Horizon X
Eventide
Eventide
Eventide
Eventide
Eventide
Eventide Horizon

Eventus
Eventyr
Ever Dark
Ever Dark
Ever Down
Ever Since
Everaftter
Everasia
Everbleed
Evercold
Evercry
Everdespair
Everdome
Evereve
Everfall
Everfest
Everflow
Everflow
Everflow
Everflow
Everfrost
Everglow
Evergrace
Evergreed
Evergreen Terrace
Evergrey
Everlasting Dark
Everlasting Reign
Everlasting Tales
Everlost
Everlost
Everlost
Everloud
Evermoore
Evermörk

Evermourn
Evermourn
Evermourning
Everon
Eversinceve
Eversor
Eversor
Eversoris
Everticum
Everwake
Everwake
Everwicked
Everwinter
Everwood
Every Bone Broken
Every Bridge Burned
Every Mother's
   Nightmare
Every Passing Hour
Everything Falls Dark
Everything's Ruined
Eve's 2nd Sin
Eve's Bringer
Eve's Downfall
Evicting the
   Testicular Squatters
Eviction
Evictus
Evidence
Evidence of Fear
Evidence of Trauma
Evidence One
Evig Blod
Evig Kveld
Evig Natt

Evighed
Evil
Evil
Evil
Evil
Evil
Evil Adam
Evil Angel
Evil Army
Evil Army
Evil Arts
Evil Attack
Evil Bards
Evil Blood
Evil Brain Food
Evil Church
Evil Conspiracy
Evil Damn
Evil Darkness
Evil Days
Evil Dead
Evil Dead
Evil Divine
Evil Emperor
Evil Empire
Evil Entourage
Evil Eternity
Evil Face
Evil Fire
Evil Genius
Evil God
Evil God Revival
Evil Holocaust
Evil Incarnate
Evil Inside

Evil Invaders
Evil Legacy
Evil Lord
Evil Machine
Evil Madness
Evil Masquerade
Evil Mayhem
Evil Never Dies
Evil Offering
Evil Omen
Evil One
Evil Pigs
Evil Poetry
Evil Power
Evil Prayer
Evil Scarecrow
Evil Silence
Evil Sinner
Evil Tardevil
Evil Trimegistus
Evil Twin
Evil War
Evil Warrior
Evil Whisper
Evil Wings
Evil Winter
   Forest Screams
Evil Witch
Evil Wrath
Evildamn
Evildead
Evildoer
Evildom
Evile
Evile

Evilion	Eviternity	Ewig Frost	Excalion	Excision	Excruciating Torment	Execution
Eviliver	EVM	Ewiges Fristen	Excarnated	Excision	Excruciation	Execution
Evilized	EVO	Ewiges Reich	Excarnation	Excision	Excruciation	Execution
Evillive	Evocation	Ewigheim	Ex-Cathedra	Excision	Excrucio	Execution
Evilnasty	Evocation	Ewigkeit	Excavated	Exciter	Excrucior	Execution
Evilness	Evocation	Ex Animae	Excavation	Exciter	Excrucior	Execution
Evilosity	Evocation	Ex Caliga	Excavation	Exciters	Excubiae	Execution Chamber
Evil's Attack	Evodia	Ex Delirium	Excavator	Exciting Vision	Excubitor Noctis	Executioner
Evil's Tears	Evohe	Ex Dementia	Excavator	eXcm	Excuriver	Executioner
Evilscent	Evoke	Ex Inferis	Exceed	Excommunication	Excurses	Executioner
Evilsmith	Evoked Curse	Ex Infernis	Exceed	Excommunion	E-X-E	Executor
EvilStorm	Evoked Doom	Ex Libris	Exceed Force	Excomulgación	Exec Justice	Exegesis
Evilthorn	Evoken	Ex Machina	Excel	Excoriate	Execrable	Exekrado
Evilusions	Evoker	Ex Machina	Excelsis	Excoriate	Exhumation	Exekrator
Evilution	Evokers	Ex Mortus	Excelsis	Excoriate	Execrandus	Exekratorio
Evilwar	Evol	Ex Nihilo	Excelsis	Excoriated	Execrate	Exekutor
Evilwinged	Evol	Ex.Danger	Excelsis Hosanna	Excoriated	Execrate	Exelsus Diaboli
Evirus	Evol Death	EX-10	Except a Few	Excoriation	Execrate	Exempla
Eviscerate	Evolotto	Exalibur	Exception	Excrement	Execrate	Exempt
Eviscerate	Evolution	Exalt	Excess	Excrementory	Execrate	Exemption
Eviscerate	Evolution	Exaltation	Excess	Grindfuckers	Execrate	Exenferis
Eviscerate	Evolution	Exaltation	Excess	Excrements	Execration	Exequia
Eviscerate	Evolution	Exalted	Excess of Cruelty	Excrements	Execration	Exequies
Eviscerated	Evolution Cancer	Exalted Demise	Excess Pressure	Excrescent	Execration	Exercet
Eviscerated	Evolution X	Exanthema	Excessive Bleeding	Excrete!	Execration	Exercitus
Eviscerated	Evolutions End	Exapathy	Excessum	Excretion	Execration	Exerion
Eviscerated	Evolved	Exarhat	Excessum	Excruciate	Execration	Exetheris
Evisceration	Evora	Exaudi	Exchased	Excruciate	Execrator	Ex-Excess
Evisceration	Evrieselaar	Exawatt	Excidium	Excruciate	Execrator	Exhale
Evisceration	Evroklidon	Excalibur	Excidium	Excruciate	Execratorio	Exhale
Eviscerator	Evthanazia	Excalibur	Excidium	Excruciate 666	Execratory	Exhaust
Eviscerator	Evtonazia	Excalibur	Excidium	Excruciating Pain	Execute	Exhaust
Eviscereecon	Evulsion	Excalibur	Excise	Excruciating Terror	Executer	Exhaust
Eviscium	Evyl	Excalibur	Excise	Excruciating	Execution	Exhaust
Evisorax	Ewe	Excalibur	Excisio	Thoughts	Execution	Exhaust Death

Exhauster
Exhaustor
Exhaustus
Exhibit A
Exhibition
Exhibition
Exhorder
Exhornal
Exhort
Exhort
Exhortation
Exhortation
Ex-hortation
Exhortation
Exhumace
Exhuman
Exhumanator
Exhumation
Exhumation
Exhumation
Exhumation
Exhumation
Exhumation
    Convulsion
Exhumator
Exhumator
Exhumator
Exhumator
Exhume
Exhume
Exhumed
Exhumed
Exhumed
Exhumed Day
Exhumer

Exhumer
Exidia
Exigence
Exile
Exile
Exile
Exile
Exile
Exile
Exile
Exile
Exile
Exile
Exile
Exile
Exiled
Exiled
Exiled
Exiled
Exiled on Earth
ExInferis
Exises
Exist
Existence
Existence
Existence
Existence Denied
Existence Denied
Existence Rising
Existench
Existentialism
Existing Threat
Exit
Exit
Exit

Exit
Exit 11
Exit 69
Exit Noise
Exit Strategy
Exit to Eternity
Exit Wounds
Exit Wounds
Exit Wounds
Exit-13
Exitium
Exitium
Exitium
Exitus
Exitus
Exitus Letalis
Exivious
Exkalibur
Exkalibur
Exkavator
Exkrement
Exlibris
EXM93
Exmortem
Exmortem
Exmortes
Exmortis
Exmortis
Ex-Nihil
Exocet
Exocet
Exocet
Exocet
Exodo
Exodus

Exodus
Exoforce
Exomortis
Exon
Exorcion
Exorcism
Exorcism
Exorcist
Exorcist
Exorcist
Exorcist
Exorcist
Exordium
Exordium
Exordium
Exordium Mors
Exordium Mors
Exordium: 418
Exorial
Exorians
Exoristoi
Exorma
Exortal
Ex-Ortation
Exosphere
Exostosis Neoplasm
Exotheria
Exotherm
Exoto
Exotoxic
Exotoxin
Exousia
Expantor
Expatriate
Expect No Mercy

Experience X
Experiment Fear
Experiments in Fear
Experimentum
    Crucis
Expiatoria
Expiration
Expiration Date
Expletive
Explicit Hate
Explicit Hate
Explicit Karma
Explicit Repulsion
Explode
Explode
Explode
Exploder
Exploder
Exploder
Exploder
Exploding
    Corpse Action
Exploding Eyeballs
Exploding Zombies
Explorer
Explorer
Explorers Club
Explosicum
Explosion
Explosive Diarrhea
Expolio
Export
Expose Your Hate
Exposed
Exposed Guts

Exposing Innards
Expozer
Expulser
Expulsion
Expulsion
Expulsion
Expulsion
Expulsive Incision
Expurgate
Expurgo
Exquisite Corpse
Exquisite Pus
Exray
Exsanguination
Exsanguis
Exscidium
Exscruciate
Exsecrator
Exsecratum
Exsecratus
Exsecror
Exsecror
Exsecror Vecordia
Exsequiale
Exsequor
Exseraphim
Exsuderia
Extaasi
Extasy
Extempore
Exterior
Exterior
Exterminance
Exterminate
Exterminate

Exterminate Messiah
Extermination
Extermination Storm
Exterminator
Exterminator
Exterminator
Exterminio
Exterminio
Extincion
Extinción Cerebral
Extinct Gods
Extinct Tradition
Extinction
Extinction
Extinction
Extinction
Extinction
Extinction
Extinction
Extinction Agenda
Extinguished Fire
Extol
Extol Vice
Extorian
Extorsion
Extraction
Extractor
Extreem Eczeem
Extrema
Extrema Uncion
Extreme
Extreme
Extreme Ambience
Extreme Deformity
Extreme Feedback

◀ Extreme Hate

Fallen Christ

Fearless Iranians from Hell	Feed Us Fetus	Fenrisulfr	Festering	Feverish Dreams	Fifth Cripples Band	Fimbulvetr
Fearload	Feedback	Fenriz	Festering Christcunt	Feylamia	Fifth Cross	Fimbulvetr
Fearlord	Feedback	Fentanyl	Festering Cunt	Feythland	5th Dawn	Fimbulwinter
FearOfHatred	Feedstuff	Fera	Festering Flesh	F-Gor	Fifth Dominion	Fimoz
Fearpleasure	Feel Burning Inside	Feral	Festering Puke	Fiarro	Fifth Reason	Fimoz
Fear's Dawn	Fegefeuer	Feral Horde	Festering Saliva	Fiave	Fifth Season	Final
Fears Missing	Fehérlófia	Ferat	Festering Sore	Fictional Prison	54	Final Aphorism
Fears of Disease	Feid	Ferdaves	Festerino	Fictional Tensions	Fifty Lashes	Final Assault
Fears Tomb	Feikn	Feretro	Festung Nebelburg	Field	Fight	Final Assault
Fearscape	Feindbild Mensch	Feretrum	Fetal Butchery	Fieldaway	Fight	Final Axe
Fearsome	Feinstein	Fermentatio	Fetal Decay	Fields of Asphodel	Fight/Delight	Final Breath
Fearsome	Fejd	Fermenting Innards	Fetal Hymen	Fields of Eternity	Fighter	Final Chapter
Fearsome	FekallicA	Fermento	Fetal Morbus	Fields of Jena	Fighterlord	Final Cry
Fearwell	Fekete Sereg	Ferngully	Fetal Mutilation	Fields of Sorrow	Fighting	Final Dawn
Feast Eternal	Feldgrau	Ferocity	Fetal Syndrome	Fields Of The Nephilim	Fighting Warriors	Final Dawn
Feast for the Crows	Felheart	Ferocity	Feticide		Figure of Hate	Final Dawn
Feast of the Zombies	Feline Melinda	Ferocity	Fetish	Fiend	Fil di Ferro	Final Destiny
Feasting Blood	Fellatia	Ferocity	Fetish 69	Fiend	Filacteria	Final Drive
Feasts of Hate	Felony	Ferocity	Feto In Fetus	Fiend	File 101	Final Edge
Februari 93	Femegericht	Ferosity	Fetocide	Fiend	Filii Nigrantium Infernalium	Final Eve
Fecal Christ	Femegericht	Ferox	Fetor of Retching	Fiendance		Final Fall
Fecal Corpse	Femgerichte	Ferox	Fetus Aftermath	Fiendish	Filsufatia	Final Fate
Fecal Corpse	Fen	Ferra Saeva	Fetus by the Pound	Fiendish Gloom	Filth	Final Gasp
Fecal Decimation	Fen Hollen	Ferro & Fogo	Fetus Christ	Fiendish Nymph	Filth	Final Heiress
Fecal Maiden	Fenestra	Ferro Ignique	Fetus Eater	Fiends Carnival of Souls	Filtheless	Final Judgement
Fecalbacteria	Fenfire	Ferrotale	Fetus in Feto		Filthy Asses	Final Prayer
Fecalized Rectal Sperm Spewage	Fenguerous	Fertilizer	Fetus in Fetu	Fierce	Filthy Charity	Final Prophecy
	Fennix	Festation	Fetuxion	Fierce Allegiance	Filthy Christians	Final Prophecy
Fecaloma	Fenria	Fester	Feu Gregeois	Fierce Atmospheres	Filthy Conscience	Final Redemption
Fecifectum	Fenria	Fester	FeuerSang	Fierce Conviction	Filthy Flesh	Final Reign
Feculent Goretomb	Fenrir	Fester 2000	Feuerstein	Fiery Dawn	Filthy Maggoty Cunt	Final Sacrifice
Fedup	Fenrir	Fester Fanatics	Feuersturm	15 Times Dead	Fimbul	Final Shower
Feeble Lies	Fenris	Fester Plague	Fever	Fifth	Fimbulthier	Final Stage
Feeble Minded	Fenris	Festerday	Fever	Fifth Angel	Fimbultyr	Final Stage
	Fenrisulfor	Festerguts	Fevered Dreams	5th Column	Fimbulvet	Final Stand

Final Tragedy
Final Underground
Final Xit
Finally Deceased
Fingernails
Fingerspitzengefühl
Finidi
Finis Africae
Finis Gloria Dei
Finish Me Off
Finisher
Finist
Finist
Finisterra
Finitude
Finngalkn
Finnthomaz
Finntroll
Finnugor
Finstere Herrscher
Finsterforst
Finsternis
Finsternis
Finsternis
Finsterwald
Fiori di Piombo
Firbholg
Fire
Fire Blade
Fire Diamond
Fire for Effect
Fire Legend
Fire Lineage
Fire Makers
Fire of Death

Fire Shadow
Fire Squad
Fire Steel
Fire Steel
Fire Strike
Fire Throne
Fire Trails
Fire Wings
Fireaxe
Fireball Ministry
Firebird
Fireborn
Firebox
Firebreathers
Fireclown
Firefly
Firefly
Firefox
Firehouse
Fireign
Firelake
Fireland
Fireland
Fireline
Firereign
Fires of Gomorrah
Fires of Hell
Firesign
Firesnakes
Firestorm
Firestorm
Firestorm
Firestorm
Firestorm
FireSword

Firevolt
Firewall
Fireway
Firewind
Firezone
Firing Squad
Firmament
Firn
First Aid
First Aid
First Aid
First Blood
First Born
First Degree Murder
First Legion
First Offence
First Reign
First Strike
First Strike
First Strike
First to Fall
Firstborn
FirstBorn
Firstborn Evil
Firstryke
Firststrike
Firth of Damnation
Fisc
Fish
Fisk Svans
Fison
Fission
Fist
Fist
Fistfuck

Fistfull
Fistula
Fistula
Fiurach
5 B Hated
5 Billion Dead
5 Days Bleeding
Five Finger
  Disintegrator
Five Foot Thick
5m3
Five Star Prison Cell
5 Symbols
Five Wheel Drive
5X
5ive's Continuum
  Research Project
Fixer
Fjalar
Fjällstorm
Fjell
Fjellsiam
Fjellsiam
Fjelltrone
Fjoergyn
Fjord
Fjörd
Flächenbrand
Flacmans Port
Flactorophia
Flactorophia
Flag
Flag of Decay
Flag of Doom
Flageladör

Flagellant
Flagellation
Flagellation
Flagellation
Flagellator
Flagellator
Flagellum Dei
Flagellum Dei
Flagelum Dei
Flagitious
  Idiosyncrasy in
  the Dilapidation
Flame
Flame
Flame Berg
Flame Exergon
Flame of War
Flameborn
Flames
Flames
Flames of Arborea
Flames of Hell
Flames of Ignorance
Flames of Misery
Flames of Revenge
Flametal
Flamethrower
Flamethrower
Flaming Anger
Flaming Entity
Flaming Frost
Flaming Skull
Flamma Aeterna
Flamma Ignis
Flammable

Flammea
Flammensturm
Flammentod
Flammentod
Flanez
Flash
Flash Fire
Flash Point
Flash Range
Flash Terrorist
Flashback
Flashback
Flashback of Anger
Flashover
Flaskavsae
Flat Ricide
Flatbacker
Flatblak
Flatline
Flatline
Flatlined
Flatulation
Flauros
Flaw
Flayel Svart
Flaying
Flayst
Flegethon
Flegethon
Flegeton
Flegeton
Flegeton
Flegma
Fleischmann
Fleischwolf

Fleret
Flesh
Flesh
Flesh Consumed
Flesh Deformation
Flesh Disgorged
Flesh Divine
Flesh Divine
Flesh Engorged
Flesh Feast
Flesh Feast
Flesh Filth
Flesh for the Beast
Flesh Gallery
Flesh Grinder
Flesh Hammer
Flesh Intoxication
Flesh Laceration
Flesh Made Sin
Flesh Mechanic
Flesh on Fridays
Flesh Parade
Flesh Removal
Flesh Temptation
Fleshart
Fleshbomb
Fleshcraft
Fleshcrave
Fleshcrawl
Fleshdance
Fleshdawn Manifesto
Fleshdoll
Flesheater
Fleshgore
Fleshgrind

Forgery

Free Corpse

Free Weed
Freebase
Freedom Call
Freefall
Freehand
Freek
Freevil
Freeway
Freewill
Freezen Blood
Freezing Darkness
Freezing Fall
Freezing Fog
Freezing Winds
Freitod
Freitod
French Maide
Frendo Absolutus
Frenetic
Frenzy
Frequency
Fret Zero
Fretboard
Freternia
Freund Hein
Frexonzo
Friar Rush
Friday the 13th
Friends
Fright
Fright Night
Fright Night
Frightful Cross
Frightmare
Frigid Bich

Frijos
Frimost
Frimost
Frodmortell
Frogskin
From a Great Height
From Ashes
From Below
From Beyond
From Beyond
From Beyond
From Beyond
From Beyond Death
From Chaos
From Citizen
  to Soldier
From Depths
From Dissension
From Exile
From Forgotten Being
From Moonshadows
  Falling
From My Grave
From My Soul
From Nowhere
From the Ashes
From the Carnival
  of Horrors
From the Dark
From the Darkness
From the Depths
From the North
From the Waters
  of Lake
From This Day

From Thy Ashes
From Under
  the Gallows
From Within
Frondescent Gout
Front
Front
Front Beast
Front Terror
Front Towards
  Enemy
Frontal
Frontears
Frontier
Front-line
FroschGott
Frost
Frost
Frost
Frost
Frost
Frost
Frost and Fury
Frost Bite
Frost Core
Frost Domain
Frost Like Ashes
Frostbeer
Frostbite
Frostbitten Kingdom
Frostblot
Frostborn
Frostburn
Frostdemonstorm
Frostdemonstorm
Frostfall

Frostfinsternis
Frosthardr
Frosthold
Frostkorp
Frostkrieg
Frostland
Frostmoon
Frostmoon Eclipse
Frostmoon Eclipse
Frostmourne
Frostnacht
Frostnatt
Frostrike
Fröstskög
Frostskogr
Frostthrone
Frostwald
Frostwind
Frosty Emotion
Frown
Frozen
Frozen
Frozen
Frozen
Frozen
Frozen
Frozen Asphyxia
Frozen Blood
Frozen Blood
Frozen Corpse
  Supremacy
Frozen Cries
Frozen Cruelty
Frozen Darkness
Frozen Death

Frozen Doberman
Frozen Embers
Frozen Embers
Frozen Eternity
Frozen Eyes
Frozen Fields
Frozen Fire
Frozen Flame
Frozen Forest
Frozen Forest
Frozen Glare
Frozen Illusion
Frozen Illusion
Frozen Infinity
Frozen Mind
Frozen Mist
Frozen Moon
Frozen Pain
Frozen Paradise
Frozen Rain
Frozen Scars
Frozen Shadow
Frozen Shadows
Frozen Soil
Frozen Soul
Frozen Souls
Frozen Sun
Frozen Sun
Frozen Tear
Frozen Tears
Frozen Tears
Frozen Tears
Frozen Tears
Frozen Throne
Frozen Throne

Frozen Time
Frozen Vein
Frozen Winds
Frozen Wings
Frozen Within
  Flames
Frozn
Fruit Tree
Frusthatred
Frustkiller
Frustradicción
Fuck Off
Fuck Off and Die!
Fuck Shit Up
Fuck the Facts
Fuck U All
Fuck... I'm Dead
Fucked With
  a Chainsaw
Fuckez-Vous
Fuckfest
Fuckin' Drill
Fucking Funeral
Fucksaw
Fucktory-X
Fucktotum
Fuego Cruzado
Fuego Eterno
Fuego Negro
Fuelblooded
Fueled
Fueled by Failure
Fueled by Fire
Fueled by Hate
Fueled by Ignorance

Fuerza Oculta
Fugitive
Fugue
Fügue
Führer
Fulci
Fulcrum Creak
Fulgor
Fulgur
Full Body
  Hemorrhage
Full Circle
Full Circle
Full Decay
Full Diesel
Full Frontal Assault
Full Metal Jacket
Full Moon
Full Moon
  Lycanthropy
Full Noise
Full of Anger
Full of Rage
Full Power
Full Strike
Fullgore
Fullmoon
Fullmoon
Fullmoon
Fullmoon Promises
Fullmoon Rise
FullMoonChild
Fullmoon's Insignia
Fulltrap
Fully Consumed

◈ Fultrack

Function Cease
Funcunt
Fundum
Funebral
Funebrarum
Funebre
Funebre
Funebre
Fúnebre
Funebre Hate
Funebre Inferi
Funebres Nuptiae
Funebria
Funebrial
Funebris
Funebrum
Funeraille
Funérailles
Funeral
Funeral
Funeral
Funeral
Funeral
Funeral
Funeral
Funeral
Funeral Age
Funeral Bitch
Funeral Bitch
Funeral Ceremony
Funeral Chant
Funeral Chant
Funeral Countess
Funeral Cult
Funeral Cult

Funeral Death
Funeral Dirge
Funeral Dirge
Funeral Dusk
Funeral Dusk
Funeral Dust
Funeral Elegy
Funeral Eucharist
Funeral Eve
Funeral Feast
Funeral Feast
Funeral Fire
Funeral Fog
Funeral Fog
Funeral Fog
Funeral For
    Rosewater
Funeral Forest
Funeral Fornication
Funeral Frost
Funeral Frost
Funeral God
Funeral Hammer
Funeral Holocaust
Funeral Howl
Funeral in Autumn
Funeral In Heaven
Funeral Inception
Funeral Inception
Funeral Lust
Funeral March
Funeral March
Funeral March
Funeral Mask
Funeral Mist

Funeral Mist
Funeral Moon
Funeral Moon
Funeral Moon
Funeral Moth
Funeral Mourning
Funeral Nation
Funeral Oath
Funeral of Life
Funeral of My Soul
Funeral of Soul
Funeral Oration
Funeral Party
Funeral Planet
Funeral Poetry
Funeral Procession
Funeral Putrid
Funeral Pyre
Funeral Pyre
Funeral Pyre
Funeral Pyre
Funeral Rape
Funeral Revolt
Funeral Rip
Funeral Rites
Funeral Rites
Funeral Rites
Funeral Ritual
Funeral Sex
Funeral Speech
Funeral Stench
Funeral Throne
Funeral Urn
Funeral Vault
Funeral War

Funeral Winds
Funeral Winter
Funeralhammer
Funerality
Funeralium
Funerarium
Funerarium
Funerarium
Funerary Dirge
Funerary Pit
Funerary Ward
Funeratus
Funerea Luna
Funereal
Funereal Dusk
Funereal Luxuria
Funereal Moon
Funereum
Funereus
Funerii
Funeris Nocturnum
Funerium
Funerius
Funerot
Funerum Mortis
    Sculptum
Funerus
Funest
Funestia
Fungal Hex
Fungoid Stream
Fungus
Funnel Head
Funny Crime
Funny Farm

Fuoco Fatuo
Fuorimoda
Furbowl
Furcalor
Furcas
Furdidurke
Furia
Furia
Furia
Furia
Furia
Furia Animal
Furia Animal
Fúria Negra
Furiatak
Furien
Furioso
Furious Barking
Furious Trauma
Furnace
Furnace
Furnaze
Further Lo
Furthest Shore
Fury
Fury
Fury
Fury Never Fades
Fury of 1000 Suns
Fury of Fire
Fury161
Furya
Furya
Furya
Furze

Fuse
Fuseboxx
fusionofhate
Futhark
Futhark 14
Futura
Future Allies
Future Darkness
Future Disorder
Future Fate
Future Is Tomorrow
Future Tense
Futureless
Fuzz Fuzz Machine
Fuzzbender
Fuzzmatica
Fuzzybearoth
Fylking
Fyrad
Fyre

G.A.T.E.S.
G.I.S.M.
G.L.A.S.
G.-L.O.C.
G.L.S.
G.O.D.
G.O.D.
G.O.E.
G.O.R.E.
G.O.R.E.
G.P.I.
G.R.I.N.D.
G.T.I.
G.U.T.
Gaahlskagg
Gabriel Amauru

Gabriel's Cry
Gabriel's Path
Gack
Gadarian
Gadget
Gaebalein
Gaeldorn Jhan
Gaffed
Gagas
Gaia
Gaia
Gaia Epicus
Gaia Fallen
Gaia Metal
Gaia Prelude
Gaia Returns

Gaias Pendulum
Gaia's Vestige
Gain
Gaisen March
Galactic Cowboys
Galactus 77
Galadriel
Galadriel
Galahad
Galaktika
Galar
Galatea
Galaxis
Galdrer
Gale
Galen
Galerna
Galexia
Galgenberg
Galgeras
Gallery of Darkness
Gallery of Dreams
Gallery of Lore
Gallery of Souls
Gallery of Sound
Gallery of Tragedies
Gallhammer
Gallia Fornax
Gallileous
Gallina Negra
Galloglass
Gallow
Gallow
Gallowmere
Gallowmere

Gallows
Gallows Eve
Gallows of Golgotha
Gallows Pole
Gallows Pole
Galneryus
Galokwudzuwis
Galope Mortal
Galskap
Galvorn
Gama Bomb
Gamalyel
Gambit
Game Over
Gamera
Gamma
Gamma Ray
Gammacide
Gammadion
Gammoth
Gandalf
Gandalf
Gandillion
Ganesha
Gang
Gang Alien
Gang Loco
Gangland
Gangrena
Gangrena
Gangrena Febrosa
Gangrena Gasosa
Ganon
Ganymed
Ganymed

Ganzmord
Gaoth Anair
Gaphia
Garant
Garbage Disposal
Garbe of Life
Garcharot
Garckus
Gardarika
Gardarika
Garden in Darkness
Garden of Autumn
Garden of Decay
Garden of Delight
Garden of Eden
Garden of Grief
Garden of Sadness
Garden of Shadows
Garden of Silence
Garden of Worm
Garden of Worm
Garden Wall
Garden White
Gardenian
Gardens of Cry
Gardens of Gehenna
Gardens of Grief
Gardens of Grief
Gardens of Obscurity
Gardens of Stone
Gardy-Loo
Gargamax
Gargamel
Gargamyrk
Gargantula

Gargara
Gargaryss
Gargauth
Gargola
Gargola
Gargoyle
Gargoyle
Gargoyle
Gargoyle
Gargravarr
Gargula
Gargullas
Garland
Garm
Garm
Garm
Garmenhord
Garmine Tango
Garnov
Garrisoned
Garrota
Garrote
Garroter
Garrotte
Garrsinn
Garstig
Garuda
Garuda
Garudas Mission
Garwall
Gary Churr and
  the Beers
Gas
Gas
Gaschamber

Gashammer
Gashed By an Axe
Gashouse Garden
Gaskin
Gaslight
Gasmah
Gasoline Baptism
Gasoline Grenade
Gasoorlog
Gaspanic
Gassturm
Gast
Gastonia
Gastre
Gastric Ulcer
Gastric Ulcer
Gastrick Burst
Gastunk
Gaszimmer
Gâte
Gate
Gate
Gate 9
Gate Crusher
Gate of Darkness
Gate of Darkness
Gatekeeper
Gates of Azharia
Gates of Dawn
Gates of Dawn
Gates of Dis
Gates of Enoch
Gates of Eternity
Gates of Holocaust
Gates of Ishtar

Gorret
Gort
Gort
Gortal
Gortauru
Gorthaur
Gorthaur
Gorthaur
Gorthaur
Gorthaur's Wrath
Gorthyrmus
Gortia
Gortician
Gorugoth
Gorvomb
Gorvomd
Gory
Gory Blister
Gory Gruesome
Gory Host
Goryfication
Goryptic
Gorysaint
Gorzb
Gosforth
Gospel of the Horns
Gospodari
  Mikrofonije
Gostwind
Goth Romance
Gotha
Gotham
Gotham
Gotham City
Gothërfall

Gothic
Gothic
Gothic Castle
Gothic Fate
Gothic Knights
Gothic Sky
Gothic Slam
Gothic Vox
Gothician
Gothmog
Gothmog
Gothmog
Gotmoor
Gotsu Totsu Kotsu
Götterdämmerung
Gottes Krieg
Gottes Vergessene
  Seelen
Gotthard
Gottlos
Gouged Eye
Govanon
Government
  of Pansies
Governmental
  Crucifixtion
Gower
Gozar
Gozarian
Gozer
Graabein
Graaf
Graal
Graal
Grabak

Graben
Grabesland
Grabesmond
Grabgesang
Grabnebelfürsten
Grabschänder
Grabschändung
Grace
Grace
Grace Force
Grace Gale
Grace of Dispair
Gracecall
Gracefallen
Gracepoint
Gracious Violence
Grade A Fancy
Gradus Pentalphae
Graf Orlock
Graf Spee
Gräfenstein
Grafenwald
Graff Spee
Graffiti 61
Grafvolluth
Grafzerk
Grail
Grailknights
Grain
Grain
Grain
Gralloch
Grålysning
Gramary
Gramheim

Grämlich
Grammaton
Gran Dia
Grand Alchemist
Grand Beast Sodomy
Grand Belial's Key
Grand Bite
Grand Design
Grand Emperor
Grand Facade
Grand Failure
Grand Illusion
Grand Lux
Grand Magus
Grand Nocturne
Grand Sermon
Grande Gremoire
Grandeur et
  Decadence
Grandma
Grandma's Vomit
Grandmother is Dead
Grang
Granhammer
Granit
Grannos
Grantig
Granulocytic
  Blastoma
Granulom
Granulosum
Graphic Violence
Graphite Symphony
Grapinherd
Grasp of Sense

Grass
Grass Harp
Grauen Pestanz
Graupel
Grausamkeit
Grausig
Grausig
Gravdal
Grave
Grave
Grave Desecration
Grave Desecration
Grave Desecrator
Grave Desire
Grave Digger
Grave Flowers
Grave Forsaken
Grave Forsaken
Grave Gore
Grave in the Sky
Grave Lord
Grave of Shadows
Grave Silence
Grave Temple
Grave Throne
Grave Worship
Grave wurm
Gravedom
GraveDroid
Gravehammer
Gravehill
Gravehole
Gravehome
Graveland
Graveless

Gravelgrinder
Graven
Graven
Graven Image
Graven Image
Graven Image
Graven Image
Gravengard
Gravenlord
Gravepig
Gravepig
Graves At Sea
Graves of the
  Endless Fall
Graveshit
Graveside
Graveslime
Gravespawn
Gravestench
Gravestone
Gravestone
Gravestorm
Gravestorm
Graveworm
Gravewürm
Graveyard
Graveyard
Graveyard BBQ
Graveyard Dirt
Graveyard Ghost
Graveyard Rodeo
Graveyard Shift
Gravferd
Gravgard
Graviora Manent

Graviter
Graviton
Gravity
Gravity
Gravity
Gravity
Gravity
Gravity
Gravity Kills
Gravlik
Gray Lines of
  Perfection
Grayblack
Grayceon
Graycode
Graymalkin
Grayscale
Grazadh
Grazed
Great American
  Desert
Great Blood
Great Coven
Great Horn
Great Master
Great Sorrow
Great Vast Forest
Great White
Grecco
Greed
Greedy Invalid
Green
Green Back
Green Carnation
Green Division
Green Miles

◀ Gruntruck

Gruntsplatter
Gruzom
Grym
Grymt
Gryn
Grynch
GS Truds
GSA
Guadaña
Guahaihoque
Guano Apes
Guarana
Guardian
Guardian Angel
Guardian Force
Guardian Heliotrope
Guardianes del
   Imperio
Guardiani di
   Frontiera
Guardian's Nail
Guardians of Dreams
Guardians of Hell
Guardians of
   Mankind
Guardians of Profane
   Secrets
Guardians of Steel
Guardians of the
   Flame
Guardians of the
   Moonlight
Guardians of Time
Guarnerius
Güdenläwd

Gudgen
Guehenom
Guenhyvar
Guerilla
Guernica
Guerra
Guerra Muerte
Guerra Santa
Guerreiros Das
   Trevas
Guerrero Inmortal
Guerreros del Metal
Guerrilha
Guerrilha
Guerrilla
Guerrilla
GUF
Guidance of Sin
Guided Cradle
Guild of Destruction
Guilhotina
Guilles de Rais
Guillotine
Guillotine
Guillotine
Guillotine
Guillotine
Guillotine
Guillotine
Guilthee
Guilty of Reason
Guiltys Law
Guinevere
Guippiud
Guitar Pete's Axe

Attack
Gulgatha
Güllethrasher
Gulu Locus
Gumbody
Gum-Hen
Gun Barrel
Gunbridge
Gunfire
Gungnir
Gungnir
Gungnir
Gunhaver
Gunmetal Grey
Gunpowder
Gunship 666
Guntlet Draw
Gurd
Gurges
Gurkkhas
Gurthang
Gurtholfinn
Gurz
Gus G.
Gush
Gust of Anger
Guszchar
Gut Absorber
Gut Instinct
Gut Thrusting
   Torment
Gutha
Gutlock
Gutrix
GutRot

Gutrot
Guts
Gutsaw
Gutslasher
Gutted
Gutted
Gutted Corpse
Gutted Pulp
Gutted Remains
Gutter Sirens
Guttersludge
Guttural
Guttural
   Engorgement
Guttural Secrete
Gutural
Gutworm
Gutwrench
Gutwrench V.B.C.
Guy Mann-Dude
Gwar
Gwen Stacy
Gwydion
Gwydyon
Gwyllion
Gwynbleidd
Gwynn Ap Nudd
GxSxD
Gynecrology
Gyöngyvér
Gyorai
Gypsy

⬦

H and H
H. Kristal
H.A.T.E.
H.A.V.O.C.
H.C. Minds
H.E.A.L.
H.E.W.D.A.T.
H.I.M.
H.I.V. Positive
H.M.P.
H.O.P.E.
H.O.S.T.I.L.E.
H.pylori
H24
H2SO4
H3O +

Ha Lela
Haar
Haat
Haatstrijd
Habacus Sucabah
Habeas Corpus
Habeas Corpus
Habitat
Habitual
Haborim
Haborym
Haborym
Haborym
Haboryn
Hacavitz
Haceldama

Hachoir
Haciendo Patria
Hacker
Hacksaw
Hacksaw to
    the Throat
Hacksore
Hacktician
Hacride
Hacusti
Hadamma
Hadan
Hadan Drailh
Hader
Hades
Hades
Hades
Hades
Hädes
Hades Adorned
Hades Almighty
Hades Archer
Hades Inc.
Hades U
Hadez
Hadiann
Hadotor
Hadúr
Haelo
Hælvete
Haema
Haemophagia
Haemophagus
Haemophilia
Haemorr Drench

Haemorrhage
Haemorrhage
Haemoth
Hæresis
Hæreticus
Hagal
Hagalar
Hagalaz
Hagalaz' Runedance
Hagall
Hagatyr
Hagelsturm
Hagen
Haggard
Hagl
Hagridden
Hagridden
Haiden
Hail
Hail Ganzir
Hail of Fire
Hail Satanas
Hail to Arms
Hailstorm
Hailstorm
Hailstorm
Hailstorm
Haimad
Haine Noire
Hair Of The Dog
Hairy Pussy
Häive
Haizum
Haji's Kitchen
Hakenkreuz

Hakenkreuz
    Nocturna
Hakenkreuzzug
HAL 9000
Halcyon
Halcyon
Halcyon
Halcyon Way
Halfirien
Halfling Thief
Halfmoon
Halford
Halfway to Gone
Halgadom
Halifax Gibbet
Halifax Gibbot
Hall Aflame
Halley
Halley
Hallion
Hallowed
Hallowed
Hallowed
Hallowed Be
    Thy Goat
Hallowed Curse
Hallowed Point
Halloween
Halloween
Hallows End
Hallows Eve
Hallows Eve
Hallstatt
Hallstatt
Hallucatus

Hallucigenia
Hallucinate
Hallucination
Hallways of
    the Always
Halmony
Halo
Halo Manash
Halo of Locusts
Halo of Shadows
Halo of Thorns
Halomachine
Halor
Halucynogen
Halun
Hamadria
Hamargroll
Hamarr
Hamartia
Hamartigenia
Hämatom
Hamburger Alien
Hamelyn
Hamerex
Hamergilde
Hamestagan
Hamingia
Hamingja
Hamka
Hamlet
Hamlyn
Hammathaz
Hammer
Hämmer
Hammer

Hammer
Hammer
Hammer
Hammer Head
Hammer of Eden
Hammer of Justice
Hammer of Revenge
Hammer of the Gods
Hammer ov Qliphoth
Hammerdown
Hammered
Hammered
Hammered
Hammerfall
Hammerhawk
Hammerhead
Hammerhead
Hammerhead
Hammerheart
Hammermauler
Hammeron
Hammeron
Hammeron
Hammers
Hammers
Hammers of
    Misfortune
Hammers Rule
Hammerschmitt
Hammerwhore
Hammerwitch
Hammodytes
Hammurabi
Hamson
Han Jin Oakland

Hatework	Hatrix	Havoc	Hazy Azure	Headless	Heartache	Heaven If
Hatework	Hatross	Havoc	Hazy Decay	Headless Christ	Heartless	Heaven Rays
Hateworks	Hats Barn	Havoc	Hazy Hamlet	Headless Cross	Heartless	Heaven Shall Burn
Hatfulder	Haunt	Havoc Mass	Hazy Hill	Headless Cross	Heartless	Heaven Ward
Hathor	Haunted	Havoc Vulture	Hazzard	Headlight	Heartless	Heavenblast
Hathor	Haunted by Angels	HavocHate	Hazzard	Headline	Heartline	Heavendeer
Hathor	Haunted Garage	HavocS	HB	Headlock	Heartscore	HeavenFall
Hathor	Haunted Gorge	Havohej	Hbattoir	Headlong	Heartwork	HeavenFalls
Hati	Haunted House	Havok	H-Bomb	Headmeat	Heartwork	Heavenly
Hatjan	Haunted Shores	Havok	He Is the Storm	Headmess	Heartwork	Heavenly Bride
Hator	Haunted Visions	Havok	He Who Corrupts	Headon	Heartwork	Heavenly Host
Hatred	Haunting Chants	Havok	Head	Head-On	Heathen	Heavenly Kingdom
Hatred	Hauntz	Havok	Head Cleaner	Headpress	Heathen Dawn	Heavenly Soldiers
Hatred	Haurmabeath	Havora	Head Control System	HeadRot	Heathen Deity	Heaven's Cry
Hatred	Haust	Havorum	Head Crusher	Heads or Tales	Heathen Fist	Heavens Edge
Hatred	Haustmyrkr	Hawaii	Head Force	Headshot	Heathen Foray	Heavens Gate
Hatred	Häväistys	Hawg Jaw	Head Hammer	Headsplosion	Heathen Hoof	Heaven's Guardian
Hatred	Havana Black	Hawk	Head Hung Low	Headstone	Heathendom	Heavens Hell
Hatred	Havarax	Hawkmoon	Head Krusher	Headstone	Heathenhammer	Heaven's Inversion
Hatred	Havayoth	Hawthorn	Head of David	Headstone	Heathen's Rage	Heavens Nearby
Hatred	Have Mercy	Hawthorn	Head On Collision	Headstone Epitaph	Heather Leather	Heaven's Rage
Hatred	Haven	Haxen	Headache	Headstrong	Heatseeker	Heavenshore
Hatred	Haven	Hayagriva	Headbanger	HeadtR.I.P.	Heave	Heavenward
Hatred	Haven	Hayras	Headbangers	Headup	Heaven	Heavenwood
Hatred	Haven Denied	Haywire	Headcage	Headwound	Heaven	Heavy and Loud
Hatred	Havengrave	Hazael	Headcrasher	Healing Sixes	Heaven Ablaze	Heavy Bones
Hatred Arouser	Havenless	Hazarax	Headfucker	Healthy Drain	Heaven Ablaze	Heavy Chainzz
Hatred Divine	Havoc	Hazard	Headgirl	Heaps of Dead	Heaven And Earth	Heavy Day
Hatred Dusk	Havoc	Hazardous Waste	Headhaunter	Hear 'n Aid	Heaven and Hell	Heavy Demons
Hatred of Wolf	Havoc	Haze	Headhunter	Hearing Impaired	Heaven and Hell	Heavy Guitars
Hatred Profound	Havoc	Haze	Headhunter	Hearken	Heaven and Hell	Heavy Load
Hatred Slave	Havoc	Haze	Headhunter	Hearse	Heaven Force	Heavy Lord
Hatred Spawn	Havoc	Haze in Flames	Headhunter D.C.	Hearse	Heaven Grey	Heavy Metal Army
Hatred Unleashed	Havoc	Hazerfan	Headless	Heart & Stone	Heaven Hill	Heavy Metal Kingdom
Hatrik	Havoc	Hazhelh	Headless	Heart of Darkness	Heaven Holocaust	

Heavy Pettin'	Hector	Heimdall	Helfahrt	Hell Bell	Hellanbach	Hellebaard
Heavy the World	Hectorite	Heimdallr	Helfield	Hell Bent For Leather	Helland	Hellectrochains
Heavy Water	Hed Planet Earth	Heimdalls Horn	Helgor	Hell Church	Hellavator	Hellegion
Heavy Weather	Hedache	Heimdalls Wacht	Helgrid	Hell Church	Hellbastard	Hellegion
Heavyness	Hedawn	Heimnar	Helgrind	Hell Denied	Hellbelly	Hellegion
Heavynessiah	Hedenskrig	Heinous Criminal	Helgrind	Hell Dormant	Hellbender	Hellen
Hebephrenic	Hedfirst	Heinous Killings	Helgrindr	Hell Dörmer	Hellbender	Hellennium
Hebosagil	Hedon Cries	Heir Apparent	Helheim	Hell Dunkel	Hellblaster	Heller
Hebrea	Hedor	Heir of Destiny	Helheim	Hell Eternal	Hellblazer	Hellewoud
Hebrea	Hedrun	Heithni	Helheim	Hell Fire	Hellblazer	Hellfire
Hebron	Heed	Hejira	Helhesten	Hell Gods	Hellblock 6	Hellfire
Hebron	Heel	Hekatomb	Helian	Hell Hound	Hellboozer Union	Hellfire
Hecadoth	Heemat	Hekatomba	Helician	Hell Icon	HellBorn	Hellfire
Hecate	Hefaistova Lyra	Hekel	Helicon	Hell In A Cell	Hell-Born	Hellfire
Hecate	Hefestos	Heksekunst	Helicon	Hell in a Cell	Hellborne	Hellfire
Hecate Enthroned	Hefeystos	Hekseri	Helion	Hell in Myself	Hellbound	Hellfire
Hecates	Hegemon	Hektcöre	Helion	Hell Mary	Hellbound	Hellfire BC
Hecatomb	Hegemoon	Hektor	Helium Head	Hell Militia	Hellbound	Hellfist
Hecatomb	Hehlock	Hekvintr	Helix	Hell 'n' Back	Hellbound	Hellfrost Armada
Hecatomb	Heia	Hel	Helizer	Hell Patrol	Hellbound	Hellfuck
Hecatomb	Heiden	Hel	Helka Hith	Hell Patrol	Hellbound	Hellfucked
Hecatomb	Heidenblut	Helangår	Helkagor	Hell Patrol	Hellbound	Hellfueled
Hecatomb	Heidenland	Helcaraxe	Helken	Hell Patrol	Hellbound	Hellgenom
Hecatomb	Heidenlärm	Helcaraxe	Helker	Hell Promise	Hellbox	Hellgoat
Hecatomb	Heidenreich	Helcaraxe	Hell	Hell Razor	Hellbreath	Hellgoat
Hecatombe	Heidentum	Helcaraxë	Hell	Hell Rot	Hellbrood	Hellhammer
Hecatombe	Heidenwald	Held in Scorn	Hell	Hell Spirit	Hellbutcher	Hellhate
Hecatombe	Heidenwelt	Held Under	Hell	Hell Terrorist	Hellchasm	Hellhaunted
Hecatombe	Heidenzorn	Held Under	Hell	Hell Trucker	Hellchild	Hellhorde
Hecatombe	Heidevolk	Heldar	Hell	Hell United	Hellcome	Hellhound
Hecatombic	Heidt	Heldentod	Hell	Hell Vomit	Hellcult	Hellhound
Hecatomic	Heifer	Heldentum	Hell & Heaven	Hell Within	Helldiver	Hellhouse
Hectic	Heiligs Blechle	Heldgard	Hell	Hellablack	Helldiver	HellHunter
Hectic 99	Heimat	Helegion	Hell Avengers	Hellacaust	Helldozer	Hellias
Hectic Patterns	Heimdall	Helevorn	Hell Baron's Wrath	Hellacious	Helldrunk	Hellicon

Hellion	Hellraiser	Hellspawn	Helpness	Hemgor	Herazz	Heretic
Hellion	Hellraiser	Hellspell	Helreið	Hemisphere	Herbst	Heretic
Hellions	Hellraisers	Hellstaff	Helritt	Hemlock	Hercules	Heretic Angels
Hellirion	Hellraizer	Hellstorm	Helrunar	Hemlock	Hercules	Heretic Blood
Hellish	Hellraper	Hellstorm	Hels	Hemlock	Here in After	Heretic Fork
Hellish	Hellraptor	Hellstorm	Hel's Crusade	Hemlock	Here Lies	Heretic Soul
Hellish Breed	Hellrazer	Hellstorm	Helsefyr	Hemlock	Herege	Heretical
Hellish Crossfire	Hellrazer	Hellstrike	Helslakt	Hemlock	Herejes	Heretical Guilt
Hellish Hounds	Hellrazor	Helltank	Helstar	Hemnur	Herejia	Heretics
Hellish Orkestra	Hellrealm	Hellthrasher	Helter Skelter	Hemogastric	Herem	Heretic's Fork
Hellish War	Hellride	Hellthrone	Helvegr	Hemoragy	Herenwen	Heretics Fork
Hellisher	Hellrider	Helltown	Helvellyn	Hemorragia	Heresi	Heretik
Hellishthrone	Hellriders	Helltrain	Helvergr	Hemorrogical Vomit	Heresia	Heretika
Hellisphear	Hell's	Hell-Train	Helvete	Hemperor	Heresians	Herezja
Hellixxir	Hell's	Hellusination	Helvete	Hëmsythreixck	Heresiarh	Herfst
Hellkult	Hells Belles	Hellvate	Helvete	Henceforth	Heresy	Hergorn
HellLight	Hell's Crack	Hellven	Helvete	Hengest	Heresy	Heritage
Hellmaggot	Hell's Dagger	Hellvetic Frost	Helvete	Henker	Heresy	Heritage
Hellmark	Hell's Eden	Hellveto	Helvete	Henker	Heresy	Heritage
Hellmasker	Hell's Infinite VI	Hellvetron	Helvete Natten	Henoth	Heresy	Heritage
Hellmasters	Hell's Kitchen	Hellvetron	Helvetets Port	Heol Telwen	Heresy	Héritage Mystique
Hellmight	Hell's Sweat	Hellvoid	Helvetica	Heorot	Heresy	Héritiers de la Haine
Hellnight	Hellsaw	HellVomit	Helvette	Heos	Heresy	Herjalf
Hellnomorf	Hellsaw	Hellwar	Helvintr	Hephaestus	Heresy	Herjan
Hello Terror	Hellscream	Hellward	Helvis	Hepheastus	Heresy	Herlathing
Helloïse	Hellsermon	Hellwitch	Helwetti	Heptameron	Heresy	Hermano
Helloween	Hellshness	Hellwrath	Helwulf	Her Enchantment	Heresy	Hermaphrodit
Hellpenis	Hellshock	Hellyeah	Hematfrost	Her Majesty	Heresyarch	Hermaphroditic
Hellpig	Hellshock	Helm of Awe	Hematit	Her Name Is Death	Heresyer	Pissparty Pleasure
Hellpreacher	Hellsing	Helmet	Hematoma	Her Rotting Ways	Heretic	Hermetic
Hellracer	Hellslaughter	Helms Deep	Hematoma	Her Seduction	Heretic	Brotherhood
Hellrage	Hellspawn	Helmskey	Hematoma	Her Warm Blood	Heretic	Hermetic Vastness
Hellraised	Hellspawn	Heloisa	Hematovore	Her Whisper	Heretic	Hermética
Hellraiser	Hellspawn	Helotry	Hemdale	Herald	Heretic	Hermh
Hellraiser	Hellspawn	Helots	Hemelbos	Heralder	Heretic	Hermit Age
				Heraldry	Heretic	

Hyoid

Ill Sanity

Illapa
Illdisposed
Illegal
Illegal Angel
Illegal Operation
Ill-Fated
Illidiance
Illminite
Illnath
Ill-Natured
Illogicist
Illogo
Illska
Illtempered
Illuminacht
Illuminandi
Illuminatus
Illuminous
Illusion
Illusion
Illusion
Illusion
Illusion of Clarity
Illusion Suite
Illusionation
Illusionists
Illusions
Illusions
Illwill
Illyrian
Ilmatar
Ilungara
Iluvatar
Ilvestgrol
Ilyes

Image
Image Beyond
Imagen Putrefacta
Images of Eden
Images of Violence
Imagika
Imaginery
Imaginoid
Imago Mortis
Imago Mortis
Imbalance
Imbecilator
Imbecile
Imbeciles
Imber
Imbleeding
Imbolc
Imbortir
Imbrue
IMC
Imein Dargor
Imindain
Imland
Immacolata
Immaconcept
Immaculate
Immaculate
   Molestation
Immanis
Immanis
Immemoreal
Immemorial
Immemorial Ages
Immemorial
   Celtic Wind

Immension
Immersed in Blood
Immersion
Imminent Psychosis
Imminentchaos
Immiserate
Immodus
Immolated
Immolation
Immolator
Immolatus
Immoral Intent
Immorally Demonic
Immorior
Immortadell
Immortal
Immortal
Immortal
Immortal
Immortal
Immortal Avenger
Immortal Choir
Immortal Corpse
Immortal Cringe
Immortal Death
Immortal Death
Immortal Destruction
Immortal Dominion
Immortal Fate
Immortal Flesh
Immortal Gate
Immortal Grain
Immortal Hammer
Immortal Hate
Immortal Legion

Immortal Possession
Immortal Pride
Immortal Remains
Immortal Remains
Immortal Rites
Immortal Rites
Immortal Sin
Immortal Slave
Immortal Soul
Immortal Souls
Immortal Suffering
Immortal Tears
Immortal Throne
Immortal Visions
Immortalis
Immortalis Machina
Immortality
Immortality
Immortally
   Committed
Immortellys
Immorten
Immotus
Immuno Affinity
Immured
Immurement
ImNotOk
Imoned
Imoonterk
Imopectore
Imortalis
Imortela
IMP
Imp
Impact

Impact
Impact
Impact
Impact Winter
Impact Wrench
Impacto Fecal
Impair
Impale
Impale
Impaled
Impaled
Impaled Angel
Impaled Nazarene
Impalement
Impalement
Impaler
Impaler
Impaler
Imparage
Impatto Frontale
Impedigon
Impellitteri
Impending Doom
Impending Doom
Impending Doom
Impending Dread
Impera
Imperador Belial
Imperanon
Imperanon
Imperator
Imperator
Imperia
Imperial
Imperial

Imperial
Imperial
Imperial
Imperial
Imperial
Imperial
Imperial
Imperial Battlesnake
Imperial Crystalline
   Entombment
Imperial Darkness
Imperial Darkness
Imperial Devastation
Imperial Domain
Imperial Doom
Imperial Empire
Imperial Foeticide
Imperial Hordes
Imperial Majesty
Imperial Rage
Imperial Sodomy
Imperial Tyrants
Imperial Wizzard
Imperiis
Imperiled Eyes
Imperio
Imperio Death
Império do Caos
Imperio Nocturno
Império Profano
Imperious
Imperious
   Malevolence
Imperium
Imperium
Imperium

Imperium
Imperium
Imperium
Imperium
Imperium
   Dekadenz
Imperium Frost
Imperium Infernale
Imperium Infernalis
Imperium Memorial
Imperium Occultum
Imperium Sacrum
Imperium Tenebrae
Imperium
   Tenebrarum
Impery
Impetigo
Impeto Paranoico
Impetuous Rage
Impetus Maleficum
Impetus Malignum
Impheria
Impherya
Impiety
Impiety
Impiety's Forest
Impious
Impious
Impious
Impious
Impious
Impious Havoc
Impish
Implacable
Implosion

❧ Implosive
  Disgorgence

Imposer
Impostor
Imprecated Destiny
Imprecation
Imprecation
Imprecatory
Imprecatory
Imprecatory
Imprekator
Improvision
Imprudence
Impudent
Impulse
Impulse
Impulse
  Manslaughter
Impulso de Tanatos
Impure
Impure
Impure
Impure
Impure
Impure Domain
Impure Possession
Impure Wilhelmina
Impureza
Impurity
Impurity
Impurity
Impurity
Impurity
Impurity
Impuro
Imunity
Imynvokad

In a Shroud
In a Spleen
In a Void
In Abeyance
In Aeternum
In Aeternum
In Aetherium
In Age and Sadness
In Aggression
In Arkadia
In Art
In Articulo Mortis
In Articulo Mortis
In Articulo Mortis
In Battle
In Between
In Blackest Velvet
In Celebration
In Chains
In Cold Blood
In Cold Eternity
In Cold Silence
In Coma
In Contempt
In Corpore Mortis
In Cunt
In Cursed Obsession
In Darkness
In Darkness…
In Darkness I Dwell
In Death We Rise
In Deaths Embrace
In Decadence
In Dementia
In Depth

In Descent
In Deum Maledicus
In Die Nacht
In Dire Need
In Disgrace
In Dread Response
In Dying Grace
In Element
In Emptiness
In Eternum
In Eternum
In Exile
In Extremis
In Extremis
In Extremo
In Extremo Spiritu
In Fieri
In Fire Baptised
In Flames
In for the Kill
In Frozen Forests
In Gremio
  Tenebrarum
In Grey
In Heaven
In Heaven's Disease
In Hell
In Human Form
In Human God
In Infernal War
In Justice
In Kairos
In Line
In Lingua Morta
In Loving Memory

In Low Spirits
In Lupus Pacis
In Malice's Wake
In Memorial
In Memoriam
In Memoriam
In Memoriam
In Memorian
In Memorium
In Memorium
In Memorium
In Memory
In Memory Of
In Misery
In Morpheus' Arms
In Mourning
In My Own Blood
In My Veins
In No Sense
In Nocte at Arras
In Nomine
In Nomine
In Nomine
In Nomine Belialis
In Ones Blood
In Pain Die
In Peccatum
In Pena
In Perpetuum
In Pulverem
  Reverteris
In Ruins
In Ruins
In Ruins
In Search of Lorelei

In Season
In Seclusion
In Silence
In Silence
In Silent
In Slumber
In Solitude
In Solitude
In Somnis
In Somnus
In Spite
In Sufferance
In Tears Bereaved
In tha Umbra
In the Casket
In the Dark Pit
In the Depth of Night
In the Mist
In the Mist
In the Name
In the Name of God
In the Nightmare
In the Profound
  Abyss
In the Shadows
In the Sight
In the Suffering
In the Woods…
In This Defiance
In Thousand Lakes
In Thy Dreams
In Tomorrows
  Shadow
In Torment
In Torment

In Torment
In Tormentata Quiete
In Twilight's Embrace
In Utero Cannibalism
In Vain
In Vain
In Vain
In Vain
In Vein
In Velvet Clouds
In Vino Veritas
In Your Face
In.Si.Dia
In.verno
In:Extremis
Inactive Messiah
Inaeternum
InAllSenses
Inamabilis
Inamentum
Inane
Inane Eminence
Inanition
Inanna
Inanna Unveiled
Inarime
Inbleeding
Inborn
Inborn Suffering
Inbreeding Sick
Incaged
Incanate
Incantation
Incantum Dilemma
Incapacity

Incarcerated
Incardine
Incarion
Incarnadine
Incarnate
Incarnate
Incarnate
Incarnate
Incarnate
Incarnate
Incarnate
Incarnate
Incarnated
Incarnated
Incarnated
Incarnation
Incarnation
Incarnation
Incarnator
Incarnatus
Incarnis
Incarrion
Incendiary
Incendium
Incendium
Inception
Inceptor
Incessant Torment
Incest
Incest
Incest
Incest
Incest
Incest
Incesto

Inch	Incrost	Indomitus	Infamous Sinphony	Infected Disarray	Infer	Infernal Blasphemy
Inchiuvatu	Incrust	Indoriath	Infamy	Infected Entrails	Inferal	Infernal Blasphemy
Incidium	Incubator	Indràzor	Infamy	Infected Flesh	Inferi	Infernal Blood
Incinerate	Incubator	InDread Cold	Infamy	Infected Intestines	Inferi	Infernal Command
Incinerate	Incubator	Inducing Terror	Infandous	Infected Malignity	Inferi	Infernal Course
Incinerate	Incubator	Indukti	Infant Bile	Infected Messiah	Inferi	Infernal Damnation
Incinerate	Incubator	Indulgence	Infant Sacrifice	Infected Mind	Inferi	Infernal Death
Incinerated Clitorial Region	Incursion	Indungeon	Infant Slug	Infected Mind	Inferi	Infernal Death
Incineration	Incursion Dementa	Industrial Noise	Infant Torso Heap	Infected Noise	Inferia	Infernal Death
Incinerator	Incursus	Indwelling	Infanticide	Infected Noise	Inferiah	Infernal Death
Incinerator	Indamnation	Indykush	Infanticide	Infected Scrotum	Inferialis	Infernäl Death
Incinerhate	Indecent	Inearthed	Infanticide	Infected Suppuration	Inferion	Infernal Decay
Incineritor	Indecent Xposure	Inebriation	Infantry of Doom	Infected Tendence	Inferion	Infernal Deity
Incinia	Indeferal	Inepsy	Infarct Focus	Infected Tendence	Inferior	Infernal Desire
Incise	Indemnity	Inequicia	Infatuation of Death	Infected Virulence	Inferior	Infernal Devotion
Incision	Indemnity	Inert	Infaust	Infection	Inferiorum	Infernal Dominion
Incision	Indesinence	Inertia	Infaustus	Infection	Inferis	Infernal Doom
Incitatus	Indesinent	Inertia	Infearior	Infection	Inferis	Infernal Dreams
Inciter	Indestroy	Inertial Mass	Infección Crónica	Infection	Inferis	Infernal Execrator
Incivism	Indestructible Noise Command	Inevitable End	Infecdead	Infection Code	Inferius Torment	Infernal Faith
Incognita	Index Librorvm Prohibitorvm	Inexile	Infect	Infection Death	Inferna	Infernal Gates
Incoming	Indian	Inexist	Infect	Infection Zero	Infernaeon	Infernal Gates
Incoming Cerebral Overdrive	Indian Fall	Inexorable	Infect	Infection Zone	Infernal	Infernal Goat
Incomprehension	Indica	Inexorable Suffering	Infected	Infectious	Infernal	Infernal Gods
Inconnu	Indicium	Inextremis	Infected	Infectious Germs	Infernal	Infernal Hammer
Incorporated	Indifferent Creation	Inextricable Entrails	Infected	Infectious Maggots	Infernal	Infernal Hate
Incorporeal	Indigent	Inextya	Infected	Infectious MG 42	Infernal	Infernal Hate
Incredible Deathforce	Indignation	Infame	Infected	Infector	Infernal	Infernal Hate
Incredible Pain	Indignation	Infame	Infected	Infectoria	Infernal	Infernal Hatred
Incredulous	Indigo Child	Infamia	Infected	Infects Humanity	Infernal	Infernal Heirarchy
Incredulus	Indoctrination	Infamia	Infected	Infectus	Infernal	Infernal Hellfire
Incremental	Indolenz	Infamis	Infected	Infekt	Infernal Angels	Infernal Holocaust
Incriminated	Indomitus	Infamous Evil	Infected	Infektor	Infernal Assault	Infernal Kingdom
		Infamous Glory	Infected Anal Fetus	Infektus	Infernal Atavism	Infernal Kingdom
		Infamous Plague	Infected Brain	Infensus	Infernal Beauty	Infernal Legion

Interferhon
Interferon
Interim
Interior
Interior Demise
Interior of Death
Interior Wrath
Interitus
Interitus
Interitus
Interitus
Interitus Dei
Interitus Dei
Interium
Interlock
Interment
Interment
Interment
Interment
Interment
Internal
Internal
   Augmentation
Internal Bleed
Internal Bleeding
Internal Corpse
   Attack
Internal Decay
Internal Decay
Internal Decay
Internal Evisceration
Internal Hate
Internal Healing
Internal Malice
Internal Putrefaction

Internal Suffering
Internal Torment
Internal Void
Internalize
Internecine
Internecine
   Exocoriation
Intero
Interphase
Interration
Interred
Interria
Interror
Interrupter
Interseed
Intervalle Bizzare
Interzone
Interzone
Intestinal Disgorge
Intestinal
   Fermentation
Intestinal Infection
Intestinal Infection
Intestinal Infestation
Intestinal Lynching
Intestinal
   Strangulation
Intestinal Ulcer
Intestine
Intestine
Intestine Baalism
Intestines
Intestines
Intestterror
Intethod

Inthefreak
Inthroned
InThyFlesh
Into Dagorlad
Into Darkness
Into Desolation
Into Eternity
Into Morphin
Into Nothing
Into Oblivion
Into Obscurity
Into the Black Forest
Into the Darkness
   My Destiny
Into the Dementia
Into the Dust
Into the Gore
Into The Moat
Into the Night
Into the Nightmare
Into the Sunless
   Meridian
Into the Void
Intoctum
Intorment Black
Intoxicate
Intoxicate
Intoxicate
Intoxicated
Intoxicated Blood
Intoxication
Intoxication
Intoxication
Intoxication
Intoxicator
Intoxicum

Intradeus
Intrepid
Intrepid
Intribe
Intricate
Intricate Division
Intrinsic
Intrive
Introitus
Intronaut
Introspección
Introspectre
Intruder
Intruder
Intrüder
Intumescence
Intus
Inui
Inumbro
Inure
Inurnment
Invadeath
Invader
Invader
Invader
Invading Chapel
Invain
Invalid Existence
Invalid Libido
Invasion
Invasion
Invasion
Invasion to Privacy
Invazija
Inveigh

Invelenitor
Inveracity
Inverna
Inverness
Inverno
Inversa Visio
Inverse Cross
Inversion
Inverted
Inverted Liturgy
Inverted Pentagram
Inverted Prophet
Inverted Saints
Inverted Trifixion
Invicta
Invicticus
Invictrius
Invictus
Invictus
Invictus
Invictus
Invidia
Inviolacy
Inviscerated
Invisius
Invocat Mortis
Invocate
Invocated Chaos
Invocation
Invocation
Invocation
Invocation
Invocation of Nehek
Invocation War
Invocator

Invoid.
Invokation
Invoke
Invoker
Invoker
Invoking Suffering
Involuntary Carnage
Inward
Inward Escape
Inward Infect
Inward Mind
Inward Path
Inward Sanctum
Inwards
In'Xight
Inzest
Inzest
Inzest
Inzight
Inzyrcle
Io
Io
Iodhar
Iodio
Iommi
Ion Britton
Ion Dissonance
Ion Drive
Ion Vein
Ionica
Iorio y Flavio
Iota Draconis
Ipalnemoani
Ipar Haizea
Ipecac

Iperyt
Iphicrate
Ipisissmus
Ipsissimus
Ipsum
Iquista Firiel
IR8
Ira
Ira
Ira
Ira
Ira
Ira Deum
Ira Divina
Ira Projeckts
Ira Regia
Ira Tenax
Irae
Iranach
Iras
Irate Architect
Irathus
Iratus Dominus
Iraven
Iraventus
Irdhing
Irdorath
Ire
Irem
I-Remain
Irencros
Irhmgaar
Iridium
Irij
Iris

J

J. Hiltunen's Wings
   of Destiny
J.B.O.
J.I.P.
Jabbar
Jack Daisy
Jack Frost
Jack Frost
Jack Glass
Jack Lord
Jack of all Trades
Jack Slater
Jack Starr
Jack the Ripper
Jackal
Jackal

Jackal
Jackal's Truth
Jackalstrain
Jackhammer
Jackhammer
Jackhammer
Jackhammer
Jackie Wulf
Jackknife
Jacknife
Jack'ost
Jackpot
Jack's Family
Jack's Hammer
Jackwave
Jacob's Dream

Jacopo Galli
Jadallys
Jade
Jaded Heart
Jaded Lady
Jads
Jag Panzer
Jagannath
Jagged Edge
Jagged Eye
Jagged Razor
Jaggernaut
Jaguar
Jahresringe
Jailbreak
Jailor
Jaksi Taksi
Jameson Raid
Jammerskrik
Jane
Jane Doe 69
Jangli Jaggas
Janine
Janus
Japanische
   Kampfhörspiele
Jarcrew
Järin Möyremä
Jarnvid
Jarojupe
Jarovit
Jarovit
Jarra
Jasad
Jasad

Jason
Jason Becker
Jason Goes to Hell
Jasun Tipton
Jati
Javelin
Javelin
Jaw
Jaw
Jawad
Jaws of Fate
Jaww
JBD
JD Bradshaw
Jealous Heart
Jeanne Dark
Jeddah
JEEL
Jeff in the Nite
Jeffrey Dahmer
Jeff's Asmodeus
Jehova
Jehovah Attak
Jehovah Barra
Jejunum
Jekazol
Jekyll
Jekyll
Jekyll
Jena
Jennifer Will Drown
Jênova
Jenovavirus
Jens Johansson
Jérémie

Jeremy
Jeremy Krull
Jerican
Jericho
Jerikó
Jerk
Jerkstore
Jernbyrde
Jerry Cantrell
Jersey Dogs
Jerusolima Est Perdita
Jeshaia
Jester
Jester Beast
Jester Cap
Jester's Crown
Jester's Funeral
Jester's March
Jesters Moon
Jesters of Destiny
Jesters of Fate
Jester's Tears
Jesu
Jesus
Jesus Anal
   Penetration
Jesus Christ
Jesus Chrysler
   Superskunk
Jesus Freaks
Jesus Joshua
Jesus Joshua 24:15
Jesus Martyr
Jesus Save
Jesus Skin

Jesus Wept
Jesusatan
Jesuside
JesusLaceration
Jet
Jevo
Jewel
Jewel
Jewicide
Jewish Juice
Jezabel
Jezabel
Jezebel Bang
Jezebel's Children
Jezebel's Tower
Jhesu Masturbator
Jig Saw
Jig-Ai
Jigsore
Jigsore Terror
Jihad
Jihad
Jihad
Jim Dofka
Jim Jones and the
   Kool-Ade Kids
Jim Martin
Jinn
Jinovatka
Jinx
Jinx
Jitterbug
Jitu
JJ's Powerhouse
Job for a Cowboy

Jodonal
Joe Granata
Joe Stump
Joe Thrasher
Joe-Erk
Joel Wanasek
Joey Tafolla
Joey Vera
Jogane Munno
Johansson
John Arch
John Christ
John Connelly
   Theory
John Jaunese
John Macaluso
   & Union Radio
John Norman Collins
John West
Johnny Lökke
Johnny Mental
Johnny Midnight
   and the Daemons
   from Hell
Johnny Truant
Johnston
Joint Depression
Jois
Joker
Joker
Jolly Roger
Jon Oliva's Pain
Jonah Quizz
Jonas Grumby
Jonas Hansson

K.A.
K.G.B.
K.I.N.
K.O.D.
K-0s
K626
Kaamos
Kaamos
Kaarnekorpi
Kaatörsnik
Kabak
Kabala
Kabarah
Kabát
Kabbal
Kabra

Kabul
Kachana
Kadakus
Kadastath
Kadath
Kadath
Kadath
Kadath
Kadath the Lost City
Kadathorn
Kadaverficker
Kadavrik
Kadenzza
Kadotus
Kadotus 609
Kaduk

Kæltetod
Kaemorph
Kaer Morhen
Kafan
Kafoth
Kafziel
Kagan
Kage
Kahtahdhen
Kahtmayan
Kaiadass
Kaiaphas
Kaihoro
Kailash
Kain
Kain
Kain
Kainabel
Kainin Lapset
Kaiphos
Kaira
Kairhia
Kairi
Kaiser
Kaiserkorps
Kaitem
Kaiżen
Kaizer
Kakadan
Kakaroth
Kaksonen
Kalaazar
Kalapács
Kalas
Kalasag

Kaldrfenrir
Kaldur
Kaledon
Kalevala
Kali Yuga
Kali Yuga
Kaliban
Kalibas
Kaliber
Kalibos
Kalijuge
Kalion
Kalisia
Kaliyuga
Kaliyuga
Kali-Yuga
Kallastir
Kallbrand
Kalm
Kalmah
Kalmah
Kalman Varjot
Kalögena
Kalopsia
Kalot Enbolot
Kalpa
Kalt
Kaltakustik
Kälte
Kalter Nebel
Kaltes
Kältetod
Kältetot
Kalvarius
Kamaedzitca

Kamala
Kamala
Kamaloka
Kamá-Merú
Kamara
Kambing
Kamchatka
Kameleontti
Kameliah
Kamelot
Kamikabe
Kamikaze
Kamikaze
KamiKazeKrieg
Kamikazes
Kaminari
Kammio
Kamo Gryadeshi
Kampf
Kampf
Kampfar
Kämpfe
Kampfzeit
Kancerbero
Kandaon
Kandela
Kandelabrum
Kandor
Kaniia
Kankra
Kantor Voy
Kaos
Kaos
Kaos
Kaos

Kaos
Kaos in Order
Kaos Rising
Kaoscentrica
KaosEngine
Kaoslord
Kaosritual
Kaoteon
Kaothic
Kaotika
Kaottick
Kaoz
Kaoz
Kapein
Kapel Maister
Kapela
Kapishcha
Kaprogöat
Kaptain Sun
Kapybara
Kar.
Kara
Kara Œmierci
Karaboudjan
Karachun
Karachun
Karakedi
Karakum
Karandash
Karantina
Karbo
Karbonized Traitor
Karcharodon
Karcinoma
Karcist of Manes

Kardahas
Karehgod
Karelia
Karelian Warcry
Karensdag
Kargvint
Karian
Kariostro
Karisma
Karkadam
Karkadam
Karkadan
Karkinoz
Karl Sanders
Karma
Karma
Karma
Karma
Karma
Karma Connect
Karma Depth
Karma to Burn
Karmage
Karmak
Karmassacre
Karmic Wheel
Karmon
Karmyne
Karna
Karnage
Karnage
Karnaj
Karnak
Karnak
Karnak

Krommodon

Kromorth
Kronet
Kronik
Kronik
Kronin
Kronium
Kronk
Kronomorph
Kronos
Kronos
Kronos
Krönös
Kronosphere
Kronow
Kroumlesh
Krovuel
Krøwührrr
Kr'shna Brothers
Kruagre
Krucifix
Krucifixion
Krucix
Krudo
Krueger
Krueger
Kruger
Kruiz
Kruizer
Kruk
Kruk
Kruk
Kruk
Krullur
Kr'uppt
Krusader

Kruschke
Krush
Krusher
Krushies
Krushya
Krux
Krv
Krvavá Práce
Krvestreb
Krwth
Kryoburn
Kryogh
Kryokill
Kryon
Krypt
Krypt Keeper
Krypta
Krypteia
Krypteria
Kryptic Kurse
Krypton
Krypton
Kryptor
Kryptos
Krysalyd
Krysaor
Kryst the Conqueror
Krýstal Sýnn
Krystal Tears
Kryzalid
Kryzees
Ksichties
Księżyc Pólnocy
Ktarsis
KteiS

Ktinodia
KTL
KTL
Ktulu
Kuafor Cengiz
Kuarentena
Kuasar
Kuazar
Kubla Khan
Kublai Khan
Kukulcan
Kulden Morket
Kulsary
Kult
Kult
Kult ov Azazel
Kult Perunov
Kult Shock
Kultheit
Kulto Maldito
Kultur
Kultus
Kultus Infernum
Kuma Rafinata
Kumkrusted
Kumshot Diesel
Kunt Destroyer
Kunt Vomit
Kuolo
Kuona
Kurator
Kurazh
Kurb Saatus
Kurgan
Kurgan

Kurgan
Kurgan
Kurgan's Bane
Kurixis
Kurnalcool
Kurtz
Kuru
Kuru
Kushantaiidan
Kutabare
Kutna Hora
Kutschurft
Kuturlat
Kuwalda
Kvazar
Kveldúlfur
Kvell
Kvellen
Kvikksølvguttene
Kvist
Kvntvr
Kwelhekse
Kyaghea
Kyala
Kybalion
Kyla
Kyla Moyl
Kylähullut
Kylesa
Kymera
Kynesis
Kyoji Yamamoto
Kyprian's Circle
Kyrie Eleison
Kyrios Sabaoth

Kyrpä
Kyrus
Kythrone
Kyuss
Kyyria

L. Mynigwal
L.A.
L.A. Guns
L.A. Hooker
L.A. Kaos
L.I.G.O.
L.O.S.T.
L.O.W.
L.S.N.
L.S.S.A.H.
L.T.K.
L6B6T6MY
La Bestia Negra
La Brigada
La Brigada
La Bruja

La Caruta di li Dei
La Cripta
La Dama Oscura
La Divina Comedia
La Division Mentale
La Era de Ophiucus
La Grita
La Hermandad
La Jaula
La Maldad
La Matanza
La Muerte
    Humana
La Naranja
La Parka
La Pestilencia

La Rumeur
    des Chaînes
Lääz Rockit
Labatut
Labei Ritual
Labeled Victims
Laberinto
Laboratory
Laboratory Sickness
Labrat
Labyrinth
Labyrinth
Labyrinth
Labyrinth
Labyrinth
Labyrinth of Abyss
Labyrinth Spell
Labyrinthus Noctis
Lace Labor
L'Acephale
Lacerate
Lacerate
Lacerate
Lacerate
Lacerated and
    Carbonized
Lacerated Defuncts
Lacerated Entrails
Lacerated Gods
Lacerated Tissue
Lacerater
Laceration
Laceration
Laceration
Lacerator

Lachesis
Lachrimatory
Lachryma Christi
Lachrymal
Lachrymal Gland
Lachrymator
Lachrymose
Lacination
Lack of Faith
Lack of Purity
Lack of Trust
Lack There Of
Lacolper
Lacrima
Lacrima
Lacrima
Lacrima Christi
Lacrima Cristi
Lacrimae
Lacrimae
Lacrimae
Lacrimae Mortalium
Lacrimae Obscurum
Lacrimal Goddess
Lacrimas Profundere
Lacrimatorium
Lacrimosa
Lacro
Lacryma Christi
Lacrymae Rerum
Lacuna Coil
Lacus Mortis
Lacus Mortis
Ladder of Creatures
Ladia

Lado Obscuro
Lady
Lady Elizabeth
Lady Killer
Lady Macbeth
Lady Reaper
Lady Sadness
Lady Temptress
Lady Winter
Ladykill
Laeta Mors'
Laethora
Laetitia in Holocaust
Lafayn
Lafordova
Lafrontera
Lagash
Lágrima Negra
Lágrima Santa
Lagrimas Negras
Lahar
Lahylat
Laid in Ashes
Laid to Unrest
Laid to Waste
Lailheb
Lair of the Minotaur
Lake of Depression
Lake of Oblivion
Lake of Tears
Lake Soul
Lakrau
Lakupaavi
Lalu
Lamacz Kosci

Lamagra
Lamb of God
Lambent
Lambotomy
Lambs
L'Ame Immortelle
Lamed
Lament
Lament
Lament
Lament
Lament Christ
Lament
    Configuration
Lamentation
Lamentation
Lamentation
Lamentations
Lamented
    Despondency
Lamented Souls
Lamento Lugubre
Lamentos Ancestrales
Laments of Silence
Lamentu
Lamia
Lamia
Lamia
Lamia Antitheus
Lamia Phantasma
Lamia Tenebrae
Lamma Sabactani
Lammashta
Lammoth
Lammoth

Lammoth
Lamort
Lampaanvapahtaja
Lamphor
Lana Lane
Lanadrid
Lance of Thrill
Land Beyond
    the Forest
Land of Anger
Land of Chaos
Land of Charon
Land of Fear
Land of Fire
Land of Frost
Land of Goshen
Land of Hate
Land of Lore
Land of Mordor
Land of Tears
Landberk
Lándevir
Landfill
Landguard
Landing
Landmine
Landmine Marathon
Lands of Past
Landscape
Landscape of Souls
Landscapes
Landsemk
Landstorm
Landvaettir
Lanfear

Lost in Blue
Lost in Darkness
Lost in Dreams
Lost in Hell
Lost in Misery
Lost in Tears
Lost in the Fire
Lost in the Shadows
Lost in Time
Lost in Time
Lost in Twilight
Lost Infinity
Lost Innocence
Lost Innocence
Lost Inspiration
Lost Legacy
Lost Legion
Lost Life
Lost Life Trouble
Lost Minds
Lost Mysteries
Lost Oblivion
Lost Patrol
Lost Realm
Lost Ritual
Lost Serenity
Lost Shade
Lost Society
Lost Soul
Lost Soul
Lost Soul
Lost Soul
Lost Soul
Lost Souls
Lost Soul's Cry
Lost Species

Lost Vital Spark
Lost Wisdom
Lostair
Lostprophets
Lotharon
Lothlorien
Lothlöryen
Lotus Cruise
Lotus Iter
Lotus Project
Lou Cyfer
Loud
Loud Crowd
Loudblast
Loudness
Loud'n'Proud
Loudrage
Louis Cypher
Loupgarou
Louwiper
Louwiper
Love Forsaken
Love History
Love Lies Bleeding
Love Lies Eternal
Love Like Blood
Love Like Waves
    Collapsing
Love/Hate
Lovecraaft
Lovecraft
Lovelorn
Lover of Sin
Loverwolf
Love's Labour's Lost

Lovex
Lovorne
Low Battery
Low Down
Low End
Low Life
Low Man's Tune
Low On Air
Low Profile
Low Twelve
Lowblow
Lowbrow
Lowdead
Lowdown
Low-Down
Lower Definition
Lower Than Zero
Lowgrown
Lowlyfe
Lowstate
LSD
Lua Negra
Luay Rifai
Lubricant
Lubrik Hate
Luca Turilli
Luca Turilli's
    Dreamquest
Lucaria
Lucera
Lucera
Luci Tristis
Lucian Blaque
Lucid
Lucid Fear

Lucid Reality
Lucid Tide
Lucidity
Lucifago Rofacale
Lucifer
Lucifer
Lucifer
Lucifer
Lucifer
Lucifer in Love
Lucifera
Luciferase
Luciferi
Luciferi Excelsi
Luciferi Glorium
Luciferian
Luciferian Dementia
Luciferian Warrior
Luciferiano
Luciferion
Luciferium
Lucifer's Friend
Lucifers Garden
Lucifer's Hammer
Lucifer's Heritage
Luciffer
Lucifixion
Lucifuego
Lucifuge Rofocale
Lucifugo
Lucifugo
Lucifugum
Lucifugum
Lucifugus
Lucika

Lucky Stiker 201
Lucretia
Luctiferu
Luctus
Luctus
Lucubro
Lucyfire
Lucy's Doll
Luddite Clone
Ludichrist
Ludicra
Ludovico Reale
Luen-Ta
Luftwaffe Raid
Lug Rexer
Lugburz
Lugburz
Lugburz
Lugburz
Lüger
Lughorn
Lugosi
Lugosis Needle
Luguber Tomb
Lugubre
Lúgubre Eclipse
Lugubrious
Lugubrious Hymn
Lugubrum
Luis Massot
Lujuria
Lukemborg
Luksferre
Lullaby
Lullacry

Lultus
Lumendei
Lumina Polaris
Luminaria
Luminous Flesh
    Giants
Luminus
Lumsk
Luna Ad Noctum
Luna Aeterna
Luna Field
Luna Inlustris
Luna Martyr
Luna Obscura
Luna Profundis
Lunacy
Lunacy
Lunacy
Lunacy
Lunacy
Lunacyde
Lunae
Lunae Dies
Lunae Nocturna
Lunar Aurora
Lunar Caustic
Lunar Dawn
Lunar Eclipse
Lunar Gate
Lunar Goddess
Lunar Onlooker
Lunar Reign
Lunar Sex
Lunar Splinter
Lunarchy

Lunaria
Lunarin
Lunaris
Lunaris
Lunarium
Lunarkult
Lunarsea
Lunarsphere
Lunatenebra
Lunatic
Lunatic Asylum
Lunatic Asylum
Lunatic Asylum
Lunatic Dictator
Lunatic Dreams
Lunatic Gods
Lunatic Hymn
Lunatic Invasion
Lunatic Paradise
Lunatic Terror
Lunatica
Lunatics Without
    Skateboards Inc.
Lunattick Fringe
Lunatycas
Lunch
Lunendei
Lungbrush
Lunglance
Lungorthin
Lungspit
Lunica Arma
Luotettava Todistus
Lupara
Lupercalia

Lupine Moon

Lupulo	Lux Eterna du Mal	Lycantrope	Lyssa
Lupus	Lux Eternæ	Lycantrophia	Lythos
Lupus Nocturnus	Lux Ferre	Lycantrophy	Lyzanxia
Lurch Killz	Lux in Tenebris	Lycaon	LZ2
Lurid	Lux Incerta	Lych Gate	
Lurid Dawn	Lux Inferium	Lydian Sea	
Lurid Trace	Lux Mortuum	Lyfthrasyr	
Lurker of Chalice	Lux Occulta	Lyijykomppania	
Luror	Lux Salutis	Lying Beneath	
Lust	Luxor	Lying Truth	
Lust	Luxt	Lykaion	
Lust	Luxúria de Lillith	Lykantrop	
Lust	Luz de Invierno	Lykantrophia	
Lust Mord	Luz Negra	Lykathea Aflame	
Lust of Decay	Luzbel	Lykeum	
Lustful	Lvpercalia	Lymentria	
Lustnotes	Lvpvs Infestvs	Lymph of Wisdoom	
Lustration	Lvzbel	Lymphatic Phlegm	
Lustrum	Lyadrive	Lymphoma	
Lusus Naturae	Lycan Thrope	Lynch Mob	
Lut	Lycanthia	Lynchmada	
Lut'	Lycanthrope	Lyndwurm Orphans	
Lutece	Lycanthrope	Lynx	
Lutemkrat	Lycanthrope	Lyon	
Luten	Lycanthrope	Lypektomy	
Luther	Lycanthropian	Lyr Drowning	
Luther Voorhees	Carnage	Lyra	
Luthien	Lycanthropy	Lyrae	
Luthier	Lycanthropy	Lyranthe	
Luthor	Lycanthropy	Lyre	
Lutomysl	Lycanthropy	Lyric Butcher	
Lux Aeterna	Lycanthropy	Lyriel	
Lux Axiomus	Lycanthropy	Lyrinx	
Lux Belle	Lycanthropy	Lyrthas	
Lux Divina	Lycanthropy's Spell	Lysets Tod	

M Virus
M.A.C. of Mad
M.A.D.
M.A.D.
M.A.D.
M.A.D: Goya
M.A.R.S.
M.A.S.A.C.R.E.
M.A.S.H.
M.A.S.H.
M.C. Blade
M.D. 45
M.D.K.
M.F.
M.F. Ragweed
M.I.C.U.I.S.A. 37%

M.ILL.ION
M.Ire
M.K.Z.
M.O.D.
M.O.R. Death
M.O.R.T.A.J.A.
M.Pheral
M.S.
M.S.I.
M.S.W.
M.T.F.
M.Y.S.T.
M.Z.
M-16
M-19
M-26

M-80
M8L8TH
M-90's
Maanelyst
Maar
Mabon
Mabus
Mabus 666
Mac Animal
Mac Beth
Mac-11
Macabius
Macabra
Macabre
Macabre Agony
Macabre End
Macabre Mementos
Macabre Minstrels
Macabre Omen
Macabre Operetta
Macabre Visions
Macabro Hallazgo
Macaroni
Macaxe
Macbeth
Macbeth
Macbeth
Macbeth
Macbeth
Macbeth
Mace
Mace
Mace
Mace To Face
Macella

Maceration
Mach 1
Machescazo
Machetazo
Machiavel
Machiavelik
Machiavellian
  Regression
Machiavellian South
Machina
Machina
Machina Deus Ex
Machinae Supremacy
Machine
Machine
Machine
Machine
Machine Called Man
Machine Dog
Machine Head
Machine Head
Machine
  Insufficiency
Machine Men
Machinemade God
Machinerie Perfect
Machinery
Machinery
Macht
Macifecation
Macification
Macrocosmic
  Emotions
Macrodex
Mactation

Mactätus
Mad Alien
Mad at Sam
Mad Axeman
Mad Brains
Mad Butcher
Mad Chyron Mob
Mad Dog
Mad Dragzter
Mad Evil
Mad Klown
Mad Lazy
Mad Machine
Mad Margritt
Mad Max
Mad Minstrel
Mad Poltergeist
Mad Reign
Mad Sanity
Mad Slaughter
Mad V
Madalena Crucified
Madam X
Madame X
Madball
Madcastle
Madd Hatter
Madd Hunter
Madder Mortem
Maddhouse
Mad-Die
Made in France
Made in Hell
Made of Iron
Madew

Madhatter
Madhouse
Madhouse
Madhouse
Madhouse
Madhouse
Madhouse
Madinside
Madison
Madjester
MadKnight
Madman is Absolute
Madman Mundt
Madmans Diary
Madness
Madness at Dawn
Madness Co.
MadNine
Madog
Madra
Madrigal
Madrigal
MadRoach
Madryal
Madryghal
Madsword
Madwork
Maegashira
Mael Morda
Mael Mórdha
Mael Mórdha
Maelstrom
Maelstrom
Maelstrom
Maelstrom

Maelstrom
Maelstrom
Maelstrom
Maelstrom
Maelstrom
Maelstrom
Maelstrom
Maelstrom
Maelström
Maelström
Maelström
Maëlstrom
Maestro
Maestus
Maeve of Connacht
Mafia
MAG
MAG
Magan
Magane
Magellan
Magellan Dream
Magenda
Maggie's Madness
Maggot Colony
Maggot Infested
Maggot of
  Putrefaction
Maggot Pigs on
  Tuesday
Maggot Shoes
Maggot Storm
Maggoth
Maggots
Maggots
Maggots

◀ Maggots

Malicious Silence	Malkbeth	Malum	Manala	Månegarm	Manias	Manitou
Maligeist	Malkuth	Malumbra	Manaroth	Manes	Maniax	Manitou
Malign	Mallet	Malummeh	Manatark	Manes	Manic	Manitou
Malign Entity	Mallet-Head	Malus	Mandala	Manetheren	Manic Depression	Manitu
Malignance	Malleus	Malus	Mandator	Manggas	Manic Movement	Mankillsman
Malignancy	Malleus	Malus Aeternus	Mandatory	Mangled	Manic Opera	Manmade God
Malignancy	Malleus	Malus Lupus	Mandatory	Mangled	Manical Rage	Mannaz
Malignancy	Malleus Maleficarum	Malveillance	Mandatory	Mangled	Manierisme	Manngard
Malignancy	Malleus Maleficarum	Malveliance	Mandatory	Mangled Atrocity	Manifescium	Mannhai
Malignant	Malleus Maleficarum	Malvento	Mandatory Death	Mangled Christ	Manifest	Mannslaughter
Malignant	Malleus Maleficarum	Malvery	Mandatory Suicide	Mangled Corpse	Manifest	Manntis
Malignant	Malmhrid	Malvo	Mandatory Suicide	Mangled Meat	Manifest	Manon
Malignant Epitaph	Malmonde	Malvoisie	Mandiga	Mangled Reality	Manifest Destiny	Manorblatz
Malignant Eternal	Malmort	Mama	Mandingazo	Mangled Torsos	Manifestation	Manos
Malignant Inception	Malnàtt	Mambo Kurt	Manditory	Mangled Whore Flesh	Manifestium	Manowar
Malignant Monster	Malnutrition	Mamilla	Mandown	Mangler	Manifesto	Man's Fall
Malignant Saviour	Malombra	Mammath	Mandragora	Manhir	Manifesto Metálico	Manslaughter
Malignant Spawn	Malón	Mammatus	Mandragora	Mania	Manifold Object	Manslaughter
Malignant Tumour	Malory	Mammon	Mandragora	Mania	Manifrest	Manslaughter
Malignity	Malphas	Mammoth	Mandragora	Mania	Manigance	Manslaughterer
Malignity	Malpractice	Mammoth	Mandragora	Maniac	Manik Thorns	Manson
Maligno	Malpractice	Mamut	Mandragora	Maniac	Manilla Road	Manstractor
Malignom	Malsain	Man	Mandragora	Maniac	Manimal	Mantak
Malignum	Malsaination	Man Among Stars	Mandragora	Maniac	Manimal	Mantapus
Malignum	Malsanus	Man Destroys	Mandragora Scream	Maniac	Manimals	Mantas
Malignus	Malstrom	Himself	Mandragore	Maniac Butcher	Maninnya Blade	Mantas
Malijam	Malsum	Man is Mostly Water	Mandrake	Maniac Frost	Manipul	Manth
Malinconia	Maltese Cross	Man Made Suicide	Mandrake	and Flames	Manipulated Slaves	Manthas
Malintent	Maltese Falcon	Man Must Die	Mandrake	Maniac Killer	Manipulation	Manthra
Malisha	Malteze	Man of the Hour	Mandrake	Maniac Winds	Manipulation	Manticora
Malitia	Malthak	Man To Man	Mandrake	Maniac Within	Manipulator	Manticore
Malkavian	Malthús	Man With Target	Mandrake Garden	Maniaca	Manitoba's Wild	Manticore
Malkavian	Malthusia	Mana	Mandrax	Maniacal	Kingdom	Manticore
Malkavian	Maltum	Mana Prime	Mandrix	Maniacal Genocide	Manitou	Manticore
Malkavian Moon	Malum	Managarm	Mandylion	Maniak	Manitou	Manticore
			Mandylion	Maniakal Torment		

Massenmord
Massenvernichtung
Masseporz
Massgrave
Massground
Masshu
Massif
Massive Appendage
Massive Assault
Massive Bereavement
Massive Carnage
Massive Charge
Massive Destruction
Massive Killing
Massive Lust
Massive Obscurity
Massive Power
Massive Punch
Massive Retaliation
Massive Roar
Massive Sound
  of Disorder
Massivepower
Massmurder
Massmurder
Mastaba
Mastaba
Mastabah
Mastectomia
Mastema
Mastema
Mastema
Mastema
Master
Master

Master
Master Damned
Master Disaster
Master Dream
Master Fury
Masterdom
Masterdomme
Masterfister
Masterguru
MasteRiff
Masterlast
Mastermind
Mastermind
Masterpiece
Masterpiece
Masterplan
Master's Child
Master's Hammer
Master's Memorial
Masters of Reality
Masterstroke
Masterstroke
Mastervoid
Masterwork
Mastery
Mastery
Mastery
Mastic Scum
Masticat
Masticate
Mastication
Masticator
Masticator
Mastifal
Mastiff

Mastiff
Mastiphal
Mastiphal
Mastix
Mastoc
Mastodon
Mastomah
Masturbace
Masturbathor
Masturbation
Masturbator
Masturbory
Masugn
Mat Sinner
Matacavalo
Matadero
Matadero
Matahero
Matakopas
Matan Boukous
Matanboukous
Matarife
Maten el Rey
Mater Hades
Mater Machina
Mater Monstifera
Mater Tenebra
Materia
Materia Grave
Materia Prima
Mathians
Mathyr
Matraz
Matriarch
Matricide

Matricide
Matricide
Matricide
Matricide
Matricide
Matricyde
Matrikhore
Matrix
Matrix
Matron
Matsudo
Matt Konfirst
Matt Lee
Matt McCourt
Mattatoio
Matthew Mills
Matthias Steele
Matutina
Matutina Noctem
Maudite Asmodée
Maudlin of the Well
Mauser
Mausoleia
Mausoleo
Mausoleum
Mausoleum
Mausoleum
Mausoleum
Mausoleum
Mausoleum
Mauthausen
Maverick
Maverick's
  Bad Breath
Maverik

Mavrik
Mawar Liar
Max Havoc
Max Lynx
Max Penalty
Max the Axe's
  Blazing Star
Maxfield Parish
Maximum Overdrive
Maximum Pentecost
Maximum
  Perversion
Maximus
Maxmillion
Maxwell Murderers
Maxx Warrior
May
May Result
Maya
Maya
Mayadome
MayDie
Mayfair
Mayhayron
Mayhem
Mayhem
Mayhem
Mayhem
Mayhem
Mayhem
Mayhem
Mayhem
Mayhem
Mayhem Inc
Mayhem Inc.
Mayhemesis

Mayhemic
  Destruction
Mayhemic Truth
May-Linn
Maze of Cako
  Torments
Maze of
  Extermination
Maze of Torment
Mazeran
Mazetorment
Mazo
Mazo
Mazo
Mazurka
M-Bush
MCB
McBrain Damage
McDeath
MCIP
MCM
MD Flush
MD.45
MDP
Mea Culpa
Meadow in Silence
Meadows End
Meads of Asphodel
Mean Geimhridh
Mean Prime
Means of Approach
Meanstreak
Meanstreak
Meantime
Measly Corpse

Measureless
Meat
Meat Missile
Meat Shits
Meat Wallet
Meatcurtain
Meatgrinder
Meatgrinder
Meatgrinder
Meat-Grinder
Meathole Infection
Meathook Seed
Meatjack
Meatknife
Meatlocker
Meatlocker Seven
Meatopathy
Me-at-us
Meatwagon
Meatyard
Mech
Mecha Messiah
Mechanica Sundown
Mechanical Chaos
Mechanical God
  Creation
Mechanical
  Manipulation
Mechanical Poet
Mechanism
Mechanix
Mechanix
Mechanix
Mechanix
Mechanix

Medallion	Medusa	Meghorash	Melancholy Cry	Melkor	Memoria	Menam
Medalyon	Medusa	Megiddo	Melancholy	Melkor	Memoria	Menarca
Medea	Medusa	Megiddo	Pessimism	Melkor	Memoria	Mendacious Messiah
Medebor	Medusa	Megiddo	Melancholyc Sunrise	Mell Rose	Memoria Mortis	Mendacity
Medecophobic	Medusa's Child	Megiddon	Melancolasi	Melliae	Memoria Vetus	Mendacity
Media in Morte	Meduseld	Megin	Melancolia	Melmoth	Memorial	Mendeed
Medical Carnage	Medussa	Megora	Melandrolia	Melodic Mayhem	Memorial	Mendeku Itxua
Medicated	Meduza	Megtorlás	Melanophorus	Melodic Meltdown	Memorial Day	Mendelb
Medication	Mefisto	Mehafelon	Melatonin	Melodica	Memorial of	Mendes
Medicine Death	Mefitic	Mehbm	Melchior	Melodrama	Desolation	Mendes
Medieval	Mega Driver	Mehfalaz	Melcorn	Melodramatic	Memorial Park	Mendes Prey
Medieval	Mega Grave	Mehkago N.T.	Melcor's Disharmony	Melody Monster	Memories Lab	Mendocide
Medieval	Mega Mosh	Mei Finis	Meldrum	Melodyact	Memories of a	Menegroth
Medieval	Megace	Meiche	Meldrum	Melpein	Lost Soul	Mengele
Medieval Art	Megadeth	Meidei	Melechesh	Melqart	Memories of Pain	Menhir
Medieval Death	Megaera	Mein Kampf	Melej	Meltdown	Memorium	Menhir
Medieval Demon	Megahertz	Meinardus	Melek Taus	Meltdown	Memorium	Menhyr
Medieval Overture	Megalith	Meinhoff	Melek Taus	Meltdown	Memorium	Mennen
Medieval Power	Megalomania 999	Mekala	Melek Tawus	Meltdown	Memorium	Menneskerhat
Medieval Sorcery	Megalon	Mekanix	Melektaus	Meltdown	Memorized Dreams	Menosgada
Medieval Steel	Megamosh	Mekano	Melek-Tha	Meltdown	Memory	Mens Sana
MediEvil	Megaslaughter	Mekhanix	Melem	Meltem	Memory Garden	Mensch Schmerz
Medieville	Megatherion	Mekong Delta	Melencolia	Melting Flesh	Men at Arms	Interaktion
Medina Azahara	Megatherion	Melan Nephos	Melencolia Estatica	Melvins	Men at Arms	Menschenbrand
Meditasi	Megathrash	Thanatou	Melencoliam	Melwosia	Men Eater	Menschenfeind
Mediterranean	Megaton	Melancholia	Melencoliasi	Mely	Men in Search of the	Menschentod
Medium	Megaton	Melancholic Art	Melets	Membaris	Perfect Weapon	Mensrea
Medium Avathar	Megaton	Melancholic Demise	Meliah Rage	Membro Genitali	Men Of War	Menstrual Blood
Medium Mortem	Megaton	Melancholic Seasons	Meliat	Befurcator	Mena Brinno	Menstrual Garbage
Medulla Nocte	Megatron	Melancholic Silence	Melisend	Memembris	Menac	Mensura
Medusa	Megattack	Melancholic Winds	Melissa	Memento Mori	Menace	Mental
Medusa	Megazetor	Melancholy	Melissa	Memfis	Menace	Mental Aberration
Medusa	Megera	Melancholy	Melissa	Memnoch	Menacer	Mental Aberration
Medusa	Meggido	Melancholy	Melkor	Memnoch	Menacer	Mental Alteration
Medusa	Meggido	Melancholy	Melkor	Memorain	Menacing War	Mental Amputation

Metal Storm	Metally Insane	Metatron	Metroz	Mictian	Midnattsol	Miecz Wikinga
Metal Storm	Metalmare	Metatrone	Metsatöll	Mictian	Midnight	Mielofon
Metal Sword	Metalmen	Metatronik	Metus	Mictlan	Midnight	Mi'gauss
Metal Virgins	Metalmilitia	Metayer	Metzeli	Mictlan	Midnight Agony	Might of Lilith
Metal Warriors	Metalmorfosis	Metempsicosis	Mevatron	Mictlan	Midnight Darkness	Might of Rage
Metal Wings	Metalmorphose	Metempsychosis	Mewithoutyou	Mictlan	Midnight Descension	Mightiest
Metal Witch	Metalmorphosis	Metempsychosis	Meyhem	Mictlantecuhtli	Midnight Dirge	Mighty
Metal Witch	Metalmorphosis	Methre	Meyvn	Mid Autumn Nights	Midnight Dirge	Mighty D.
Metal Wizard	Metalmorphosis	Methadol	Meza Virs	Mid Evil	Midnight Dream	Mighty Goat Obscenity
Metal Wolf	Metalourd	Methadrone	Mezadura	Midas	Midnight Forces	Mighty Goathorns
Metalakord	Metalrain	Methanol	Mezarkabul	Midas Touch	Midnight Fullmoon	Mighty Scepter
Metalasia	Metalsteel	Metharia	Mezzerschmitt	Middian	Midnight Idöls	Mighty Thor
Metalchrist	Metalstorm	Methedras	Mezzrow	Midevil	Midnight Mass	Mighty Wings
Metaldeath	Metalucifer	Methedrine	Mezzula	Midevil	Midnight Reign	Migul
Metalepsia	Metalvetia	Methius	MG-15	Midgard	Midnight Scream	Mike Fillius
Metalförge	Metalwar	Method	MG-34	Midgard	Midnight Scream	Mike Madness
Metalgods	MetalWar	Method	Mgla	Midgard	Midnight Sun	Mike Terrana
Metalhead	Metalwolf	Method	MH LMTH	Midgard	Midnight Sun	Mikill
Metalhead	Metamorph	Method	Mharbh	Midgard	Midnight Symphony	Miksha
Metalhead	Metamorph	Methodic	Mhirage	Midgard	Midnight Thunder	Miktlantekutly
Metalheadz	Metamorphose	Methodust	Mhorgen	Midgard	MidnightDate	Miles Beyond
Metalian	Metamorphosis	Methonia	Mhorgl	Midgard	Midnightmare	Milice Française
Metalinda	Metan	Methos	Miasis	Midgard	MidNightSerenity	Milimetrica
Metalist	Metano	Methusalem	Miasma	Midgard.	Midnightstorm	Milit
Metalium	Metanoia	Methuselah	Miasma	Midgard.upgraded	Midnite Overture	Militant
Metalium	Metanoon	Methuselahs	Miasthenia	Midget Parade	Midnite Snake	Militant Mass
Metalize	Metanoya	Metower	Michael Angelo	Midian	Midryasi	Military Wife
Metall	Metao	Metralion	Michael Gapys	Midian	Midvinter	Militia
Metallic Fury	Metaphor	Metranks	Michael Harris	Midian	Midwar	Militia
Metallica	Metaphysics	Metro	Michael Knight	Midian	Midway	Militia
Metallien	Metastasis	Metro Society	Michael Pinnella	Midian	Midwinter	Militia
Metallisk Escl Hives	Metástasis	Metrock	Michael Romeo	Midian	Midwinter	Militia of Death
Metalloid	Metastasys	Metrock	Michel Peyronel	Midian	Midwinter	Millarca
Metalius Maximus	Metastises	Metropolis	Microcosm	Midland	Midwinter Storm	Millenia
Metallust	Metatron	Metropolis	Mictian	Midmortemtorment	Midwynter	Millenium

Misery	Missing	Mistreated	Mitrium	Moby Dick	Molehill	Monarchia
Misery	Missing in Action	Mistreater	Mitrumothy	Mock	Molek	Daemonium
Misery	Missing Link	Mistreater	Mitten Spider	Mock the Innocent	Molest	Monarchie Infernale
Misery	Missió	Mistress	Mitternacht	Mockery	Molestation	Monarque
Misery	Mission of One	Mistress	Mittwinter	Modar	Molestation of Beauty	Monasterial Crypt
Misery	Missionary	Mistress of the Dead	Mixomatosis	Modbolt	Molested	Monasterio
Misery	Missionary One	Mistrust	Mixophagia	Moder	Molested Entrails	Monasterium
Misery	Misspend Noise	Mistrust	Mizar	Moderix	Molested Senses	Monasterium
Misery Inc.	Mist	Mistur	Mizery	Modern Funeral Art	Molester	Pisanum
Misery Index	Mist	Mistwander	Mizraab	Modessa	Molestia	Monastery
Misery Loves Co.	Mist	Mistward	Mjöllnir	Modifidious	Molestiah	Monastery
Misery Machine	Mist Enticer	Mistweaver	Mjöllnir	Modilium	Molestor	Monastery
Misery of Insomnia	Mist of Eternity	Mistweaver	Mjöllnirs Destiny	Modorra	Moloch	Monastery
Misery Remains	Mist of the Maelstrom	Mistweaver	Mjölner	Modulus	Moloch	Monastery
Misery Speaks	Mistake	Mistwrath	Mjölnir	Modus Delicti	Moloch	Monastery
Miserycore	Mistaken Element	MistyFate	Mjölnir	Modus Operandi	Moloch	Monastyr
Misery's Omen	Misteltein	Misumena	MMFHL	Modus Vivendi	Moloch	Mondocane
Misfire	Mister Bones	Misvita	Mnaga A Zoorp	Moëvöt	Moloch	Mondocane
Misfortune	Mister Kite	Mitad Oscura	MNDWRX	Mog Ruith	Molokh	Mondragon
Misgivings	Mister Scarry	Mithotyn	Mnemic	Mogorva	Molosse	Mondwolf
Misguided Aggression	Misteria	Mithra	Mnemonic	Mogoutre	Molot	Monestery Brew
Mishere	Misterium	Mithra	Mnich	Mogradem	Molot Vedim	Monev
Misleading Ways	Misterium	Mithrandir	Mo Rage	Moho	Molotov Solution	Money
Misled by Lies	Mistery	Mithras	Moahni Moahna	Mohomax	Molphar	Money Power
Misogi	Misthaufen	Mithril	Moaning Wind	Mohortum	Molten Lava	Mongolian Death
Misogyny	Mistheria	Mithril	Moat	Moi dix Mois	Death Massage	Worm
Misopsychia	Misticia	Mithril	Mob Rules	Moira	Molten Steel	Mongoloid Witchcraft
Misos	Misticona	Mithril	Mob Scene	Moiré	Moltencore	Moñigo
Mispaganthropy	Mistigo Varggoth	Mithril Hall	Mobchild	Moisture	Moment After Scarlet	Monitor
Misquamacus	Darkestra	Mithrubick	Mobile Home	Moker	Moment Maniacs	Monkey Business
Miss Daisy	Mistik	Mitika	Massacre	Mokoma	Momentary Sickness	Monkey Cave
Missa Mercuria	Mistral	Mitochondrion	Mobilizer	Moksha	Moments of Despair	Monkey Head
Missão Metal	Mistral	Mitosis	Mobilizer	Moksha	Moments of Gore	Monoblock
Missfoster	Mistralth	Mitra	Moby Dick	Molar	Momentum	Monoceros
Misshapen Hatred	Mistreated	Mitra	Moby Dick	Molecular Repulsion	Monarch	Monogono

Morbius	Mordant	More Majorum	Morgenstern	Moria	Moriturus	Mornament
Morbius	Mord'A'Stigmata	More Noise For Life	Morgenstern	Moria	Moriturus	Morne
Morblast	Mordaz	More of Myself to Kill	Morggorm	Moria	Moriturus	Morning
Morbosidad	Mordaz	More Than Fear	Morgh	Moriah	Moriturus	Morning After
Morbovia	Mordaz	More Than Hate	Morgion	Moriah	Moriturus	Morning Rise
Morbus	Mordecai	Moredhel	Morgoth	Morian	Mörk Gryning	Morning Rise
Morbus	Mordeth	Moredhel	Morgoth	Moriar	Mork Minnesmerke	Morning Star
Morbus	Mordgier	Moredhell	Morgoth	Moribound	Mörk Munin	Morningless
Morbus	Mordgrim	Morena's Ire	Morgoth	Moribund	Mork Skog	Morningstar
Morbus	Mordgrund	Morerock	Morgoth	Moribund	Morkal	Morningstar
Morbus	Mordhell	Morfetic	Morgudul	Moribund	Morke	Moroi
Morbus Deus	Mordibathor	Morfeus	Morgue	Moribund	Mørke	Moroi
Morbus Gravis	Mordichator	Morfeus	Morgue	Moribund	Morke Helvetes	Morok
Morbus Inferno	Mordichrist	Morfium	Morgue	Moribund	Morkegjemsel	Morók
Morbus Kronn	Mordicus	Morfolk	Morgue	Moribund Oblivion	Mørkekunst	Morokh
Morbus Mortifer	Mordiggan	Morg	Morgue	Moribund	Morkelvyz	Moron
Morbus Mundi	Mordis	Morg	Morgue	Tremendous	Morkem	Morose
Morbusdown	Mordium	Morg	Morgue	Orchestra	Mörker	Morose Vitality
Morbydia	Mordor	Morgaelian	Morgue	Moriendi	Mörkersinnad	Morpha
Morcegos	Mordor	Morgain	Morgue	Morier	Morkeum	Morphal
Morcrof	Mordor	Morgan	Morgue	Morifade	Mørkheim	Morphales
Mord	Mordor	Morgan Lefay	Morgue	Morigan	Morkill	Morphayne
Mord	Mordor	Morgana	Morgue Fetus	Morion	Mörkö	Morpheus
Mord	Mordor	Morgana	Morgue Inc.	Morion	Morkret	Morpheus
Mord	Mordor	Morgana	Morgue Supplier	Morion	Mørkriket	Morpheus
Mord	Mordor	Morgana Lefay	Morgueazm	Morionor	MorkSkogen	Morpheus
Mord Umysłu	Mordorn	Morgana's Kiss	Morgue's Last Choice	Morior	Mörksvamp	Morpheus
Morda	Mordorzhög	Morganatische	Morguetology	Morior	Morlock	Morpheus
Mordacis	Mordrak	Machenschaft	Morguewhore	Morior	Morlock	Morpheus
Mordacum	Mordred	Morgart	Morgul	Morior Axis	Morlock	Morpheus
Mordaehoth	Mordred	Morgatory	Morgum	Morior Ergo Sum	Morlog	Morpheus
Mordak	Mordskog	Morgenes	Morgus	Moriorr	Morlok	Morpheus
Mordancy	Mordslag	Morgengry	Morgus Down	Moriquendi	Mormaugoth	Morpheus Descends
Mordancy	Mordulv	Morgenstern	Morhogg	Moris Exire	Morna	Morpheus Embrace
Mordant	Mordum	Morgenstern	Moria	Moritura	Mornaland	Morphia
	More	Morgenstern	Moria	Morituri		Morphia

Morphosia	Morsek	Mortal Fear	Mortal Trace	Morte Súbita	Mortifer	Mortiphobia
Morphosis	Mörser	Mortal Fear	Mortal Treason	Mortellez	Mortifer	Mortis
Morphosis	Morsgatt	Mortal Fear	Mortal Wish	Mortem	Mortifer	Mortis Dei
Morphoss	Morstice	Mortal Flesh	Mortala	Mortem	Mortifer Rage	Mortis Deveia
Morphosys	Morsun Diaboli	Mortal Form	MortalDread	Mortem	Mortifera	Mortis Mephisto
Morphus	Morsüre	Mortal Fungus	Mortalia	Mortem	Mortifera	Mortis Nex
Morphyn	Morsus	Mortal Gaze	Mortalis	Mortem	Mortiferia	Mortiturus
Morquido	Mort	Mortal God	Mortalis	Mortem Animalium	Mortiferik	Mortivore
Morr	Mort	Mortal Grudge	Mortalitas	Mortem Christ	Mortiferus	Mortjuri
Morrah	Mort	Mortal Illusion	Mortalitus	Mortem Occumbere	Mortifest	Morto Festy
Morranaphab	Mort	Mortal Immunity	Mortality	Mortemstorm	Mortification	Mortofobia
Morridan	Morta Skuld	Mortal Impact	Mortality	Mortenos	Mortification	Mortogtre
Morrigan	Mortage	Mortal Intention	Mortality	Morterix	Mortificy	Morton
Morrigan	Mortaja	Mortal Love	Mortality	Morterra	Mortified	Mortophilia
Morrighan's Cry	Mortal	Mortal Madness	Mortality	Mortes Saltantes	Mortified	Mortorion
Morrigu	Mortal	Mortal Massacre	Mortality	Mortes Vivendi	Mortified	Mortos
Morrigu	Mortal	Mortal Mutilation	Mortalized	Mortfontaine	Mortified	Mortoss
Morris	Mortal Affliction	Mortal Pain	Mortalized	Morthar	Mortified Saint	Mortox
Morrow	Mortal Agony	Mortal Passion	Mortally Infected	Mortharm	Mortifier	Mortridan
Mors	Mortal Agony	Mortal Profecia	Mortal's Dream	Morthem	Mortifier	Mortridden
Mors	Mortal Cannabis	Mortal Reign	Mortandad	Morthifer	Mortifilia	Morttus
Mors Amara	Mortal Coil	Mortal Remains	Mortar	Morthirim	Mortifix	Mortu Noferacius
Mors Atra	Mortal Decay	Mortal Remains	Mortar	Morthona	Mortifixion	Mortualia
Mors in Tabula	Mortal Decay	Mortal Remains	Mortar	Morthond	Mortify	Mortualia Nocturnum
Mors Liberatrix	Mortal Dezire	Mortal Remains	Mortare	Morthor	Mortify	Mortuaria
Mors Omnia Solvit	Mortal Discipline	Mortal Remains	Mortarion	Morthor	Mortify	Mortuario
Mors Osculi	Mortal Dread	Mortal Sanctuary	Mortaris	Morthra	Mortify	Mortuário
Mors Principium Est	Mortal Dread	Mortal Scream	Mortavik	Morthvargr	Mortify	Mortuarium
Mors Silens	Mortal Dream	Mortal Scream	Mortbrand	Mortician	Mortify	Mortuary
Mors Subita	Mortal Enemy	Mortal Sin	Morte Aeterna	Mortician	Mortigena	Mortuary
Mors Subita	Mortal Enemy	Mortal Sin	Morte Genesis	Morticinum	Mortigor	Mortuary
Mors Summa	Mortal Enemy	Mortal Slaughter	Morte Incandescente	Morticious	Mortiis	Mortuary
Mors Tua	Mortal Eyes	Mortal Terror	Morte Interna	Morticus	Mortiis Daemonium	Mortuary
Mors Ultima	Mortal Factor	Mortal Torment	Morte Sicuro	Mortifer	Mortimer Dipthong	Mortuary
Morse Death	Mortal Fear	Mortal Torment	Morte Silmoris	Mortifer	Mortinatum	Mortuary

Murder in Art	Murha	Mutala	Mutilation	My Demons Diversity	My Silent Wake	Myrddraa
Murder in the Red	Murhmur	Mutant	Mutilation	My Dying Bride	My Sister's Machine	Myrddraal
Light District	Murinus	Mutant	Mutilation	My Empty Room	My Sixth Shadow	Myriad
Murder Ink	Murk Exorbitance	Mutant Soldier	Mutilation	My Enchantment	My Son	Myriad
Murder Intentions	Murkla	Mutant Speed	Mutilation	My Eye	My Executioner	Myriad
Murder of Crows	Murkna	Mutant Terror	Mutilation	My Fallen Father	My Therapy	Myriads
Murder of God	Murmur	Mutated	Mutilation	My Fallen Garden	My Threnody	Myring
Murder One	Muro	Mutated	Mutilation Nation	My Fate	My Thrusting Crown	Myrk
Murder One	Murrain	Mutation	Mutilator	My First Knife	My Tide	Myrkal
Murder One	Murrain	Mutha Corpse	Mutilator	My Friend Rudra	My Uncle the Wolf	Myrkgrav
Murder Persons	Murw	Mutha Corpse	Mutilator	My Funeral	My Victim	Myrkr
Murder Practice	Musaka	Muthas Pride	Mutilator	My Funeralmarch	My Will	Myrkskog
Murder Rape	Museros	Muthellation	Mutilhate	My Garden	Myatan	Myrkur
Murder She Wrote	Museum of	Muthurlode	Mutilus Mucous	My Hate	Mydgard	Myrkvar
Murder She Wrote	Transient Lights	Mütiilation	Mutiny	My Horsey	Mydra	Myrkvid
Murder Squad	Mushroom	Mutilación	Mutiny	My Infinite Kingdom	MyGRAIN	Myrkvidr
Murderaim	River Band	Mutilador	Mutum	My Insanity	Myiasis	Myrkwid
MurderBurg	Mushroomhead	Mutilador	Muunnos	My Lament	Myin Sanity	Myrmidion Creed
Murdercar	Mushy Mind Surgery	Mutilage	MVP	My Last Identity	Mykorrhiza	Myrmidon
Murderdolls	Music Hates You	Mutilarium	MWS	My Last Keen	Mylidian	Myrmidon
Murdered at Random	Musical Massacre	Mutilate Corpse	MX	My Last War	Myndkill	Myrmidon
Murderer	Muslimcorpse	Mutilate Myself	MX	My Life With	Myndsnare	Myrrdin
Murderers Row	Muspelheim	Mutilated	MX Machine	Her Ghost	Mynedarion	Myryad
Murdergoat	Múspell	Mutilated	My Bitter End	My Life's Despair	Mynjun	Myself
Murdergod	Muspellsheim	Mutilated Cadaver	My Cold Embrace	My Mind's Mine	Myocarditis	Myself Am Hell
Murdermass	Mussorgski	Mutilated Christ	My Courtyard	My Own Grave	Myoclon	Mysera
Murderous Rampage	Must Missa	Mutilated Christ	My Craving	My Own Mess	Myokastor	Mysotheisme
Murdershock	Musta Kappeli	Mutilated Corpses	My Cross to Bare	My Own Victim	Myon	Mysstress
MurderWorld	Musta Surma	Mutilated Remains	My Dark Half	My People's Suicide	Myopia	Myst
Murdock	Mustain	Mutilated Remains	My Dark Mind	My Pet Demon	Myopia	Mystere de
Murdread	Mustan Kuun Lapset	Mutilated Soul	My Dark Sin	My Plague	Myosotis	Notre Dame
Muren	Mustasch	Mutilated to	My Darkest Dream	My Ruin	Myproof	Mysterhydden
Murgost	MustDie	Perfection	My Darkest Hate	My Sanctuary of Hate	Myra	Mysteria
Murgunstrum	Mustpain	Mutilated Undead	My Dawn	My Shadow	Myra	Mysteria
Murha	Mutación	Mutilation	My Deepest Inner	My Shameful	Myracle	Mysteria

Mysteriarch

Mysteries
Mysteriis
Mysteriis
Mysteriis
Mysteriis
Mysterion
Mysterion
Mysterion Noctum
Mysterious Eclipse
Mysterium
Mysterium
Mysterium
Mysterium
Mystery
Mystery
Mystery
Mystery
Mystery
Mystery
Mystery Blue
Mysterya
Mystes
Mysth
Mystheria
Mystherium
Mysthical
Mystic
Mystic
Mystic
Mystic
Mystic
Mystic Alliance
Mystic Atrocity
Mystic Charm
Mystic Circle

Mystic Death
Mystic Death
Mystic Force
Mystic Forest
Mystic Moon
Mystic Opera
Mystic Prophecy
Mystic Rage
Mystic Realm
Mystic Shadows
Mystica
Mystica
Mystica
Mystica
Mystical
Mystical Death
Mystical Dreams
Mystical End
Mystical Fate
Mystical Fire
Mystical Frost
Mystical Fullmoon
Mystical Fullmoon
Mystical Gate
Mystical Nightcharm
Mystical Warning
Mystice
Mysticism
Mysticism Black
Mystictorment
Mysticum
Mystification
Mystification
Mystifier
Mystik

Mystik Trace
Mystique
Mystiria
Mysto Dysto
Mystress
Mystrez
Mystria
Mysttral
Mystura
Mystyca Odyssea
Mytes Gradel
Myth
Myth
Myth 410
Myth of Freedom
Mythanos
Mythem
Mythiasin
Mythic
Mythic Force
Mythica
Mythistory
Mythlorian
Mytholic
Mythologic
Mythologica
Mythological Cold
   Towers
Mythology
Mythology
Mythology
Mythopoeia
Mythos
Mythos Nord
Mythra

Mythrill
Mythus
Mythyca
Mytile Vey Lorth
Mytox
Mytra
Myzterion

◀ Nasav

Nascitus
Nasferatu
Nasha Vaina
Nashama
Nashehrhum
Nasheim
Nashwuah
Nastik
Nastrandir
Nåstrond
Nasty Disaster
Nasty Rose
Nasty Savage
Nasum
Natan
Natas
Natas
Natas
Natas Demonic
  Regime
Natassievila
Natastor
Natek
Nathan P. Holly
Nathania
Nathania
Nathaniel
Nathicana
Nation
Nation
Nation A.D.
Nation X
National Napalm
  Syndicate
National Suicide

Nations of Death
Natisk
Native
Native FX
Native in Black
Native Instinct
Nativo
Nator
Natrach
Natrium
Natron
Natt
Natt
Nattas
Natte Ulf
Nattefrost
Nattegaahl
Nattemork
Nattens Barn
NatterVrede
Nattestid
Nattetid
Náttfari
Nattferd
Nattfrost
Nattkvad
Nattsmyg
Nattstrid
Nattstrype
Nattsvart
Nattvarg
Nattvind
Nattvindens Gråt
Natural Death
Natural Disaster

Natural Selection
  Agency
Natural Spirit
Naturaleza Muerta
Naturemorte
Nature's Elements
Naty
Nauar
Naught Around
Naughty Naughty
Nauglath
Naumachia
Nausea
Nausea
Nausea Gods
Nauseant
Nauseating
  Tepid Whiff
Nauseous Surgery
Nauseum
Nauthis
Nauthisuruz
Nautiluss
Nav'
Navar
Naverhalvete
Naven
Navij
Navja
Nawak
Nawia
Nayled
Nazarene Deceiver
Nazca
Nazghul

Nazgul
Nazgul
Nazgul
Nazgul
Nazgul
Nazgul Rising
Nazgulum
Nazhand
Nazhgul
Nazroth
Nazxul
Nazzaq
NB-604
NC Death Grind
N-Carkade
NDE
Ne Obliviscaris
Ne Plus Ultra
Neaera
Neaera
Neandertahl
Neandertal
Neandertal
Neanderthal2069
Neanderthalia
Neant
Neantiel
Near
Near Dark
Near Dark
Near Death Condition
Near Death
  Experience
Near Life
Near Mataron

Neasit
Neat001
Neath
Nebadom
Nebel
Nebel
Nebel
Nebel Torvum
Nebelbanner
Nebelborn
Nebelburg
Nebelgrab
Nebelheer
Nebelheim
Nebelheim
Nebelhexë
Nebelhorn
Nebelkorona
Nebelkrähe
Nebelkrieger
Nebelmacht
Nebelmythen
Nebelsturm
Nebeltor
Nebelwald
Nebelwerfer
Nebiras
Nebiros
Nebiros
Nebiros
Nebiros
Nebirus
Nébirus
Neblina
Nebória

Nebrae
Nebron
Nebucadnezzer
Nebuchadnezzar
Nebukadnezza
Nebula
Nebula
Nebula
Nebula
Nebula 666
Nebula Carmine
Nebula Gates
Nebula Soturna
Nebulae31
Nebulah
Nebulah
Nebulah of Destiny
Nebulah X
Nebular Carpathians
Nebular Frost
Nebular Moon
Nebular Mystic
Nebularaven
Nebulizer
Nebulosa
Nebulosus Fatum
Nebunam
Nec Timide
Necare
Necator
Necessary Evil
Nechbeyth
Nechist
Nechrist
Nechrist

Necis
Neck
Neckbreaker
Neckrofight
Neckropolis
Necra
Necrafh
Necramyth
Necraphilia
Necreous
Necrid
Necris Dust
Necrite
Necro
Necro Holocaust
Necro Paris
  Catacombes
Necro Phoenix
Necro Ritual
Necro Sadist
Necro Schizma
Necro Sentient
  Mortis Feed
Necro Strike
Necro Tampon
Necroabortion
Necroart
Necrobass
NecroBeast
Necrobiosis
Necrobiosis
Necrobiosis
Necrobiosis
Necrobiosis
Necroblaspheme

Necrocannibal	Necrófago	Necrokult of Kronos	Necromancy	Necronomicon	Necropia	Necropsy
Necrocannibal	Necrófago	Necrokulture	Necromancy	Necronomicon	Necroplasma	Necropsy
Necrocannibalistic	Necrófago	Necrolatreia	Necromancy	Necronomicon	Necropolaris	Necropsy
Vomitorium	Necrofeast	Necrolatry	Necromancy	Necronomicon Beast	Necropolis	Necropsy
Necroccult	Necrofeast	Necrolatry	Necromandus	Necronomitron	Necropolis	Necropsy
Necrocultus	Necrofemmè	Necrolatry	Necromanicide	Necronslaught	Necropolis	Necropsy
Necrocest	Necrofest	Necrolatry	Necromanicider	Necrony	Necropolis	Necropsy
Necrochrist	Necrofilia	Necrólisis	Necromansy	Necropath	Necropolis	Necropsy Room
Necrocide	Necrofilia	Necrolith	Necromant	Necropedophagia	Necropolis	Necropsya
Necrocide	Necrofilia	Necrologi	Necromantia	Necropedophile	Necropolis	Necropsya
Necrocide	Necrofilia	Necrologist	Necromantic	Necropedophilia	Necropolis	Necrorgasm
Necrocide	Necrofilia	Necrology	Necromantic	Necrophacus	Necropolis	Necrorgasm
Necrocifer	Necrofily	Necrology	Necromass	Necrophagia	Necropolis	Necrorgy
Necrocite	Necrofist	Necrology	Necromemisis	Necrophagia	Necropolis	Necrorising
Necrocock	Necroflesh	Necrolord	Necromessiah	Necrophagist	Necropolis	Necrorrosion
Necrocomium	Necrofobia	Necrolord	Necromicon	Necrophagous	Necropolis	Necros
Necrocorpse	Necrofobia	Necrolust	Necromion	Necrophagus	Necropolis	Necros Christos
Necrocult	Necrofog	Necrolust	Necromis	Necropher	Necropolis Rising	Necrosadic
Necrocult	Necroforge	Necrolust	Necromonica	Necrophil	Necropollis	Necrosadist
Necrocult	Necrofrost	Necrolust	Necromorbus	Necrophile	Necropsia	Necrosadist
Necrocunt	Necrofuck In Hell	Necrolust	Necromorph	Necrophile	Necropsia	Necrosadistic
Necrodaemon	Necrofuckinglicious	Necrolust	Necromorten	Necrophilia	Necropsia	Goat Torture
Necrodaemon	Necrofurya	Necrolytic	Necromortica	Necrophilia	Necropsia	Necrosanct
Necrodaemon	Necrogay	Necromance	Necromortis	Necrophiliac	Necropsia	Necrosanity
Necrodaimon	Necrogenesis	Necromance	Necromortum	Necrophiliac	Necropsia	Necroscope
Necrodead	Necrogenous	Necromancer	Necron	Necrophiliac	Necropsia	Necrose
Necrodeath	Necrogore	Necromancer	Necron	Necrophiliac	Necropsia	Necrosearch
Necrodeit	Necrogorica	Necromancer	Necronaut	Necrophilism	Necropsia	Necrosia Delectus
Necrodemon	Necrogrim	Necromancer	Necronemesis	Necrophilisma	Necropsia	Necrosis
Necrodemon	Necrohellbugs	Necromancer	Necronoclast	Necrophobia	Necropsy	Necrosis
Necrodochion	Necroholocaust	Necromancer	Necronom	Necrophobia	Necropsy	Necrosis
Necrodoom	Necroid	Necromancia	Necronomic	Necrophobia	Necropsy	Necrosis
Necro-E	Necroid	Necromancia	Necronomical	Necrophobia	Necropsy	Necrosis
Necrofago	NecroK.I.L.L.Dozer	Necromancy	Crucifixion	Necrophobic	Necropsy	Necrosis
Necrofago	Necrokiller	Necromancy	Necronomichrist	Necrophobic	Necropsy	Necrosis

Necrosis
Necrosis
Necrosis
Necrosis
Necrosis
Necrosist
Necroslaughter
Necrosleezer
Necrosorth
Necrosphere
Necrost
Necrostasis
Necroster
Necrosynthesys
Necrotaph
Necroterio
Necroternal
Necrotesticvs
Necrotic
Necrotic
Necrotic Chaos
Necrotic
   Disgorgement
Necrotic Flesh
Necrotic Mutation
Necrotic Trust
Necrotica
Necrotician
Necrotician
Necroticism
Necrotion
Necrotize
Necrotized Flesh
Necrotomie
Necrotomy

Necrotomy
Necrotomy
Necrototure
Necrotos
Necrovation
Necroverdose
Necrovile
Necrovile
Necrovomit
Necrovomitor
Necrovore
Necrovorous
Necrowar
Necrowar
Necrowinter
Necrowitch
Necrowizard
Necrown
Necrozzz
Necryptic
Nedgeva
Nee
Need
Needless God
Needleye
Needs for Flesh
Neetzach
Nefandus
Nefario
Nefarion
Nefarious
Nefarious
Nefarious
Nefarious
Nefarious

Nefarious
Nefarious
Nefarious
Nefarious
Nefarious Azarak
Nefarious Baptism
Nefarium
Nefarius
Nefas
Nefas
Nefast
Nefasta Dies
Nefasto
Nefasto
Nefastum
Nefastus Abbatia
Nefastus Diès
Nefaustium
Nefelheim
Nefelim
Neferion
Nefertum
Neffheim
NEFormat
Nefroptosis
Neftaraka
Negarobo
Negation
Negationist
Negativ
Negativ Pólus
Negativa
Negative
Negative Creed
Negative Creep

Negative Face
Negative Four
Negative Plane
Negative Reaction
Negative Theory
Negativity
Negator
Negatron
Negazione
Neglected Faith
Neglected Fields
Negligence
Negligent Collateral
   Collapse
Negorgodon
Negramagia
Negras Visiones
Negro Altar
Negură Bunget
Nehëmah
Nehemiah
Nehpalese
Nehyam
Neige et Noirceur
Neige Noire
Neil Hess
Neil Turbin
Neimes
Neithal
Neithan
Neither
Neither
Nekantropy
Nekhrôsis
Nekkrosis

Nekra Souvlakia
Nekrad
Nekro Khaos
Nekro Vinterstrom
Nekrofilet
Nekroforest
NekroFuk Kvlt
Nekrogoblikon
Nekroholocaust
Nekrokaos
Nekrokrist SS
Nekrokult
Nekrolog
Nekromantheon
Nekromantie
Nekromantik Kurse
Nekronom
Nekropol
Nekropoland
Nekropolis
Nekros
Nekrós
Nekros Pervertor
Nekrosis
Nekrosis
Nekrotiis
Nekro-Torso
Nekrovoid
Nektra
Nekysia
Nelchael's Throne
Neldoreth
Neldöreth
Nema
Nema

Nema
Nemain
Neman
Nematon
Nemavze
Nembience
Nembrionic
Nembrionic
   Hammerdeath
Nemedian
Nemesant
Nemesea
Nemesi
Nemesis
Nemesis
Nemesis
Nemesis
Nemesis
Nemesis
Nemesis
Nemesis
Nemesis
Nemesis
Nemesis
Nemesis
Nemesis
Nemesis
Nemesis
Nemesis
Nemesis
Nēmesis
Nemesis Aeterna
Nemesis Inferi
Nemesis Irae
Nemesis Occulta

Nemesis Ocvlta
Nemesy
Nemesys
Nemeton
Nemeton
Nemeton
Nemetona
Nemhain
Nemo Ante
   Mortem Beatus
Nemontemi
Nemossos
Nemrael
Nemrod
Nemrod
Nemus
Nemus
Nemus Mortuum
neNasty
Nenavist
Nenia
Neo Cultis
Neo Prophecy
Neo Shark
Neoandertals
Neochrome
Neocori
Neocosmic
Neocracy
Neocracy
Neocrima
Neófito
Neofobia
Neolith
Neolithic

Neomortem
Neon
Neon
Neon Cross
Neon Cross
Neon Dream
Neon God
Neon Night
Neon Sunrise
Neonatal Death
Neophitus
Neophobia
Neophron
Neophyte
Neophyte
Neoplasia
Neoplasmah
Neoshine
Neotruth
Nepal
Nepauz-Had
Nepenthe
Nepenthe
Nepenthe
Nepenthe
Nepenthes
Nepharitus
Nephasth
Nephastus
Nephastus
Nephele
Nephelium
Nephenzy
   Chaos Order
Nephesh

Nephilim
Nephilim
Nephilim
Nephilim
Nephragorious
Nephrite
Nephritis
Nephtys
Nephusim
Nephwrack
Neptune
Neptune
Neptune
Neptune Towers
Nequicia
Nera
Neraia
Nerakain
Nergal
Nergal
Nergal
Nergal
Nergal
Nergalkult
Nerkroth
Nerlich
Nero Circus
Neron
Neron
Neronia
Neronoia
Nerraka
Nerthus
Nerthus
Nerumia

Nerun
NERV
Nerve
Nerve Gas Tragedy
Nervecell
Nervekiller
Nervengas
Nervochaos
Nervous
Nervous Playground
Neshamah
Nessun Dorma
NeSSuS
Nest
Neter
Netherbird
Netherealm
Netherelm
Netherkin
Nethermancy
Nethervoid
Netherworld
Netherworld
Nethescerial
Netra
Netrist
Netter
Nettlecarrier
Nettlethrone
Netvil
Neue Regel
Neuma
Neuntoter
Neural Booster
Neural Implosion

Neurasthenia
Neurasthenia
Neurasthenia
Neurasthenie
Neuraxis
Neuri
Neuria
Neurinome
Neuro Toxin
Neuro Visceral
   Exhumation
Neurobex
Neurodeliri
Neurodelirium
Neuromist
Neuronia
Neuronomicon
Neuropath
Neuropathia
Neurosis
Neurosis
Neurosis
Neurosis Inc.
Neurosphere
Neurothing
Neurotic
Neurotic Decay
Neurotic of Gods
Neurotic Serenity
Neurotica
Neurotomy
Neurotoxin
Neuro-Visceral
   Exhumation
Neus

Neuthrone
Neutron Hammer
Nevelheim
Nevelrijk
Never
Never Azkt
Never Comes Silence
Never Die Alone
Never Ending Beauty
Never Ending Hate
Never Light Horizon
Never Say Die
Never Sleep
Never Sunrise
Never the Sunshine
Never Void
Neverborn
Neverborn
Neverdead
NeverDream
Neverend
Nevergreen
Neverise
Neverkrist
Neverland
Neverland
NeverLand
Neverland
Neverland
Neverland
Neverland
Nevermore
Nevermore
Neveroad
Nevid'

Nevolution
Nevralgia
New Age
New Black Widow
New Blood
New Born Chaos
New Dawn
   Foundation
New Disease
New Eden
New Eminence
New Family
New Flesh Coming
New Land
New Machine
New Mexican
   Erection
New Millennium's
   End
New Order
   of Messiah
New Project
New Religion
New Religion
New World
New World
   Depression
New World Order
New World Psychos
New York
Newborn Nemesis
NewBreed
Newtrodyne
Nex
Nex Aestatis

Nex Mortalis
Nex Perpetui Regis
Nexis
Next
Next Domination
Next in Line
Next Pain
Nexum
Nexus
Nexus
Nexus
Nexus
Nexus
Nexus
Nexus
Nexxo
Nexxt
Nezgaroth
Nezhegol
Neznaboh
NFC 15-100
N-Fin
NG26
Ngeloth
Nhaavah
Nhadar
Nhuvasarim
Niagara
NIB
Nibdem
Nibelheim
Nibelung
Nibiru
Nibiruth
Nicaraguan
   Death Squad

Nitroseed	No Man's Land	No Spiritual	Noctiferia	Nocturnal Altar	Nocturnal Howling	Noddegamrah
Nitrous	No Man's Land	Surrender	Noctifier	Nocturnal Arts	Nocturnal Impulse	Node
Nitroxyde	No Man's Land	No States Spirits	Noctiflorous Thorns	Nocturnal Blasphemy	Nocturnal Invocation	Nodens
Nivaira	No Man's Land	No Stress	Noctiluca	Nocturnal Blasphemy	Nocturnal Majesty	Nodens
Njafrar	No Mark	No Trouble	Noctis	Nocturnal Breed	Nocturnal Necropsy	Nodes of Ranvier
Nme Within	No Mercy	No Utopia	Noctis	Nocturnal Crown	Nocturnal Orchestra	Noekk
No	No Mercy	No Warning Shot	Noctis Imperium	Nocturnal Crypt	Nocturnal Plauge	Noenum
No Armor	No Mercy	No Way	Noctis Invocat	Nocturnal Damnation	Nocturnal	Noesis
No Blest	No Mercy	No Way Out	Noctivago Misantropo	Nocturnal Death	Procreation	Nofear
No Body	No Mercy	Noah's Flood	Noctophilia	Nocturnal Decay	Nocturnal Prophecy	Nofek
No Bros	No Mercy	Nobassak	Noctos	Nocturnal Decay	Nocturnal Raven	Nofertum
No Candy	No Mercy	Nobilitas Nigra	Noctpherah	Nocturnal Delusion	Nocturnal Rites	Nofuck
No Choice	No Morality	Noble Savage	Noctran Demanto	Nocturnal Depression	Nocturnal Ritual	Nogbold's Palace
No Class	No More	Nobody	Noctu	Nocturnal Desire	Nocturnal Sin	Nohellia
No Comply	No More Fear	Noche Eterna	Noctuary	Nocturnal Devotion	Nocturnal Soul	Nohmad
No Credits Left	No More Lies	Nocratai	Noctuary	Nocturnal	Nocturnal Supremacy	Noia
No Creeps	No More Pain	Nocta	Noctum	Domination	Nocturnal Supremacy	Noid
No Dawn	No Pride	Nocta	Noctumbre	Nocturnal Dominium	Nocturnal Supremacy	Noir
No Destiny	No Promises	Noctambulant	Nocturn	Nocturnal Doom	Nocturnal Symphony	Noise Forest
No Direction	No Quarter	Noctambulant	Nocturn	Nocturnal Earth	Nocturnal Symphony	Noise Is Not Enough
No Emotions	No Raza	Grimness	Nocturn	Nocturnal Eclipse	Nocturnal Venus	Noise Killer
No Empathy	No Remission	Noctambulath	Nocturn	Nocturnal Emissions	Nocturnal Voices	Noise Kommando
No Empathy	No Remorse	Noctambulism	Nocturna	Nocturnal Emissions	Nocturnal Vomit	Noise Machine
No Excuse	No Remorse	Noctarabulant	Nocturna	Nocturnal Empire	Nocturnal Winds	Noise of Silence
No Exit	No Remorse	Nocte Obducta	Nocturna	Nocturnal Evil	Nocturnal Winter	Noise Sickness
No Fate	No Return	Noctem	Nocturna	Nocturnal Faith	Nocturnal Worshipper	Noisear
No Fate	No Rules	Nocterminus	Perambulant	Nocturnal Fear	Nocturne	NoiseCult
No Fate	No Scrap	Nocternity	in Tenebris	Nocturnal Fear	Nocturne	NoiseField
No Fear	No Second	Nocternity	Nocturnal	Nocturnal Fears	Nocturnes Mist	Noisehunter
No Flesh Spared	Chance	Nocternity	Nocturnal	Nocturnal Feast	Nocturnia	Noisekiller
No Future	No Sense	Noctes	Nocturnal	Nocturnal Feelings	Nocturnia	Noiselust
No Hand Path	No Sign of Life	Nocti Vagus	Nocturnal	Nocturnal Funeral	Nocturno	Noiser Gate
No Identity	No Silence	Nocticula	Nocturnal	Nocturnal Grace	Nocturno Culto	Noism
No Inner Limits	No Sissy Stuff	Noctifer	Nocturnal Aar	Nocturnal Graves	Nocturnus	Noitavalkea
No Love Lost	No Sobriety	Noctifer	Nocturnal Addiction	Nocturnal Horde	Noctus	Noitawaimo
	No Souls Lost					

Nokemono
Nokthe
Noktiis Eterna
Nokturn
Nokturnal
Nokturnal
Nokturnal
Nokturnal Mortum
Nokturnal Rust
Nokturnal Summoner
Nokturne
Nokturnel
Nol
No-Lokost
Noltem
Nomad
Nomad
Nomad
Nomad Barbie
Nomad Conqueror
Nomad Soul
Nomada
Nomans Land
Nome
Nomed
Nomedeht
Nomenclature
  Diablerie
Nomenmortis
No-Mercy
Nomicon
Nomin
Nominon
Non Aeternus
Non Compos Mentis

Non Compos Mentus
Non Divine
Non Grata
Non Immemor Mei
Non Iron
Non Negotiable Life
Non Omnis Moriar
Non Omnis Moriar
Non Opus Dei
Non Serviam
Non Serviam
Noname
Nonchristian
Nonconformity
Non-Divine
Nondivine
None
None
None Divine
None More Evil
None Shall Defy
Noneptahsir
Noneuclid
Nonexist
Nonexistence
Non-Existence
Non-Fiction
Non-Human Level
Nonhumental
Nonpoint Factor
Nonsakrum
Nonsense
  Premonition
Noom
Noosebomb

Nooses for Neckties
Noothgrush
Nopheleth
Noplacetohide
Noplies
Nopresion
Noquenth
Nora
Norace
Nord
Nord
Nord
Nord
Nord av Snaefells
Nord 'N' Commander
Nord Ulv
Nordafrost
Nordavind
Nordblod
Norden
Nord-Est
Nordfrost
Nordglanz
Nordheim
Nordheim
Nordic Blood
Nordic Mist
Nordic Necropolis
Nordic Netheren
Nordic Terror
Nordica
Nordicwinter
Nordisches Blut
Nordischreik
Nordishavet

Nordisk Velde
Nordkampf
Nordlicht
Nordlys
Nordmen
Nordor
Nordream
Nordreich
Nordschrei
Nordsturm
Nordum
Nordvargr
NordVinter
Nordvrede
Nordvykk
Nordwind
Norgard
Norgathaal
Norgoth
Norhyth
Norinian
Norm Rejection
Norma Jeanne
Norman Bates
Norman K. Anderson
Norn
Nornir
Norns
Noromi Lucalen
Noroses
Norot
Norphelida
Norrsken
Norrsken
Norse

Norsekrieg
Norseman
Norseth
Norske Synder
Norstarah
Nortada Gelada
Nortavlaggh.377
North
North
North of Eveywhere
North Sindrom
Northaunt
Northcrown
Northdark
Northeast
Norther
Norther
Northern Alliance
Northern Blaze
Northern Breeze
Northern Damnation
Northern Darkness
Northern Discipline
Northern Empire
Northern Flame
Northern Frost
Northern Gods
Northern Invasion
Northern Kataklysm
Northern Lights
Northern Lights
Northern Lights
Northern Myst
Northern Myst
Northern Oak

Northern Storm
Northern Tales
Northern Tod
Northern Werewolves
Northgate
Northland
Northrend
Northrone
Northside
Northstar
Northstream
Northwail
Northwalls
Northwind
Northwind
Northwind
Nörthwind
Northwinds
Northwinds
NorthWorld
Nortron
Nortt
Norwegian Evil
Norxcal
Norz Feuer
Nos Vrolok
Nosce Teipsum
Nosdrama
Nose Amputation
Nosferatos
Nosferatu
Nosferatu
Nosferatu
Nosferatu
Nosferatu

Nosferatu
Nosferatus XIII
Nosferiel
Nosferion
Nosgoth
Nosgoth
Noslom
Nosophoros
Nosophoros
Nosphares
Nospheratu
Nostalgia Dreams
Nostalgiczna
  Wędrówka Słońca
Nostaria
Nostra Turma
Nostradameus
Nostradamus
Nostradark
NostraDrama
Nostredame
Nostromo
Nostromo
Nostromo
Nostrovia
Nostrum
Nostrum
Nosvampyram
Nosvrolok
Nosvyr
Not Eyeless
Not Fragile
Notanga
Notarium
Nothing

Nothing Left For Tomorrow	November Grief	Noxious	Nuclear Tribunal	Nullsake	Nyctanthous
Nothing Less	November Leaf	Noxious Faith	Nuclear Vengeance	Num Skull	Nycticorax
Nothing More	Novembers Doom	Noxius	Nuclear Vomit	Numen	Nyctophobia
Nothing Remains	Novembers Fall	Noxx	Nuclear Warfare	Numen	Nyctophobic
Nothing Sacred	Novembre	Nozghot	Nuclear Winter	Numenor	Nydvind
Nothing Sacred	Noverca	NPC	Nuclear Winter	Numic	Nyia
Nothingface	Novgorod	Nrocinu	Nuclear Winter	Numinous	Nyktalgia
Nothingfaith	Novilunion	Nth	Nuclear Winter	Numortevok	Nykteros
Nothingness	Novistador	Ñu	Nuclear Winter	Nunca Mas	Nylis
Nothingness	Novocaine	Nü World Disorder	Nuclearhammer	Nunkthul	Nympha
Nothing's Grace	Novon	Nu.Clear.Dawn	Nucleon	Nuns With Guns	Nympha
Nothum	Novum Organum	Nuclear	Nucleus Torn	Nunslaughter	Nymphalis
Notorica	Novy Zavet	Nuclear	Nuctemeron	Nunwhore Commando 666	Nymphea Aurora
Notorious	Nów	Nuclear Anticristo	Nuctemeron		Nyne
Notr	Now It's Dark	Nuclear Assault	Nuctemeron	Nüpfelgard	Nyogtha
Notre Dame	Nowen	Nuclear Blast Allstars	Nuctemeron	Nuquerna	Nyogthaeblisz
Nott	Nowhere	Nuclear Crucifixion	Nuctemeron	Nûr	Nyomor
Nottingham	Nowogrodek	Nuclear Crucifixion	Nudge	Nurgle	Nyseius
Notung	Nowonmai	Nuclear Death	Nueairea	Nürn	Nysrogh
Notung	Nox	Nuclear Death	Nuestra Familia	Nurnen	Nysrogh
Noturna	Nox Aderat	Nuclear Desecration	Nuestros Derechos	Nurse Ratched	Nytemare
Noumena	Nox Aeterna	Nuclear Devastation	Nueva Etica	Nuse	Nythro
Nous	Nox Aeterna	Nuclear Hammer	Nuevo Poder	Nusuth	Nytrix
Nova Art	Nox Eterna	Nuclear Hell	Nugatory	Nuthin' Pritty	Nyx
Nova Epica	Nox Intempesta	Nuclear Holocaust	Nugatory	Nutskab	NZZN
Nova Era 555	Nox Invicta	Nuclear Holocaust	Nuisance	Nux	
Nová Rùže	Nox Invictus	Nuclear Massacre	Nuisance	Nux Vomica	
novAct	Nox Lunaris	Nuclear Nature	Nuit Noire	Nuxvomica	
Nova-Era	Nox Mortis	Nuclear Nights	Nuits Eternelles	Nvlvs	
Novalis	Nox Perpetua	Nuclear Punishment	Nuke-O-Rama	Nyarlathotep	
Novathor	Nox Pestes	Nuclear Ravager	Nuklear Annihilation	Nyarlathotep	
Novel Feeling	Noxa	Nuclear Shadow	Nuklear Antikrist	Nyarlathotep	
Novelty	Noxious	Nuclear Simphony	Null	Nyarlathotep	
November Death	Noxious	Nuclear Storm	Nüll	Nyarlathotep	
	Noxious	Nuclear Terror	Nullkern	Nybras	

Obsidian
Obsidian
Obsidian
Obsidian
Obsidian
Obsidian Aspect
Obsidian Chamber
Obsidian Empire
Obsidian Gate
Obsidian Halo
Obsidian Kingdom
Obsidian Reign
Obsidian Throne
Obsidio
Obsidion
Obsin
Obskene Sonare
Obskur
Obskur
Obskure
Obskure Torture
Obskurum
Obsta
Obstetrical Palsy
Obstinacy
Obstinacy
Obstruction
Obstruo
Obstsalat
Obtain
Obtained
  Enslavement
Obtenebratum
Obtenebris
Obtest

Obtruncation
Obtuse
Obús
Obzidian
Ocanthus
Occams Razor
Occasus
Occasus
Occasus
Occidens
Occisas
Occision
Occision
Occisor
Occult
Occult
Occult Astral
Occult Corpse
Occult God
Occulta
Occulta Struttura
Occultism
Occultum
Occultus
Occultus
Occultus
Occurrence
Ocean
Ocean
Ocean Chief
Ocean Machine
Ocean of Sorrow
Ocean Soul
Oceana
Oceano
Océano de Sangre
Oceans Afire

Oceans of Sadness
Ocelot
Oconnor
Octagon
Octagon
Octagon
Octagon
Octave
Octavia
Octavia Sperati
Octinimos
Octinomos
October
October 31
October Falls
October Rust
October Thorns
October Tide
October's End
Octopus
Octoria
Ocularis
Ocularis Infernum
Ocultan
Oculus
Odal
Odal
Odal Rune
Odd Dimension
Odd Heathenish
Odd Logic
Oddameatr
Oddech Buntownika
Oddity
Oddmongers

Odds
Odds
Oddskabbcatz
Ode Odium
Ode of Eternity
Odeiross
Odelegger
Odem Arcarum·
oden
Odenwrath
Odeon
Odeon
Odes of Ecstasy
Odhinn
Odi Profanum Vulgus
Odin
Odin's Court
Odins Forest
Odin's Law
Odious
Odious
Odious
Odious Mortem
Odious Sanction
Odisea
Odisea
Odisséia
Odium
Odium
Odium
Odium
Odium
Odium
Odium
Odium

Odium
Odium Hominum
Odium Immortalis
Odium Inc.
Odium Incarnate
Odium Perpetuum
Odius Embowel
Odor Mortis
Odo'Sha
Odpad
Odroerir
Odyssea
Odyssey
Odyssey
Odyssey
Odyssey
Odyssey
Odyssey
Oestre
Œwiętoróg
Of Aeons
Of Agony and
  of Death
Of Angels And
  Gravediggers
Of Darkness
Of Darksome Origin
Of Dream and Drama
Of Forsaken Divinity
Of Grator
Of His Own Hand
Of Human Bondage
Of Infinity
Of Mara
Of Parting Words

Of Pure Blood
Of Rytes
Of the Archaengel
Of the Fallen
Of the Wand
  and the Moon
Of Trees and Orchids
Off With Her Head
Offal
Offal Stench
Offalmincer
Offbach
Offender
Offending
Offense
Offensive
Offerblod
Offertorium
Office of Strategic
  Influence
Officium Triste
Officum
OffRoad
Offtall
Ofring
Ofryskje
Ofsoski
Ogmias
Ogmios
Ogneslav
Ogre
Ogre
Ogre
Ogress
Ogun's Will

Oh Marita
Ohron
Ohtar
Ohura Mazdo
Ohvrikivi
Oil
Ojos Negros
Okkultum
  Magnificentia
Okkultum Threat
Okrozom
Oksanat
Oksymoron
Oktagon
Oktober
Oktober
Oktor
Okult
Okulus Diaboli
Ol' Scratch
Ol Sonuf
Olam Ein Sof
Olc Sinnsir
Old
Old Black Majestic
Old Forest
Old Funeral
Old Goat
Old Goats
Old Grandad
Old Legacy
Old Legend
Old Maid
Old Man Gloom
Old Man's Child

Osobrom	Otkroveniya Dozhdya	Outburst	Outworld	Overload	Overshadow	Oxyrius
Ossarium	Otyg	Outcast	Over Death	Overload	Oversoul	Oyhra
Ossarium	Oubliette	Outcast	Over Dose	Overload	Oversoul	Oz
Ossastorium	Oubliette	Outcast	Over Faith	Overload	Overstatement	Oziris
Ossian	Ouija	Outcast	Over Speed	Overload	Overstep	Ozirisz
Ossian	Oulanem	Outcast	Over the Coals	Overload	Overstolz	Ozlomoth
Ossian	Ounce of Self	Outcast	Over the Top	Overload	Overt Hostility	O-Zone
Ossuaire	Ounis	Outcasts	Over Us Eden	Overload	Overthrash	Ozzy Osbourne
Ossuarist	Our Dying Souls	Outcome	Overaction	Overload	Overthrone	
Ossuary	Our Grace	Outcrop	Overblood	Overloaded	Overthrow	
Ossuary	Our Lady of	Outcry	Overcast	Overlord	Overthrow	
Ossuary	Bloodshed	Outcryfire	Overcast	Overlord	Overthrowing	
Ossuary	Our Requiem	Outer Edge	Overdeth	Overlord	Overture	
Ossuary	Our Survival	Outer Orgasm	Overdose	Overlord	Overture	
Ossuary	Depends on Us	Outer Skin	Overdose	Overlord	Overture	
Ossuary	Our Terrible Sickness	Out-Kri	Overdose	Overlord	Overturn M	
Ossuary Insane	Ouroboros	Outlander	Overdose	Overlord	Overvibes	
Ossyris	Ouroboros	Outlaw	Overdose	Overlord	Ovoian	
Ostracised	Out Body Experience	Outlaw Order	Overdozed	Overlord	Ovskum	
Ostracized	Out for a Kill	Outrage	Overdream	Overlord	Ovskum-Mørke	
Ostrogoth	Out For Blood	Outrage	Overdrive	Exterminator	Ovvercross	
Oswenzim	Out for Blood	Outrage	Overdrive	Overlord Industries	Owl Sees All	
Osyris	Out for Blood	Outrage	Overdrive	Overlorde	Ox	
Otargos	Out in the Cold	Outrage	Overdrunk	Overlorde	Oxblood	
Otep	Out of Area	Outrage	OverFaith	Overlord's Perpetual	Oxbow	
Otesanek	Out of Order	Outrage	Overfiend	Overmars	Oxenkiller	
Othala	Out of the Lair	Outrage	Overflash	Overmeind	Oxidised Razor	
Othendara	Out of the System	Outrage	Overgard	Overmind	Oxido	
Other Side	Outbreak	Outremer	Overgarven	Overnoise	Oxido	
Other Side	Outbreak	Outshine	Overheat	Overoth	Oxiplegatz	
Other World	Outbreak	Outside	Overkill	OverPoweR	Oxnkiller	
Otherside	Outbreak	Outside	Overkill	Overrider	Oxus	
Otherwise	Outburst	Outsider	Overkill	Overrun	Oxyacanthous	
Othyrworld	Outburst	Outsider	Overkill L.A.	Overseer	Oxym	
Otila	Outburst	Outta Line	Overlife	Overshadow	Oxymor	

◄ Panic Room

Panikos
Pánikroham
Panitrator
Panndora
Pannychida
Panomania
Panonski Sindrom
Panopticum
Panphage
Pansament
Panssarinyrkki
Pantáculo
  Místico
Panteon
Pantera
Panteu
Pantheion
Pantheism
Pantheist
Pantheon
Pantheon
Pantheon
Pantheon
Pantheon
Pantheon
Pantheon
Pantheon I
Panther
Panther
Panther
Pantianak
Pantokrator
Pantokrator
Pantokrator

Pantokratur
Pantokreator
Pantommind
Panychida
Panza Division
Panzer
Panzer
Panzer
Panzer
Panzer Angriff
Panzer Storm
Panzer X
Panzerchrist
Panzerdivision
Panzerfaust
Panzerfaust
Panzerfaust
Panzerfaust
Panzerfaust
Panzer'Faust
Panzerfrost
PanzerFrost
Panzergreif
Panzerhitler
Panzerium
Panzerkampf
Panzerkrieg
Panzerkvlt
Panzerschranzpoet
Panzerschreck
Panzerskrekk
Panzersturm
Panzram
Papercut Homicide
Papsmear

Para a Glória de Teu
  Nome Lúcifer
Para Tu Eterno
  M.M.J.P.G.A.
Parabellum
Parabellum
Parabellum
Parabellum
Paracels
Paracoccidioidomi-
  cosisproctitissarco-
  mucosis
Parade of Souls
Parade of
  the Lifeless
Paradigm
Paradigma
Paradise in Flames
Paradise in Tears
Paradise Lost
Paradox
Paradox
Paradox
Paradoxx
Paradoxxa
Paragon
Paragon Belial
Paragon Impure
Paragon of Beauty
Paragon X
Parakletos
Paralegic
Paralex
Paralisis
Paralisy

Parallaxe
Paralyser
Paralysis
Paralysis
Paralysis
Paralytic Of...
Paramaecium
Paramecium
Paramedics
Paramoure
Paranaut
Paranoia
Paranoia
Paranoia
Paranoia
Paranoia
Paranoia
Paranoia
Paranoia
Paranoia
Paranoia
Paranoid
Paranoid
Paranoiz
Paranormal Activity
Paranormal
  Disposition
Paranormal Infusion
Paranormal Misteria
Paranormal Waltz
Paraphernalia
Paraphilia
Paraphrenia
Paraplegic
Parasite

Parasite Crowd
Parasitic
Parasitic Infection
Parasitoid
Parasma
Parasophisma
Parastos
Parasynapthikus
Paratyfus
Paraxism
Parazide
Parchment
Paréidolia
Parental Advisory
Pareo Mortuus
Paria
Paria
Paria
Pariah
Pariah
Pariah
Pariah
Pariah
Pariah Flame
Pariah Theory
Paris Daane
Parish
Parity Boot
Parnassus
Parodie Sacrass
Päronballe
Paroxysm
Paroxysm
Paroxysm
Parracide

Parricide
Parricide
Parricide
Parricide
Parricide
Parricide
Parricide
Parricide Eve
Parryzide
Partakrist
Partenos Petras
Parusie
Parvati
Pas Infinit
Pasca Tragedy
Pascal
Pascal Allaigre
Passage
Passage Temple
Passenger
Passion
Passion In Twilight
Passive Aggressive
Past Redemption
Pastor Brad
Patan
Patecabra
Pater Noster
Path
Path of Chaos
Path of Debris
Path of Golconda
Path of Needles
Path of the Blind

Pathetic
Pathetic Madness
Pathogen
Pathogen
Pathogen
Pathogenic
Pathogenic
  Dysentery
Patholog
Pathologic Noise
Pathological
  Splatter
Pathologist
Pathologist
  Department
Pathology
Pathology
Pathology
Pathology Stench
Pathos
Pathos
Pathosray
Paths of Possession
Patisserie
Patologicum
Patriarca
Patriarch
Patriarch
Patricide
Patrick Rondat
Patunum
Paul Carcass
Paul Chain
Paul Di'Anno
Paulo Barros

Pavementsaw	Pelican	Pentdragon	Perfect Maggots	Perpetua	Persecution	Perverse Monastyr
Pavlov's Dogs	Peligrosso	Pentecost	Perfect Maggots	Perpetual	Persecutor	Perverse Souls
Pavor	Penance	Penthause	Perfect Mind	Perpetual	Persecutor	Perverse Suffering
Pavor Nocturnus	Pencil Lead Syringe	Penumbra	Perfect Symmetry	Perpetual	Persecutor	Perverseraph
Pavouk	Pendemia	Penumbra	Perfect Symmetry	Perpetual	Persecutor	Perverseum
Paw	Pendulum	Penumbra Leal	Perfect Symmetry	Perpetual	Persefone	Perversion
Pax Mortis	Pendulum	Penumbras	Perfidia	Perpetual Burn	Perseidan	Perversist
Pax Satana	Pendulum	Penyangak	Perfidy Biblical	Perpetual Darkness	Persephone	Perversor
Payable on Death	Pené Grandé	Penzzer	Performances	Perpetual Death	Descending	Perversor
Payak	Penetralia	People	Pergamen Luciferian	Mode	Persephone's Dream	Perversus Stigmata
Paybak	Penetralia	Peordh	Pergament	Perpetual Demise	Persepolis	Pervertico
Paymon	Penetrate	Peorth	Pergamon	Perpetual Dilemma	Perseus	Perverts
Payne's Gray	Penetrator	Peorth	Pergamon	Perpetual Disgrace	Perseverance	Pervertum
Paysage d'Hiver	Penetrator	Pequod	Pergolos	Perpetual Doom	Perseverance	Pervertum Obscurum
Pazuzu	Penetrator Hammer	Per Aspera	Periadam	Perpetual Dreams	Persian Risk	Perverze
Pazuzu	Penge	Per Sepulcra	Pericardium	Perpetual Dusk	Persian Risk	Pervezija
Pazuzu	Penis Leech	Per Tenebras	Perifa	Perpetual Flame	Persistense	Pervogoat
Pazuzu	Penitence	Perception	Peril	Perpetual Hate	Persona	Perzonal War
PC Death Squad	Penitence	Perceptions	Perimeter	Perpetual Infestation	Persona Grata	Peso Eterno
PCP	Penitència	Perceverance	Period of Silence	Perpetual Maddness	Personal Advisory	Pessimist
Pcyst	Penitent	Percival Schuttenbach	Perish	Perpetual Solitude	Personal Demon	Pessimist
PD SS Totenkopf	Penitenziagite	Percutor 1708	Perish	Perpetual Suffering	Personal War	Pessimistic
Peaceful Tomb	Pentacle	Perdition	Perished	Perpetual Tears	Persophone	Pessimus
Peaceless	Pentacost	Perdition	Perished	Perpetual Winter	Persuader	Pessimyst
Pecatorium	Pentacrostic	Perdition	Perishing Mankind	Perpetual Witness	Perterricrepus	Pessonha
Peccatum	Pentaface	Perdition	Perisynti	PerpetualFire	Perth	Pest
Pechal'	Pentagon	Perdition	Perkele	Perpetuance	Pertness	Pest
Pederasty	Pentagoria	Perdition	Perkos	Perpetuum	Perturbador	Pest
Pedifile	Pentagory	Perdition Hearse	Permafrost	Perrished	Perun	Pesta
Pedro Botero	Pentagram	Perditism	Permafrost	Perro Negro	Perun'	Pesta Porcina
Pegasus	Pentagram	Perditor	Permanent Midnight	Perryside	Perunica	Peste Noire
Pegasus	Pentagram	Perennial	Permian	Persecution	Perunwit	Pesten
Pegazus	Pentagram	Perfect Chaos	Pernicious	Persecution	Perverse	Pesten 1349
Pek	Pentaslave	Perfect Crime	Pero Defformero	Persecution	Perverse	Pester
Pekari	Pentatonik	Perfect Engine	Perpectual Hate	Persecution	Perverse Bat	Pesthauch

Plague Bearer	Plasmic Ocean	Plutonium Desaster	Point Blank	Polymetal	Porta Inferna	Possessed
Plague Bearer	Plastic Earth	Plutonium Nyborg	Point Blank	Polymorph	Porta Salomoniis	Possession
Plague Bringer	Plastic Grave	Plutonium Orange	Point of No Return	Pomaranca	Portal	Possession
Plague Divine	Plastic Whore	Pneuma	Point of View	Pomerania	Portal	Possession
Plague Impaled	Plastilinovy Jinn	Po.O.L.S.	Poison	Ponce Pilate	Portal	Possessor
Plague Majestic	Platanus	Poccolus	Poison	Pond Of Death	Portal 7	Possuído Pelo Cão
Plague Marine	Platfform	Pocket Pussy Hash	Poison Asp	Pontius Pilate	Portall	Post Deus
Plague Martyr	Platform Black	Pipe	Poison Mosh	Pontius Pilate	Portentous	Post Mortem
Plague of Ages	Platina	Pod People	Poisonblack	Pontius Prophet	Portikus	Post Mortem
Plague of Excrement	Platinum	Poder	Poisoned Gift	Poostew	Porto Pak	Post Mortum
Plague of Man	Platitude	Poder Oculto	Poisoned Leaves	Pope Death Threat	Portrait	Post Scriptum
Plague of Sheol	Platonic Disease	Poem	PoisonGod	Pope Heathen Scum	Portrait	Post Scriptum
Plague of Sorrow	Platypus	Poema Arcanus	Poisonhead	Poppy Seed Grinder	Portrait	Post Trevor
Plague Project	Play Dead	Poem's Death	Poizon Green	Popular Belief	Portrait	Posthumous
Plague Rages	Playground	Poems of Shadows	Pokolgép	Population Reduction	Portrait of Beyond	Posthumous
Plague Ridden	Pleasant Valley	Poena Dare	Polaris	Porcelain God	Portrait of Pain	Posthumous
Plague.	Please Remember	Poënarii	Polaris	Porcupine Tree	Portraits of Murder	Blasphemer
Plaguebearer	Pledge Sin and the	Poesia per Aurem	Polaris	Pore	Portrayal	Post-Life Disorder
Plaguelord	Painful	Poeticus Severus	Polarized	Porfiria	Poseidon	Postmorte
Plagues	Plenilunio	Poetry	Pole Position	Porfiriah	Poseidon	Postmortem
Plaguewielder	Plenty Suffering	Poetry of Chaos	Poles Apart	Porfyria	Poseidon	Postmortem
Plaguewielder	Pleural Effusion	Poetry of Dreams	Polestar	Porn	Poseidon	Postmortem
Plamen Iskona	Pleurisy	Poet's Cry	Polidicks	Pornea	Poseidons Anger	Post-Mortem
Plan B	Pleuritic	Poets of the Plague	Polimetro	Porno	Poser Disposer	Postmortem
Planar Evil	Pleurosis	Pofony	Polinove Pole	Porno Coma	Posesión	Disembowelment
Planet AIDS	Plexus	Pogrom	Polluted	Pornocracy	Posession	Postmortem Fabulae
Planet Alliance	Plowshare	Pogrom	Polluted Inheritance	Pornoise	Poseydon	Postmortem Promises
Planet Gemini	Pluck	Pogrom	Pollution	Pornucopia	Poseydon	Postmortem
Planet Hate	Plugger	Pogrom	Pollution	Poropetra	Posguerra	Postmortom
Planet Rain	Pluie Noire	Pogrom	Polterchrist	Porosity of Mind	Posidom	PostNecrum
Planet X	Plunder & Pillage	Pogrom 1147	Poltergeist	Porphyria	Posithrone	Postnuclear
Plankton	Pluribus Impar	Pohakka	Poltergeist	Porphyria	Position	Deathmass
Planta Cadaver	Plutocracy	Pohjoinen Kuri	Polterkrist	Porphyria	Positiv Hate	Postwar
Plasma	Plutonia	Point Blank	Poltus	Porphyria	Pösk	Potabilisadora
Plasma Pool	Plutonium	Point Blank	Polvo de Estrella	Porrada	Posmrtna Liturgija	Potential Threat

◀ Proclamation

◀ Psi.Kore

Putrefaction	Putridity	Pyrifleyethon
Putrefaction	Putridity	Pyriphlegethon
Putrefactive Necrosis	Putrifact	Pyrocide
Putrefacto	Putrilage	Pyrolyse
Putrefactor	Putritorium	Pyromania
Putrefaktor	Putrocorpse	Pyromania
Putrefaxion	Putsch	Pyromaniac
Adipocere	Puya	Pyron
Putrefest	Puzzle of Flesh	Python
Putrefied	Pwcca	Pyuria
Putrefied	PWR	Pyvoli
Putrefied Flesh	PX-Pain	
Putrefied Genitalia	Pyad	
Putrefukation	Pyad	
Putrefy	Pyaemia	
Putrefying God	Pyathrosis	
Putregod	Pyatnitza 13	
Putregore	Pyesis	
Putrescence	Pygmalion	
Putrescence	Pyl' Sotvorenia	
Putrescent	Pylaghian	
Putricid	Pylon	
Putrid	Pyogenesis	
Putrid Carnage	Pyopoesy	
Putrid Decay	Pyorrhoea	
Putrid Flesh	Pyöveli	
Putrid Inbred	Pyphomgertum	
Putrid Mass	Pyracanda	
Putrid Morgue	Pyracantha	
Putrid Offal	Pyramaze	
Putrid Pile	Pyramid	
Putrid Pile	Pyramide	
Putrid Resurrection	Pyre	
Putrid Scum	Pyre	
Putride	Pyrexia	

Q.W.A.N.
Q5
Qabr
Qhafir
Qhwertt
Qliphoth
Qliphoth
Qojau
Qoph
Qrujhuk
Q-Squad
QÜ
Quadrivium
Quadruple
Quadryss
Quaet Gespuys

Quake
Quandary
Quandary
Quantum
Quaoar
Quark 7
QuarterBurn
Quartz
Quasar
Quasi Modo
Quasimodo
Quasy Modo
Queef Huffer
Queen Absinthia
Queen Adreena
Queen Bitch

Queen Evil
Queen of
   the Elves Land
Queensrÿche
Queer Circle
Quehanna
Queiles
Queiron
Quejidos Del Seol
Quel Che Resta
   Della Cresta
Quell
Quelonio
Quemar
Quercus
Querimonia
Querubes
Ques Ans
Quest
Quest
Quest
Quest
Quest Haven
Quest of Aidance
Questionmark
Question-Mark
Questions
Questor
Quick Change
Quick Fix
Quicksand
Quicksand Dream
Quiema
Quiet Absence
Quiet Outcry

Quiet Riot
Quietflower
Quietus
Quietus
Quijote
Quill-pen
Quilmess
Quilter's Bane
Quimera
Quimera
Quinta Essentia
Quintessence
Quintessence
Quintessence
Quintessence
   of Flesh
Quintessence of Hate
Quintessenza
Quisling
Quix
Qumran
Quo Vadis
Quo Vadis
Quod Demonstratum
   Est
Quorthon
Quoth the Raven
Quötta Pas
Qwestion

R & R	Raa Hoor Khuit
R.A.I.C.E.S.	Raakku
R.A.V.A.G.E.	Raate
R.A.W.	Rabalder
R.A.W.W.A.R.	Rabbath Ammon
R.D.B.	Rabbits
R.E.T.	Rabbit's Carrot
R.H.D.	Rabe
R.I.P.	Rabennacht
R.I.P.	Rabia
R.I.P.	Rabid
R.U. Dead?	Rabid
R.U. Deadly	Rabid Captor
R:I:P	Rabies Caste
R2	Race Against Time
Ra	Racer X

Races	Rage N Revenge	Railway	Raising Fear	Ramses
Rachel Mother Goose	Rage Of Achilles	Rain	Raising Messiah	Ramses
Rachels Coven	Rage of Angels	Rain	Raism	Ramzes
Rad Kick	Rageborne	Rain	Rajas	Ram-Zet
Radaghast	Rageborne	Rain	Rajavyöhyke	Ranber Jack
Radakka	Ragedate	Rain Delay	Rajawali	Rancid Christ
Radar	RagenHeart	Rain Fell Within	Rajfajh	Rancid Decay
Radegast	Rager	Rain 'n' Steel	Rajna	Rancor
Rademassaker	Rager	Rain·Novelty	Rake	Rancorous
Radialdrop	Ragestorm	Rain of Ashes	Rake Sodomy	Rancour
Radiathor	Raggradarh	Rain of Pain	Ra-Kish	Randagi
Radiation 4	Raging Angels	Rain of Sorrow	Rakoth	Randall Flagg
Radiation Dust	Raging Blood	Rain Paint	Rakun	Random Acts of
Radiation Sickness	Raging Force	Rain Skiktlu	Ralmador	Violence
Radical	Raging Fury	Rainbird	Ralph Santolla	Random Conflict
Radical Corps	Raging Speedhorn	Rainbow	RAM	Random Damage
Radigost	Raging Storm	Raincarnation	Ramagarhh	Random Eyes
Radio Camboja	Ragnar	Raindream	Raman Gifta	Random Man
Radio Criminals	Ragnarok	Rainfall	Rambokk	Random Mullet
Radioactive	Ragnarok	Rainfall	Ramesses	Random Riot
Radioactive Danger	Ragnarok	Raining	Ra-M-Ha	Random Violence
Radiocamboja	Ragnarok	Rainoise	Ramhorn	Randomize Timer
Radium	Ragnarok Fate	Rainroom	Rammer	Randy
Radium	Ragnarökr	Rainspawn	Rammpage	Randy Tri
Radius	Ragnor	Raintime	Rammwurst	Randy Uchida Group
Radogast	Ragor	Rainwill	Ramp	Randy Weitzel
Radogost	Rahovart	Rainwound	Rampage	Rangda
Radon	Rahowa	Rainy Night	Rampage	Rankelson
Raff	Raices Muertas	Raise Cain	Rampage	Rankor
Rafflesia	Raices Torcidas	Raise Hell	Rampage	Rankor
Raga	Raid	Raise the Dead	Rampage	Rann
Raga	Raider	Raise the Shield	Rampage	Rape On Mind
Ragadozók	Raidshelter	Raised Banner	Rampancy	Raped Ape
Rage	Rail	Raising Cain	Ramrod	Raped God
Rage	Railsplitter	Raising Fear	Ramses	Raped Toad

Regurgitate
Regurgitate
Regurgitated Terror
Regurgitation
Regurgitation
rehtaF ruO
Reich
Reichsblood
Reichsradio
Reido
Reifen 14
Reifriesen
Reign
Reign
Reign
Reign in Blood
Reign IV
Reign of Decay
Reign of Erebus
Reign of Pestilence
Reign of Shadows
Reign of Terror
Reign of Terror
Reign of Terror
Reign of Vengeance
Reigncarnation
Reignterror
Reincarnate
Reincarnate
Reincarnated
Reincarnation
Reincremation
Reinfection
Reinforced
Reinless

Reino de Baphomet
Reino Ermitaño
Reino Fatal
Reinwen
ReinXeed
REISM
Reizgas
Rëkiem
Rekuiem
Relative Silence
Relaypse
Release
Release
Released Anger
Relentless
Relentless
Relentless Assault
Relentless Attrition
Relevant Few
Relic
Relics
Relik
Relikt
Relikvia
Reliquium
Rellik
Rellik
Rellik
Rellik
Relva de Sangue
Remain
Remain
Remaining
    Anonymous
Remains

Remains
Remains
Remains
Remains of Eden
Remains of Silence
Remains of the Fallen
Remains of the
    Grotesque
Remasculate
Remember Arlington
Remember November
Remember Twilight
Remembrance
Remembrance
Remembrance of Pain
Remmirath
Remnant
Remnants of a Deity
Remorse
Remove The Veil
Renacer
Renaissànce
Renascence
Renascent
Renavera
Renazcore
Rendan Tluin
Render
Renegade
Renegade
Renegade
Renegade
Renegade
Renegade
Renegade

Renégadeth
Renegado
Renewal
Renfield
Rennaissance
Renno
Rentgen
Reo
Reos
Repeated Trauma
Repent
Repentance
RephaSword
Replica
Replica
Replica
Replica
Replica
Replica X
Replicant Zero
Replika
Repossessed
Repressed Crusader
Repression
Reprieve
Reprisal Scars
Reprobate
Reprobation
Repsel
Reptil
Reptilian
Reptilian Death
Repudiate
Repudilation
Repugnance

Repugnance
Repugnant
Repugnant
Repugnant Gore
Repugnant
    Inebriation
Repugnant Pigs
Repugnant Stench
Repulsa
Repulsa
Repulsao Explicita
Repulse
Re-Pulse
Repulsed
Repulsion
Repulsive
Repulsive Depravity
Repulsive Dissection
Repulsive Exhume
Repulverizer
Repvblika
Requem
Request Denied
Requested Sufferings
Requiem
Requiem
Requiem
Requiem
Requiem
Requiem
Requiem
Requiem
Requiem
Requiem
Requiem

Requiem
Requiem
Requiem
Requiem
Requiem
Requiem
Requiem
Requiem
Requiem
Requiem
Requiem
Requiem Aeternam
Requiem Aeternam
Requiem Aeternum
Requiem K626
Requiem Laus
Requiem Mass
Requital
Requital
Rerfind
Research
Resection
Resentment
Resentment
Resentment
Reset
Residual Effect
Residvvm
Resigned to Fate
Resistáncia Terminal
Resistance
Resistance
Resistance
Resistance

Resistant Culture
Resistence
Resistencia
Resleep
Resolution15
Resonant
Resound
Respawn
Respawn Inc.
Respawn the Plague
Respawned
Respect
Respite
Response Negative
Ressonância Mórfica
Rest in Darkness
Rest in Gore
Rest In Pain
Rest In Pain
Rest In Pain
Rest in Peace
Rest in Peace
Rest in Peace
Restart
Restless
Restless
Restless Dead
Resurrected
Resurrected
Resurrection
Resurrection
Resurrection
Resurrection
Resurrection
Resurrection

S
S&L
S.A. Adams
S.A. Slayer
S.A.D.
S.A.D.O.
S.A.R.
S.A.S.
S.C.A.L.P.
S.C.A.R.D.
S.C.E.P.T.R.E.
S.C.U.M.
S.D.I.
S.D.I.D.
S.D.S.
S.F.D.

S.G.R.
S.I.D.E.
S.I.L.U.R.
S.I.S.T.
S.I.T.E.
S.K. Krow
S.K.N.S.
S.L.G.
S.L.R.
S.L.U.T.
S.M.D.
S.M.E.S.
S.M.I.
S.N.F.
S.N.O.T.
S.N.P.

S.O.B.
S.O.C.M.D.
S.O.H.
S.O.K.
S.O.S.
S.O.S.
S.O.S.
S.P.O.R.K.
S.P.Q.R.
S.Pam
S.Pollution
S.R.L.
S.T.A.B.
S.T.I.
S.U.N.D.S.
S.V.D.
S.W.O.R.D.
S:t Erik
S1ft
Sławia
Sa Meute
Saatanan Marionetit
Saatkrähe
Saattue
Sabachthani
Sabacthani
Sabaism
Sabaium
Sabaoth
Sabaothic Cherubim
Sabatan
Sabathan
Sabathan
Sabathon
Sabathory

Sabaton
Sabazius
Sabazz
Sabbat
Sabbat
Sabbatariam
Sabbath Knights
Sabbathan
Sabbatic Feast
Sabbatical Goat
Sabbatical Rites
Sabbatical Throne
Sabbrabells
Sabbtail
Saber Tiger
Sabhankra
Sabinas Rex
Sable
Sable
Sabnack
Saboath
Sabotage
Sabotage
Sabotage
Sabotage
Sabrax
Sabre
Sabre
Sabre
Sabretung
Sabroz
Sacarius Noctis
Sacerdoth
Sachsenhausen
Sachta

Sackrace
Sacra Arcana
Sacra Entropía
Sacradis
Sacrafice
Sacral Death
Sacralis
Sacrament
Sacrament
Sacrament
Sacrament
Sacrament
Sacrament
Sacrament A.D.
Sacrament L.A.
Sacramental
    Awakened
Sacramental Blood
Sacramental Fusion
Sacramental Sachem
Sacramentary
    Abolishment
Sacramentum
Sacraphyx
Sacrario
Sacrarium
Sacrarium Execratus
Sacrasphemy
Sacrater
Sacrecy
Sacred
Sacred
Sacred Alien
Sacred Blade
Sacred Blood

Sacred Blood
Sacred Chao
Sacred Child
Sacred Crucifix
Sacred Curse
Sacred Curse
Sacred Dawn
Sacred Death
Sacred Few
Sacred God
Sacred Heart
Sacred Moon
Sacred Night
Sacred Oath
Sacred Outcry
Sacred Reich
Sacred Reign
Sacred Rite
Sacred Serenity
Sacred Sin
Sacred Sinner
Sacred Slaughter
Sacred Spell
Sacred Steel
Sacred Storm
Sacred Tears
Sacred Warrior
Sacreligious Torment
Sacretomia
Sacrificalis
Sacrification
Sacrifice
Sacrifice
Sacrifice
Sacrifice

Sacrifice
Sacrifice Slaughtered
    Jesus
Sacrificed
Sacrificed
Sacrificed
Sacrificed
Sacrificed Moloch
Sacrificer
Sacrificia Mortuorum
Sacrificial
Sacrificial Blood
Sacrificial Dagger
Sacrificial Genocide
Sacrificial Slaughter
Sacrificial Totem
Sacrificio
Sacrificio Sumério
Sacrificium
Sacrificium
Sacrificium Sacralis
Sacrifist
Sacrifix
Sacrifixio
Sacrilege
Sacrilege
Sacrilege
Sacrilege
Sacrilege B.C.
Sacrilegeous
Sacrilegio
Sacrilegio
Sacrilegio
Sacrilegio
Sacrilégio

◀ Sacrilegion

Sacrilegious
Sacrilegious
 Impalement
Sacrilegist
Sacrilegium
Sacrilegium
Sacrilegium
Sacrilegium
Sacrilium
Sacrist
Sacristy
Sacritual
Sacriversum
Sacro
Sacro
Sacro Blade
Sacro Fuego
Sacrom
Sacrophobia
Sacrosanct
Sacrosanct
Sacrosanct Moon
Sacrosanctum
Sacrum
Sacrum
Sacrum
Sacrum
Sacrum
Sacrum
Sacrum
Sacrum
Sad
Sad
Sad Entheus
Sad Fact
Sad Harmony

Sad Iron
Sad Legend
Sad Moon's Grief
Sad Reality
Sad Siberia
Sad Theory
Sad Whisperings
Sad Wind
Sad Wings
Sada
Sadako
Sadauk
Saddam's Family
Saddleback Shark
Sades
Sadhara
Sadhu
Sadis
Sadis Euphoria
Sadism
Sadist
Sadist
Sadist
Sadistic
Sadistic 666
Sadistic Blood
 Massacre
Sadistic
 Brainslaughter
Sadistic Feast
Sadistic Gore
Sadistic Grimness
Sadistic Humor
Sadistic Intent
Sadistic Kill

Sadistic Noise
Sadistic Pain
Sadistic Penetrations
Sadistic Souls
Sadistic Spell
Sadistic Torment
Sadistic Undertorture
Sadistic Vision
Sadistic Vision
Sadistik Exekution
Sadistik Mutilation
Sadistis
Sadistis
Sadium
Sadizmo
Sadiztik Impaler
Sadness
Sado Massakist
Sado Sathanas
SadoCrawl
Sadogoat
Sadok
Sadom
Sadomaniac
Sadomasochism
Sadomasochrist
Sadomator
Sadometatron
Sadorass
Sadrith Mora
Sadus
Sadwings
Saeculum
Saed
Saeko

Sael
Saevus
Saevus Somnia
SAF
Safe Haven
Safer Than Sleep
Safir e Arsh
Saga
Saga
Saga Inferna
Saga`s Needle
Sagaris
Sagaris
Sage
Sage
Sagenland
Sagitta
Sagittarius
Sagittarius
Sagittarius
Sagittarius
Sagn
Sagntid
SagoMetal
Sagoth
Sagrada Blasfemia
Sagrado Inferno
Sagraliege
Sagros
Sagu
Sahar
Sahara
Sahara Dust
Saharra
Sahg

Sahhar
Sahib
Sahin feat. Ludvik
Sahon
Sahsay
Sahsnotas
Saidian
Saigneur
Saigon
Saigon
Saigon Kick
Saikon
Sailendra
Saint
Saint Infection
Saint Spirit
Saint Vania
Saint Vitus
Saintly Sinner
Saints & Preachers
Saints Anger
Saints Everlasting
 Rest
Saints of Pain
Saintsbleed
Saintsinner
Saiph
Sakahiter
Sakaratul Maut
Sakkuth
Sakrament
Sakramortem
Sakramoth
Sakrefix
Sakrificer

Sakrificial
Sakrificio
Sakrilegio
Sakrogoat
Sakurai
Salacious Gods
Salamandra
Salário Mínimo
Salem
Salem
Salem
Salem
Salem
Salem
Salem
Salem
Salem Fires
Salem Justice
Salem Orchid
Salem Orchid
Salem Spade
Salem`s Wych
Salem's Childe
Salem's Law
Salem's Lot
Salem's Lot
Salem's Wych
Salient
Saligia
Sally
Salman Teloch
Salmos Luciferi
Salt of the Earth
Salt the Wound

Salt the Wound
Saltanat
Saltatio Mortis
Salted Wounds
Saltério
Saltus
Salupa
Salutary
Salute
Salvage
Salvaged
Salvanor
Salvation
Salvation
Salvation
Salvation666
Salvator Carlino
Salvus
Sam Black Church
Sam Kazerooni
Sam Thunder
Samael
Samael Tears
Samain
Samain
Saman
Sámán
Samar
Samaritan
Samarkanda
Samartary
Samas
Samayoi
Samchung
Samech

Sargatanas
Sargatanas Reign
Sargeist
Sarghnagel .
Sargnagel
Sargo Fvck
Sargon
Sargon
Sargoth
Sargträger
Sarin
Sarin's Gift
Sariola
Sarissa
Sarkasm
Sarkastic Demons
Sarkastica
Sarkel
Sarkom
Sarkoma
Sarkophag
Sarkus
Sarlatán
Sarmak
Sarna
Sarnath
Sarnath
Sarnath
Sarnath
Sarolf
Saros
Saros
Sarpanitum
Sarpedon
Sarratum

Sarrgh
Sars
Sars Infected
Sarsekim
Sartan
Sartess
Sartinas
Saruman
Sarvari
Sarvela
Sarx
Sasamaso
SA-Sanctuary
Saskatchewan
Sasquatch
Sat
Sata
Satacass
Satan
Satan
Satan
Satan
Satan Crux
Satan Jokers
Satan Maleficarium
Satan Sluts
Satan Soldier
Satan´s Laughing
  Generation
Satanachia
Satanachia Agliareth
Satanachristy
Satanail
Satanaquia
Satanarchy

Satanas
Satanas
Satanas Macabre
Satanasshole
Satanel
Satangra
Satani Infernalis
Satania
Satanic
Satanic Angel
Satanic Apostate
Satanic Army
Satanic Blood
Satanic Blood
Satanic Christ
Satanic Darkness
Satanic Death
Satanic Destroyer
Satanic Dirge
Satanic Evil
Satanic Funeral
Satanic Grounds
Satanic Hellslaughter
Satanic Lust
Satanic Massacre 666
Satanic Prophets
Satanic Rites
Satanic Rites
Satanic Ritual
Satanic Sacrifice
Satanic Sega Genesis
Satanic Slaughter
Satanic Storm
Satanic Temple
Satanic Terror Cult

Satanic Torment
Satanic Verses
Satanic Warfare
Satanic Warmaster
Satanic Wizard
Satanic Woods
Satanica
Satanica
SatanicBlack
Satanicon
Satanicum Tenebrae
Satanik Art
Satanik Priest
Satanik Terrorists
Satanize
Satanized
Satanized
Satanizer
Satanochio
Satan's Almighty
  Penis
Satan's Blood
Satans Claw
Satan's Doom
Satans Elite
  Kommando
Satan's Empire
Satans Helvete
Satan's Holocaust
Satan's Host
Satan's Massacre
Satans Penguins
Satan's Pharynx
Satan's Saints
Satans Sign of War

Satan's Soldiers
Satans Vind
Satan's Warriors
SatanSSoldierS
Satarial
Satariel
Satellights
Sater
Sathanafago
Sathanas
Sathord
Satin Steel
Satira
Satira
Satisfying Suicide
Satoata
Sator
Sator Marte
Satori
Satorium
Satriani
Satrias
Satsugai
Saturate
Satureye
Saturno
Saturnus
Saturus
Satus
Satyagraha
Satyr
Satyra
Satyre
Satyrian
Satyriasis

Satyrica
Satyricon
Satyrium
Satyron
Satyrus
Saudade
Saunter
Saurian
Saurom
Saurom Lamderth
Sauron
Sauron
Sauron
Sauron
Sauron
Sauron
Sausage
Sauts Alastor
Savage
Savage
Savage Annihilation
Savage Butchery
Savage Circus
Savage Crow
Savage Death
Savage Grace
Savage Harmony
Savage Heart
Savage Maniacs
Savage Rage
Savage Rites
Savage Skülls
Savage Steel
Savage Thrust

Savagers
Savagery
Savagery
Savallion Dawn
Savan
Savant
Savant
Savaot
Savaoth
Savatage
Savatan
Save
Save Our Souls
Savers
SavinGraces
Savior
Savior Sect
Saviour
Saviour Machine
Saviour to None
Saviours
Savras
Saw
Saw You Drown
Sawchain
Sax
Sax Piják
Saxana
Saxer
Saxnot
Saxo
Saxon
Saxorior
Saxxas
Sayn

Sexx	Shadeworks	Shadowcaster	Shadows Dance	Shághrádh	Shaolin Death Squad	Shattered Nothing
Seyer	Shadow	Shadowcaster	Shadows Emperor	Shagidiel	Shapat Terror	Shattered Realm
Seyiren	Shadow	Shadowchord	Shadows Eve	Shagnum	Shape of Despair	Shattered Soul
Seyminhol	Shadow Cult	Shadowcraft	Shadows Fall	Shah	Shape Shifter	Shattered Sunrise
Sezarbil	Shadow Cut	Shadowdance	Shadow's Far	Shaigon	Shapeshift	Shattered Within
Sezession	Shadow Demon	Shadowdance	Shadows FX	Shaiklock	Shaphal	Shatterpoint
Sfagnum	Shadow Division	Shadowdancer	Shadow's God	Shaitan Mazar	Sharatan	Shatterproof
SFH	Shadow Gallery	Shadowdances	Shadows Ground	Shakespeare	Shardenmyth	Shattersphere
Sflexia	Shadow Host	ShadowDivine	Shadows Land	Shakespeare in Hell	Shardless	Shatterwrath
SFN	Shadow Hunter	Shadowdream	Shadows of Dawn	Shakhan	Share The Suffering	Shaxul
SFR	Shadow Image	Shadowed Beneath	Shadows of Eden	Shakin' Street	Sharkrage	Shayol Ghul
SGM	Shadow Keep	Shadowen	Shadows of Iga	Shakra	Sharks	She Cries
SGP Projekt	Shadow Magus	Shadowfax	Shadows of Paragon	Shall Suffer the	Sharks	She Said Destroy
Sgt. Carnage	Shadow Mask	Shadowfost	Shadows of Steel	Eclipse	Sharp Blade	She the Murderess
Shaaman	Shadow Moon	Shadowgate	Shadows of Sunset	Shallow Grave	Sharpened Razor	Sheades
Shaarimoth	Shadow of Death	Shadowheart	Shadows of the	Shallow Water Grave	Sharpness	Sheavy
Shaark	Shadow of Demise	ShadowHost	Unseen	Shaltev	Sharrowe	Shed This Blood
Shab	Shadow of Doom	Shadowings	Shadows Past	Sham Rain	Shatargat	Shedding Old Skin
Shabash	Shadow of Doubt	ShadowKeep	Shadows Time	Shaman	Shathanas	Shedim
Shackle Jack	Shadow of Sadness	Shadowlit	Shadows Toward	Shaman	Shatriya	Sheepgrinder
Shackles	Shadow of Soul	Shadowlit Mind	My Sky	Shaman Macabre	Shatter Messiah	Sheephead
Shadar Logoth	Shadow of the Beast	Shadowlord	Shadows Under Arms	Shamanic Rites	Shatterbone	Sheer Greed
Shadar Logoth	Shadow Pointe	ShadowLord	Shadow's Veil	Shamash	Shatterd Image	Shehine
Shade	Shadow Reichenstein	Shadowlord	Shadows Within	Shambles	Shattered	Sheilan
Shade	Shadow Season	Shadowlord	Shadowseeds	Shambless	Shattered	Sheitan
Shade Empire	Shadow Vexillum	Shadowlord	Shadowside	Shamed	Shattered	Sheky & the
Shade of Black	Shadow Warriors	Shadowlord	Shadowsphere	Shamelady	Shattered	Bloody Boys
Shaded Enmity	Shadow Willber	Shadowlorde	Shadowsphere	Shamharoth	Shattered	Shelder
Shadegrown	Shadow Zone	Shadowlore	Shadowsreign	Shammash	Shattered	Shelf
Shadembrace	Shadowblade	Shadowolf	Shadowthrone	Shamway	Shattered Dream	Shell Shock
Shades of Deep Water	Shadowbreed	ShadowPlay	Shadowthrone	Shane Gibson	Shattered Dreams	Shelley
Shades of Dusk	Shadowbuilder	ShadowRealm	Shadowwind	Shangai Blue	Shattered Existence	Shellshock
Shades of Grey	Shadowbuilder	Shadows	Shady Glimpse	Shanghai	Shattered Eyes	Shellshock
Shades of Grey	Shadowcast	Shadows Abyss	Shafott	Shannacai	Shattered Hope	Shellyz Raven
Shadeweaver		Shadows and Chaos	Shaftdrive	Shannara	Shattered Hope	Shelob's Lair

Shemaforesh
Shemamphor
Shemhamforash
Shemhamphorash
Shemhamphorash
Shenen
Shenine
Sheol
Sheol
Sheolgeenna
Shepherd
Shepherd of Sheol
Sheratán
Shere Khan
Shermann Soldiers
Sherpa
Sherwood
She's Gore
shEver
Shide
Shieldwall
Shiftlight
Shigai
Shigella
Shihad
Shimera
Shine in Darkness
Shining
Shining
Shining Abyss
Shining Blade
Shining Edge
Shining Fear
Shining Force
Shining Fury

Shining of Kliffoth
Shining of...
Shining Star
Shire
Shiri
Shismopathic
Shisser
Shit for Brains
Shitlust
Shitstorm
Shiva
Shiva
Shiva
Shiva
Shiva in Exile
Shival Vah
Shivan
Shiver
Shiver
Shock
Shock
Shock Box
Shock Machine
Shock Opera
Shock Split
Shock Tilt
Shock to the System
Shock Treatment
Shock Troopers
Shockcode
Shockplate
Shockwave
Shockwave
Shockwave
Shoctaw

Shoggoth
Shoggoth
Shoggoth
Shoggoth
Shogun
Shok Paris
Shooting Gallery
Shooting Hemlock
Shoreborn
Shores of Sheol
Shores of Tundra
Shorgon
Short Life Crisis
Short Sharp Shock
Shortfuse
Shorts and
    Churchbells
Shot at Dawn
Shot Injection
Shotgun
Shotgun
Shotgun Justice
Shotgun Sodomy
Shotgun Stallion
Shotgun Wedding
Shout of Destiny
Shoutline
Show Me on the Doll
Show No Mercy
Show No Mercy
Shower
Shrapnel
Shrapnel
Shrapnel
Shrapnel

Shrapnel Pill
Shredded
Shredded Corpse
Shredded Head
Shredmaster
Shredmill
Shreds Of Flesh
Shrettled Illusions
Shrieker
Shrine
Shrine
Shrine
Shrine
Shrine of Scars
Shrine of the Monkey
Shroud
Shroud
Shroud
Shroud of
    Bereavement
Shroud of
    Despondency
Shroud of Silence
Shroud of Tears
Shroud of Turin
Shrouded Deity
Shroudshifter
Shrum
Shryke
Shtriga
Shub Niggurath
Shubend
Shud
Shuddersome
Shumma Martum

Shunt
Shuriken
Shuriken Cadaveric
    Entwinement
Shutdown
Shworchtsechaye
Shylock
Shylock
Shyva
Shywolf
Siam
Siaurys
Siax
Sibet
Sibila
Sibimortem
Sibylline
Sic Luceat Lux
Sic Seed
Sic(k)reation
Sicamol
Sicarios
Sick
Sick
Sick
Sick Death
Sick Fantasy
Sick Flesh
Sick Human Art
Sick Mind
Sick Pop Parasite
Sick Room 7
Sick Sins
Sick Society
Sick Terror

Sick996
Sickbag
Sickblast
Sickening
Sickening Art
Sickening Gore
Sickening Horror
Sickenside
Sickleave
Sickmath
Sickmath
Sickness
Sickness
Sickness
Sickness
Sickness
Sickness
Sickness
Sickness
Sickness
Sickness
Sickness
Sickness
Sickness
Sicknote
Sicksouls
Sickspeed
SickSyco
Sick-U-R
Siculicidium
Side Effect
Side Effects
Side of Side
Side Winder
Sideblast
Sideburn

Sideffects
Sideline
Sider
Sidereal
Sideshow
Sideshow Zombies
Sidewinder
Sidinex
Sidius
Sidonia
Sidus Tenebrarum
Sie Sterben
Siebenbürgen
Siechtum
Siecrist
Sieg
Sieg Oder Tod
Siege
Siege of Hate
Sieged Mind
Sieges Even
Siegfried
Siegfried
Sieghetnar
Siegrid Ingrid
Siegtruppen
Sielwolf
Sierpe
Sifilis
Sifilis
Sifon
Sifr
Sig
SIG:AR:TYR
Sigel

Sigh
Sighisoara
Sight of Emptiness
Sightless
Sightless
Sigil
Sigil
Sigillum Diaboli
Sigillum Diaboli
Sigillum Diabolicum
Sigis
Sigismund
Sigma
Sigma
Sigma 5
Sigma Cero
Sigma Draconis
Sigma Elementa
Sigma Sentinel
Sign
Sign
Sign
Sign of Hate
Sign of KatuMarus
Sign of Sorrow
Sign of the Goat
Signal Blade
Signos
Signs of Cain
Signs of Collapse
Signs of Darkness
Signs of Dying
Signs of the Evil
Signum Diabolicum
Signum Diabolis

Signum Pugnae
Sigrblot
Sigtyr
Siinner Serpent
Siissisoq
Sikarikin
Sikfuk
Siksa Kubur
Siksakubur
Sikth
Sil Khannaz
Sil Veth
Silas
Silberbach
Silence
Silence
Silence
Silence
Silence
Silence
Silence
Silence
Silence Dead
Silence Death
Silence Enshroud
Silence Erebus
Silence Means Death
Silence of Moonset
Silence of Tranquility
Silence Within
Silence...
Silencer
Silencer
Silength
Silent
Silent Agony

Silent Agony
Silent Blast
Silent Call
Silent Civilian
Silent Confusion
Silent Cry
Silent Darkness
Silent Death
Silent Death
Silent Death
Silent Decay
Silent Device
Silent Devotion
Silent Dream
Silent Dreams
Silent Edge
Silent Exile
Silent Eye
Silent Eyes
Silent Force
Silent Forest
Silent Grief
Silent Kingdom
Silent Listener
SIlent Lucidity
Silent Memorial
Silent Moon
Silent Obedience
Silent Overdrive
Silent Rain
Silent Raven Fell
Silent Scream
Silent Scream
Silent Scream
Silent Scream

Silent Scream
Silent Scream
Silent Scream
Silent Scream
Silent Scythe
Silent Secrets
Silent Slip
Silent Sorrow
Silent Souls
Silent Spring
Silent Strain
Silent Stream of
  Godless Elegy
Silent Strike
Silent Tales
Silent Terror
Silent Threnody
Silent Tomb
Silent Tower
Silent Vanquish
Silent Victory
Silent Voices
Silent Winter
Silent Winter
Silentdecay
Silentium
Silentium
Silentium
Silentium Est
  Aureum
Silentium Noctis
Silentree
Silenxce
Silenzio
Silesia

Silester
Silexater
Silhaven
Silicon Head
Silk Gloves
Silkhannaz
Silly Twats
Silo
Silovanje
Silva Nigra
Silvanus
Silvara
Silver Back
Silver Blade
Silver Blade
Silver Cry
Silver Cypher
Silver Eagle
Silver Fist
Silver Grave
Silver Lady
Silver Mountain
Silver Seraph
Silverdollar
Silverlane
Silvershades
Silversteel
Silvertrain
SilverWing
Silveth
Simargal
Simbelin
Simbiose
Simbiotic
Simbioz

Simmetry
Simone Fiorletta
Simonia
Simphonia
Simple Aggression
Simple Kulto
Simply Death
Simson
Simulacrum
Sin
Sin
Sin
Sin
Sin Dizzy
Sin Driven Tide
Sin of Angels
Sin of God
Sin of Kain
Sin of Silence
Sin on Skin
Sin Origin
Sin Theorem
SIN.thetic
Sin:Overflow
Sinaatra
Sinah
Sinai Beach
Sinamore
Sinaria
Sinaside
Sinasylum
Sinate
Sinathrop
Sinawe
Sinbolic

Since the Flood
Sincere Darkness
Sincerity Green
Sinch
Sinclined
Sincronisity
Sindecade
Sindikate
Sindios
Sindone
Sindrome
Sindrome Motoria
Sindustry
Sine Anima
Sine Nomine
Sin-Eater
Sinedrion
Sinequanon
Sinergia
Sinergy
Sines of Life
Sinescent
Sinestesia
Sinful
Sinful
Sinful Bliss
Sinful Lust
Single Bullet Theory
Singularis Y Spheria
Singultus
Singur Fiinta
Siniac
Sinikil
Sinis
Sinister

Solifugia	Solus	Somnolentia	Sonicmind	Soothsayer	SoreLoser	Sorrows
Soliloquy	Solution 13	Somnus	Soniminos	Sophia's Eye	Soreption	Sorrow's End
Soliloquy	Solution Suicide	Somnus Cadaversus	Sonnenkreuz	Sophistes	Sorg	Sorrows Lament
Soliloquy	Solutions	Somrak	Sonnentod	Sophistication	Sorg	Sorrows Path
Solipsism	Solve et Coagula	Son et Lumiere	Sonny Red	Sophus	Sorg	Sorrowsend
Solipsist	Som Triturador	Son in Curse	Sonorous Din	Sopor	Sorg Innkallelse	SorrowStorm
Solitaire	Soma	Son of a Bitch	Sonorous Reluctance	Sorath	Sorgerth	Sors Immanis
Solitarium	Soman	Son of Dog	Sons of Azrael	Sorath	Sorghegard	Sort Vokter
Solitary	Somber	Son of Lilith	Sons of Belial	Sorbon	Sorgnatt	Sorthug
Solitary	Somber	Sonata	Sons of Chaos	Sorcerer	Sorgsen	Sortilege
Solitary	Somber Blessings	Sonata Arctica	Sons of Death	Sorcerer	Sorgsvart	Sortilege
Solitary	Somber Serenity	Sonata Nocturna	Sons of Fenris	Sorcerer	Sorhin	Sortilégio
Solitary Confinement	Somberlain	Sonata Soturna	Sons of Jonathas	Sorcerer	Soriben	Sortilegium
Solitary Confinement	Sombras del Destino	SonDamned	Sons of Kyuss	Sorcerer	Sorkkarauta	Sortokausi
Solitary Torture	Sombre Chemin	Sonder Grämen	Sons of Lioth	Sorcerer	Sororicide	Sorts
Solitude	Sombre Haine	Sønderfall	Sons of Madness	Sorcery	Sorrogate	Sortsind
Solitude	Sombre Labyrinthe	Sondor	Sons of Mars	Sorcery	Sorrow	Sostran
Solitude	Sombre Nostalgie	Song of Melkor	Sons of Musspellheim	Sorcery	Sorrow	Sotajumala
Solitude	Sombre Presage	Songe d'Enfer	Sons of Nihil	Sorcery	Sorrow	Sotavuohi
Solitude	Sombres Forêts	Sonheillon	Sons of Otis	Sorcery	Sorrow	Soter
Solitude	Sombriu	Sonic Agitation	Sons of Poseidon	Sorcery	Sorrow	Soter
Solitude	Some Won Spit	Sonic Annihilation	Sons of Satan	Sorcery	Sorrow and Tears	Soterion
Solitude	Someone Inside	Sonic Brew	Sons of Satan	Sorcier Des Glaces	Sorrow Bequest	Sothis
Solitude	Something Beautiful	Sonic Debris	Sons of Serpent	Sorcoror	Sorrow Born	Sothis
Solitude Aeturnus	Something Must Die	Sonic Flower	Sons of Seth	Sordid	Sorrow Breed	Sothoth
Solium XI	Something to Think About	Sonic Lord	Sons of Slaughter	Sordid	Sorrow Decadence	Sotos
Sollen	Somewhere in Nowhere	Sonic Pulsar	Sons of Thunder	Sordid	Sorrow Filled	Sottotomba
Solmath	Somniae Status	Sonic Reign	Sons of Tomorrow	Sordid Death	Sorrow of Tranquility	Soturna
Solnorth	Somniator	Sonic Stone	Sons of Vikings	Sordid Doctrine	Sorrow Sphere	Soturnus
Solomon Kane	Somnifere	Sonic Structure	Sons of War	Sordid Ideas	Sorrowed	Soul Assassins
Sólstafir	Somnium Mortuum	Sonic Syndicate	Sontsevorot	Sordide	Sorrowfall	Soul Blades
Solstice	Somnolence	Sonic Violence	SonX	Sore	Sorrowfield	Soul Cages
Solstice	Somnolent	Sonichaos Aeon	Soomdrag	Sore Plexus	Sorrowful God	Soul Casket
Solstice		Sonicide	Soon To Be Forgotten	Sore Sight	Sorrowful Winds	Soul Cellar
Solstice of Suffering		Sonick Plague	Soot		Sorrowind	Soul Chamber
Solstis						

Soul Devoured	Soul Terror	Soulitary	Souls on Fire	Sounds of Sim	Sovereign	Spastic Mime
Soul Devourer	Soul Transition	Soulitude	Souls That Fade	Soundshok	Sovereign	Spawn
Soul Devourer	Soul Vomit	Souljur	Soulscar	Soundstem	Sovereign	Spawn
Soul Dissector	Soul's Damnation	Soulkeep	Soulscarred	SoundStorm	Sovereign Serafin	Spawn
Soul Embodiment	Soulash	Soulless	Soulscourge	Soundstorm	Sovereign Steel	Spawn
Soul Embraced	Soulbender	Soulless	Soulsearch	Sounpictures	Sovereignty	Spawn
Soul Erosion	Soulblaze	Soulless	Soulseasons	Source	Sovijus	Spawn of Evil
Soul Exile	Soulbreach	Soulless	Soulset	Source of Deep	Sovran	Spawn of Possession
Soul Existence	Soulburn	Soulless	Soulsgate	Shadows	Sovversivo	Spawn of the
Soul Factor	Soulburner	Soulless	Soulsick	Source of Demise	Sower	Matriarch
Soul Flayer	Soulburner	Soulless	Soulside	Source of Sorrow	sOy bOmb	Spawned by Rot
Soul Forlorn	Soulcage	Soulless	Soulskinner	Source of Tide	Soziedad Alkoholika	Spazmosity
Soul Forsaken	Soulcide	Soulless	Soulskinner	Sourground	Space Billiard	Spazztic Blurr
Soul Fracture	Soulcide	Soulless	Soulslide	Sourpuz	Space Eater	Speak No Evil
Soul Grind	Soulcut	Soulless Heart	Soulspell	Sourreal	Space Mirrors	Speaking to Stones
Soul Hunter	SoulDæmon	Soulless Symphony	Soulsteeler	Sourvein	Space Odyssey	Spear of Longinus
Soul In Pain	Souldrainer	SoulLine	Soulstice	South of Heaven	Space Patrol	Spearhead
Soul Inquisition	Souldust	Soulmaker	Soulstitia	Southern Black Sand	Space Raven	Spearhead
Soul Less Divine	Souledge	Soulmine	Soulstorm	Southern Cross	Space Time	Spearhead
Soul Mask	Souless	Soulpit	Soulstorm	Southern Forest	Spade Shovel Atrophy	Spearhead
Soul Obsolete	Souless	Soulpreacher	Soulstream	Southern Hate	Spancer	Special Experiment
Soul of the Machine	Soulfade	Soulquake System	Soultaker	Southern Isolation	Sparagmos	Special Forces
Soul of the Savior	Soulfallen	Soulreaper	Soultorn	Southern Realm	Spare	Special Guest
Soul Reaper	Soulfield	Soulreaver	Soultrack	Southern Storm	Sparkling Pain	Specimen 32
Soul Sacrifice	Soulfly	Soulrest	Soulwound	Southern Storm	Sparks and Flames	Speckmann
Soul Sacrifice	Soulforge	Soulriver	Sound Barrier	of Evil	Sparrow Mutant	Speckmann Project
Soul Sailor	Soulforger	Souls Astray	Sound Mind	Southern Whiskey	Sparta	Spectator
Soul Saver	Soulfracture	Souls at Zero	Sound of Frailty	Rebellion	Spartacus	Specter
Soul Scrape	Soulfuckingblight	Souls Demise	Sound of Silence	Southfork	Spartan Warrior	Specters
Soul Sinner	Soulgate	Souls Domain	Sound of Silence	Southpaw	Sparto	of Madness
Soul Skinner	Soulgates Dawn	Soul's Dying Path	Sound Pollution	Southule	Sparzanza	Spectra
Soul Sound Day	Soulgrind	Souls' Gallery	Sound the Alarm	Southview	Spasme	Spectral
Soul Source	Soulgrind	Souls in Apocalypse	Soundbringer	Southwake	Spasmodic	Spectral
Soul Takers	Soulhate	Souls of Emptiness	Sounder	Sovako	Spasmophilius	Spectral Birth
Soul Tempest	Soulhavoc	Souls of the Departed	Soundmynd	Sovereign	Spastic Ink	Spectral Forest

Spectral Impunity

◀ Squealer

T.A.O.	Taakeferd	Taetre	Talas	Tanat	Tantrom	Tarkus
T.A.R.	Taakeheimen	Tagraht	Talavet	Tanatossis	Tantrum	Tarland
T.H.C.	Taarenes Vaar	Tahiraã	Talbot	Tanatron	Tantrum	Tarm
T.H.G.	Taarma	Tai Pan	Tales of Blood	Tandjent	Tantrum	Tarot
T.H.O.R.N.S.	Tabbasa	Tai-A	Tales of Dark	Tandus	Tantrum	Tarot
T.I.T.	Taberah	Taia	Tales of Darknord	Tandus	Tanzwut	Tarot
T.M.A.	Tabes	Taifa	Tales of Destiny	Tanelorn	Taog Susej	Tarot's Myst
T.M.K.	Tabularasa	Taiga	Tales of Fate	Tanelorn	Taor	Tarpeia
T.N.T.	Tacere	Taigetos	Tales of Hate	Tanelorn	Tapa!	Tarpit
T.O.M.B.	Tachy	Taiho	Tales of Medusa	Tanelorn	Tapetum Lucidum	Tarrabazza
T3chn0ph0b1a	Tacit Fury	Taija Rae	Tales of Sorrow	Tang Dynasty	Tarabas	Tartaros
T55	Tactics	Tailgunners	Tales of Twilight	Tangaroa	Taramantia	Tartaros
T666	Tactile Gemma	Taine	Talesien	Tangled in Tangerine	Taramis	Tartarus
Taagefolket	Tad Morose	Tainted	Taliándörögd	Tangorodream	Taran	Tartarus
Taak	Taddart	Tainted Rych	Taliensin	Tangorodrim	Taranis	Tartarus
Taake	Taedeat	Tainted Saint	Taliesin	Tangrycan	Taranis	Tartessos
		Taipan	Taliesin	Tanha	Taranis	Tartharia
		Taipan	Talion	Tanhauser Gate	Taranis	Tartness
		Tairach	Taliön	Tanis	Taranis	Tartosgardh
		Taish	Talisman	Tanist	Tarantist	Tarturis
		Taist of Iron	Talisphere	Tank	Tarantula	Tarzen
		Takara	Tallboy Shotgun	Tankard	Tarantula	Taste
		Takashi	Talleron	Tankard Noble Tea	Tarantula	Taste of Blood
		Take Death	Talon	Tankcsapda	Tarantula Hawk	Taste of Doom
		Take Zero	Talon	Tanke	Tarask	Taste of Fear
		Taken by Wolves	Talos	Tanker	Taraxacum	Taste of Insanity
		Takeover	Talvella	Tankred Best	Tarbatu	Taste of Tears
		Takeover	Talvisota	Tanktrap	Tarchon Fist	Tasteless
		Takeru	Tamerlán	Tankwart	Target	Tasty Gore
		Taketh	Tamisra	Tanner	Target	Tasyim
		Tal Dorgar	Tammiyön kilta	Tannheyn	Target	Tathagata
		Talamasca	Tamnus	Tanqeray	Target	Tatir
		Talamasca	Tamoto	Tantal	Targost	Tattered Salvation
		Talamyus	Tampon Crucifix	Tantalos	Tarihan	Tattoo
		Talan	Tanahauzer	Tantalus	Tarkus	Taufane

◀ Taunt

Taunusheim	Tears	Teatr Teney	Temnozor'	Temple of the Absurd	Tenebrae	Tenever
Taur Nu Fuin	Tears	Technakill	Tem-Ohp-Ab	Temple of Tiphareth	Tenebrae	Tenfold Truth
Taurin	Tears for the	Technikill	Temperament	Templegate	Tenebrae	Tengereken
Taurine	Dead Gods	Technocracy	Temperance	Templerion	Tenebrae in	Tengeri Püspök
Tauro	Tears from the Sky	Tectonic	Tempered Steel	Templo de lo Absurdo	Perpetuum	Tengkorak
Tauron	Tears in Vain	Ted Bundy	Tempest	Templo del Rey	Tenebrae Oboriuntur	Tengwar
Taurus	Tears of a Mourning	Ted Maul	Tempest	Templo Negro	Tenebrare	Tengwar
Taurus	Angel	Tedd Deireadh	Tempest	Templum	Tenebrário	Tenhi
Tauthr	Tears of Anger	Teelus	Tempest	Templum Slavus	Tenebrarum	TenHornedBeast
Tavaron	Tears of Beggar	Teeth of Lions	Tempest	Tempo Tantrum	Tenebrarum .	Tenochtitlan
Tavion	Tears of Blood	Rule the Divine	Tempest	Temporary Insanity	Tenebrarvm	Tenotitlan
Tavú	Tears of Christ	Teeth of the Hydra	Tempest Reign	Temptamentum	Tenebras Omnia	Tenowar
Taxi Karlo	Tears of Decay	Tefilla	Tempesta	Tempter	Vincit	Tenshy of Death
Taxidermist	Tears of Ea	Tefra	Tempesta	Tempus Fugit	Tenebre	Tenside
Taxidermist	Tears of Eden	Tefrosis	Tempestad	Tempus Mori	Tenebre	Tension
Tayga	Tears of Euphony	Tegen Hart	Tempestas	Temtris	Tenebre	Tension
Taylan Ayýk	Tears of Evil	Tehace	Tempestilence	Temujin	Tenebreant	Tension
Tayohuac	Tears of Fire	Tehenet	Tempestine	Ten	Tenebres	Tension Head
Tazumal	Tears of Glory	Teitan	Tempestt	10$ Head	Ténèbres	Tension Point
Tchandala	Tears of Grief	Teitanblood	Templar	1080	Tenebrha	Tentamentum
Tchildres	Tears of Israfel	Teka Phobia	Templaria	10Eyes	Tenebricosus	Tenval
Tchort	Tears of Joker	Telegram	Templario	Ten Feet From Murder	Tenebrion	Teofobia
Tchort	Tears of Mankind	Telidemon	Templarius	10 Kingdoms	Tenebris	Teogoniya
TDW	Tears of Martyr	Telis	Temple	Ten Rail Cell	Tenebris	Teophania
Te Deum	Tears of Melody	TellTaleHard	Temple of Ascension	10-67 P.D.O.A.	Tenebris	Teos
Te Devm	Tears of Misery	Tellurian	Temple of Baal	Tendencia	Tenebrium	Teotwawki
Teabag	Tears of Mystigma	Tellurian	Temple of Baphomet	Tendencia Extrema	Tenebrium	Tepheret
Tear Gas and	Tears of Rain	Temblor	Temple of Baphomet	Tenderizer	Tenebrosa Escuridão	Tephra
Plate Glass	Tears of Seraphim	Temeluchus	Temple of Blood	Tenderness	Tenebrosa Invidia	TER
Tear Her Eyes	Tears of the Sun	Temenon	Temple of Brutality	Tendr	Tenebrosity	Terafirmer
Tearabyte	Tears of Wrath	Temenos	Temple of Chaos	Tenebra	Tenebrosus	Terakil
Teardown	Tearstained	Temnich	Temple of Eternity	Tenebra	Tenebrous	Teramaze
Tearfall	Teasanna Satanna	Temnohor	Temple of Not	Tenebra	Tenebrum	Terapon
Tearful	Teaser	Temnojar	Temple of Oblivion	Tenebrae	Tenebrum Infectus	Teräsbetoni
Tearful Heaven	Teaser	Temnozor	Temple of Shadows	Tenebrae	Tenet	Teräsvilla

Teratism	Terra Caput Mundi	Terror	Terrorthrone	Teth	Thamuz	The 3rd and the Mortal
Teratogenic	Terra Cotta	Terror	Terrortory	Tethuo	Thanateros	The 4th Is Eligor
Teratoma	Terra Firma	Terror	Terrorust	Tetragon	Thanatheros Rites	The 69 Eyes
Teratos	Terra Mortis	Terror	Terrorwheel	Tetragrammaton	Thanathron	The 7th Gate
Teratosis	Terra Noir	Terror 2000	Terrorythm	Tetraktys	Thanatoid	The 8th Sin
Teratosts	Terra Obscura	Terror Ascends	Terrorzone	Tetraplegic God	Thanatopsis	the 9th Cell
Tercios	Terra Prima	Terror by the Lake	Térsivel	Tetriconia	Thanatopsis	The 9th Plague
Terdor	Terra Rosa	Terror Engine	Terteros	Tetsukabuto	Thanatopsus	The Abodox
Terem	Terra Rossa	Terror Fector	Tervahauta	Tetsuo	Thanatos	The Abominable Iron Sloth
Tereza	Terra Sur	Terror Is a Man	Tervaskanto	Teufel	Thanatos	The Absence
Terhen	Terra Tenebrae	Terror of the Trees	Terveet Kadet	Teufelblut	Thanatos	The Abyss
Terminal Bliss	Terra::POLARIS	Terror Organ	Tesla	Teufelswerk & Narrentanz	Thanatos	The Abyssaria
Terminal Cancer	Terracide	Terror Scum	Tess	Teurgia.	Thanatos Inc.	The Accident
Terminal Confusion	Terracuda	Terror Squad	Tessaract	Teut	ThanatoSchizo	The Accursed
Terminal Death	Terrae Sole Calentes	Terror Strike	Tessila	Teuta	Thanatosis	The Accused
Terminal Descent	Terragon	Terror Throne	Tesstimony	Teutates	Thandus	The Aerium
Terminal Disease	Terrahsphere	Terror Tractor	Test Fobii	Teuton	Thane	The Affected
Terminal Function	Terramortis	Terrorama	Test of Faith	Teutonic	Thanelorn	The Afterglow
Terminal Grace	Terraphobia	Terrorbeer	Test of Faith	Texidor	Thangelic	The Aftermath
Terminal Lovers	Terrathorn	Terrorblade	Test Switch Isolator	Textures	Thanius	The Age
Terminal Plan	Terratomb	Terrorcorpse	Testament	Tezarchaeon	Tha-norr	The Aging Harbor
Terminal Reign	Terremoto	TerrorCreation	Testament	Tezcatlipoca	Thanos Nocturnum	The Agony Scene
Terminal War	Terrenal	TerrorCult	Testicle Cancer	Tezcatlipoca	Tharaphita	The Alex Parche Project
Terminally, Your Aborted Ghost	Terrencial Embrace	Terrordrome	Testicle Disease	Tezkatlipoka	Thargos	The Alfredo Contract
Terminated Rite	Terrible	Terrorgoat	Testicle Vomit	Thade	Tharithimas	The Allknowing
Terminator	Terricon	Terrorgod	Testification	Thagirion	Tharn	The Allseeing I
Terminator	Terrific Verdict	Terrorist	Testify	Thalarion	Tharna	The Almighty
Terminator	Terrify	Terrorist Kommando	Testimony	Thalarion Lati	Tharsis	The Almighty Punchdrunk
Terminus	Terrify	Terroristic Professy	Testimony	Thales	Tharsis	The Alphes
Terminus	Territory	Terrorizer	Testimony	Thalia	Tharsys	The Amenta
Terminus 5	Terrodrown	Terrorkult	Testimony	Thalidomide	Thastment	The Ancient Queen
Terminus Ex	Terror	Terrormachine	Testisment	Thalion	That Old Black Magic	
Terra Blachorum	Terror	TerrornymmpH	Testor	Thallium	Thatcher	
	Terror	Terrorspawn	Testosteron	Thallium	Thaurorod	
	Terror	Terrorstorm	Tétano		Thaurval	

The Answer
The Anti Doctrine
The Anti-Human
The Anti-Human
The Aphelion
The Apostasy
The Apparatus
The Arcane
The Arcane Order
The Archaic Terror
The Armada
The Arrival
The Arrival of Satan
The Arrow
The Arrs
The Arson
The Arsonist's
  Daughter
The Art of Blasphemy
The Art of Butchery
The Art of Chaos
The Art of Jor
The Ascension
The Ashes
The Athiarchists
The Atmosfear
The Austrasian Goat
The Autumn Offering
The Autumn Winds
The Avatar
The Awakened
The Awakened One
The Awakening
The Awakening
The Awakening

The Away
The Awful Truth
The Axis of Perdition
The Banner
The Barque of Dante
The Batallion
The Beast
The Beast
The Beast
The Beast
The Beast
The Beauty of Death
The Becoming
The Bedlam
The Beheading
The Being Blind
The Belonging
The Bereaved
The Berzerker
The Beyond
The Beyond
The Bezerker
The Bizarre
  Blue Spectre
The Black
The Black
The Black Acadia
  Mourning
The Black Arts
  Movement
The Black
  Dahlia Murder
The Black Death
The Black Gate
The Black League
The Black Order

The Black Pest
The Black
  Symphony
The Blackest
  Incarnation
The Bleeding
The Bleeding
The Bleeding
The Bleeding Sun
The Bleedout
The Blessed
  Deception
The Blinding Light
The Blizzard
The Blood Divine
The Blood of
  Transylvania
The Bloodcult
The Bloodless Dead
The Bloodline
The Bloody Dicks
The Bloody Earth
The Blue Season
The Body
The Body Bag
  Romance
The Body Beneath
The Body Snatcher
The Book of Death
The Bottle Doom
  Lazy Band
The Braindead
The Brained
The Bräts
The Breath Of Life

The Breathing
  Process
The Breathing
  Process
The Breeding
The Broken Souls
The Bronx
The Bronx Casket Co.
The Brood
The Bubonic Plague
The Bulemics
The Burning
The Burning
  Cathedral
The Burning Issue
The Cable Car Theory
The Cage
The Caktus
The Call
The Call of the
  Four Gates
The Candle
The Candles
  Burning Blue
The Carnival
The Cascades
The Casket Crew
The Cauterized
The Cave
The Cavernous
The Cellts
The Centre of Gravity
The Cerastine Order
The Chaos Nether
  Silence

The Chapter
The Chargers
The Chasm
The Chasm Chateau
The Chicken Okkült
The Children
The Choir of
  Vengeance
The Chosen
The Church Bizzare
The Circle
The Circle
  of Zaphyan
The Citadel
The Clan Destined
The Clan of Steel
The Classic Struggle
The Claymore
The Cleaner
The Cold Beyond
The Communion
The Company
The Company
  Of Snakes
The Concubine
The Confederacy
The Conquering
The Continuum
The Contradiction
  of Christ
The Corpse
The Corpse Grinders
The Council
The County Medical
  Examiners

The Coven
The Coven
The Coven
The Covent
The Coventry
  Sacrifice
The Cranium
The Crap
The Crashing Falcon
The Craving
The Crazies
The Creed
The Crescent
  and the Cross
The Crescents
The Crest
The Crestfallen
The Crew
The Crimson Divine
The Crimson
  Syndicate
The Cromptons
The Cross
The Cross
The Crown
The Crucified
The Crypt
The Cryptosy
The Culling Song
The Cult Occult
The Cumshots
The Cursed
The Damascus
  Intervention
The Damnation

The Dark Arts
The Dark Beyond
  Conception
The Dark Fury
The Dark One
The Dark Regions
The Darkening
The Darkest Blood
The Darkness Within
The Darksend
The Dawning Project
The Day Everything
  Became Nothing
The Day of the Beast
The Dead
The Dead
The Dead
The Dead Beginners
The Dead Eat Worms
The Dead Is Tired
  When the Morning
  Comes
The Dead Musician
The Dead Youth
The Deadly
The Deafening
  Silence
The Deathbed Gospel
The Defaced
The Deformity
The Deliverance
The Demonstration
The Denial
The Destro
The Destro

The Device	The Embalmers Daughter	The Evil Cell	The Fifth One	The Funeral Orchestra	The Guardian	The Hour of Reckoning
The Devout	The Ember Tide	The Evil Solstice	The Fifth Season	The Funeral Pyre	The Guff	The Hourglass
The Difference	The Embodiment	The Evolution	The Fifth Season	The Furious Horde	The Hag	The House of Capricorn
The Disciples of Zoldon	The Embowel	The Exalted Piledriver	The Fifth Sun	The Furor	The Hand of Doom	The Howl
The Dismal	The Embraced	The Excrementory Grindfuckers	The Filthy Creeps	The Fury	The Handshake Murders	The Howl
The Divining	The Enchanted	The Exile	The Filthy Rich Band	The Fuzz	The Handsome Beasts	The Howling
The Doctor	The End	The Exorial	The Final Burden	The Gallery	The Hate Within	The Human Condition
The Dogma	The End	The Experience	The Final Holocaust	The Garcia	The Hatred Machine	The Hunt
The Doomsday Cult	The End	The Exploited	The Final Journey of the Seer	The Garden of Martyrs	The Haunted	The Hunt For Ida Wave
The Downward Candidate	The End	The Eye	The Final Season	The Gate	The Haunting	The Hypochondriacs
The Dreamside	The End	The Eyes	The Final Sign	The Gates of Slumber	The Headbangers	The Ill Over Death
The Drop of Water That Can Wear Through a Stone	The End 666	The Fabulous Concerto	The Fireball	The Gateway	The Heat	The Immortal
The Drowned	The End of All Reason	The Face	The First Lie	The Gathering	The Heavils	The Impact
The Drowning	The End of Six Thousand Years	The Faceless	The Firstborn	The Gault	The Henchmen	The Implicate Order
The Dunwich Horror	The Endoparasites	The Fact	The Flaw	The Gersch	The Henchmen	The Inbreds
The Duskfall	The Enemy	The Fadal	The Flesh	The Gladiator	The Heretic	The Index
The Dust Connection	The Entity	The Fading	The Flinkstoneds	The Glassmode	The Hidden	The Insomnia
The Dying Light	The Entropy	The Falcon	The Flying Hat Band	The God Machine	The Hidden	The Irons
The Dying One	The Equinox ov the Gods	The Fall of Eden	The Fools of Christ	The Goddamned	The Hidden	The Ivory Tower
The Earthfall	The Eschaton Creed	The Fall of Every Season	The Foot	The Goddess	The Hidden Hand	The Jack
The Ebola Projekt	The Esoteric Movement v: 6.660	The Fallen	The Forensic	The Golden Age	The Hidden Project	The Jam Session
The Edge	The Essence Embraced	The Fallen	The Foreverlorn	The Gorewar	The High Council	The Jelly Jam
The Eldflames	The Eternal	The Fallen	The Forgotten	The Grand Phoenix	The Highlanders	The Johansson Brothers
The Electric Hellfire Club	The Eternal	The Fallen Angel	The Forgotten Grace Theory	The Grasshopper Lies Heavy	The Hirvi	The Joint Chiefs
The Element	The Eternal Blade	The Fallen Sons	The Formori	The Gravity Guild	The Hollow	The Jones
The Element	The Eternal Pain	The Famous-X	The Forsaken	The Great Deceiver	The Hollow Earth Theory	The Jonestown Syndicate
The Eleventh Room	The Ethereal	The Fantastikol Hole	The Fortuna	The Great Kat	The Hope Conspiracy	The Juliet Massacre
The Elysian Fields	The Everdawn	The Farewell Fields	The Four Chapters	The Green Evening Requiem	The Hordes	The K
The Embalmed	The Evermind	The Fellowship of the Ring	The Four Horsemen	The Grey Calamity	The Host	The Kabal
	The Everscathed	The Fieldz	The Frost	The Grief	The Hostage Heart	
			The Fuck Machine	The Grieving Process	The Houdini Complex	
			The Fucking Champs			

- The Quest
- The Quiescent
- The Quiet Room
- The Quill
- The Quintessence
- The Rain
- The Rain
- The RamDo Connection
- The Ransack
- The Rape of Lucrece
- The Raunchous Brothers
- The Raven
- The Ravenous
- The Ravens
- The Rays of the Sun
- The Real Massacre
- The Reality
- The Reaper
- The Reaper
- The Rebel Wounded
- The Rebirth of Humanity
- The Reckoning
- The Reckoning
- The Rectum Satans
- The Red Chord
- The Red Death
- The Red Strike
- The RedFlux
- The Reefer Hut
- The Regime
- The Reign of Terror
- The Remnant
- The Renewed
- The Republic of Desire
- The Resonance Association
- The Resonant Strain
- The Return
- The Revenge Project
- The Reverie
- The Reviled
- The Revival
- The Ring
- The Rising Force
- The Rite of Retaliation
- The River
- The RMS
- The Roadcrew
- The Rocking Dildos
- The Rods
- The Roxx
- The Royal Blood
- The Rudes
- The Ruins of Beverast
- The Sabians
- The Sad Sun
- The Salvation Crusade
- The Sarcophagus
- The Satan's Scourge
- The Saviours
- The Scarr
- The Scavenger
- The Sceptic
- The Scourger
- The Scream of the Guillotine
- The Scrubs
- The Scythe Divine
- The Season
- The Seasons of Wither
- The Second Coming
- The Second Moon
- The Secret Life
- The Senseless
- The Sequel
- The Serpent Kiss
- The Serpent Son
- The Serpent Sun
- The Seven Deadly Sins
- The Seven Gates
- The Seventh
- The Seventh Cross
- The Seventh Gate
- The Seventh Seal
- The Shadow Order
- The Shattering
- The Shitheadz
- The Showdown
- The Shrink
- The Sickening
- The Siege of Kvatch
- The Silenced
- The Silent Agony
- The Sinful Ensemble
- The Sinkage
- The Sins of thy Beloved
- The Sixth Incubator
- The Skarekrow
- The Sleepfarmers
- The Soil Bleeds Black
- The Solution
- The Sorcerer
- The Souls Unrest
- The Sound of Sirens
- The Soundbyte
- The Southpaw Jinx
- The Spawn of Satan
- The Spektrum
- The Spill of Infinity
- The Sprawlcosm
- The Steel Empire
- The Stone
- The Stone
- The Storcings
- The Storm
- The Storm
- The Stormrider
- The Storyteller
- The Suffering
- The Suffering
- The Sun of Weakness
- The Sundial
- The Sunset
- The Supremacy
- The Swarm
- The Sweet Leaf
- The Sword
- The Sygnet
- The SymphOnyx
- The Synaptic Dissent
- The Taken
- The Tantalizor
- The Taste of Silver
- The Temple
- The Temple of Azoth
- The Tempter
- The Tenth Circle
- The Thinking Principle
- The Third Collision
- The Third of the Storms
- The Thorn
- The Threat
- The Tombers
- The Tora Tora Tourettes
- The Torment
- The Traceelords
- The Tragedians
- The Trasten Traste
- The Trauma
- The Tri-Star Embodiment
- The Truckers
- The True Beltez
- The True Black Dawn
- The True Dark Lord
- The True Endless
- The True Frost
- The True Warriors
- The True Werwolf
- The Tyrant of Manchester
- The Ugly
- The Unborn
- The Unchallenged
- The Uncreation
- The Undead Family
- The Undertaken
- The Undertakers
- The Ungrateful
- The Unholy
- The Unholy Warlock
- The Unjust
- The Unsane
- The Unspeakable Cult ov Goatpenis
- The Vala
- The Vast
- The Vein of Lunacy
- The Venting Machine
- The Very End
- The Villain
- The Violent Breed
- The Vision Bleak
- The Visions of Burning Saints
- The Voice
- The Void
- The Void
- The Von Frankensteins
- The Vultures
- The W.O.R.S.T.
- The Wake
- The Walk of the Shadows
- The Walruz
- The Warning
- The Warslain
- The Watch
- The Watch
- The Way of All Flesh
- The Weeds
- The Werewolves of Venice
- The Whip
- The Whisper
- The Whorehouse Massacre
- The Wicked
- The Wicked Chambers
- The Wild Mild
- The Wind
- The Wise
- The Witches Sabbath
- The Wizard
- The Wizards of Gore
- The Wolves Age
- The Wood's Silence
- The World We Knew
- The Worst
- The Wounded
- The Wounded
- The Wrath
- The Wrathful and the Sullen
- The Wreckage
- The Wretched
- The Year of Our Lord
- The Zephyr
- The Zeronaut
- The Ziggurat

Tiburon	Time Escape	Tini Zabutih Predkiv	Titarius	Toad the Wet	Tolerance	Tomorrows Victim
Tidal Wave	Time Haven Club	Tinieblas	Titus	Sprocket	Tolerant	TON
Tides	Time Kills Everything	Tinieblas	Tiwanaku	Toadliquor	Tol-In-Gaurhoth	Tonantzin
Tides of Darkness	Time Machine	Tinnitus	Tiwaz	Toadstool	Tollwut	Tondra
Tides of Eternity	Time Not Forgotten	Tintagel	Tixotropia	Toby Knapp	Toluol	Tonerlow
Tides Within	Time of Death...	Tion	Tjern	Toccata Magna	Tom Abella	Tonka
Tidfall	Time of Plague	Tipheret	Tjolgtjar	Tod	Tom Angelripper	Tonus
Tieflader	Time of the Wolf	Tipper Gor	Tkhort	Today Is The Day	Tomahawk	Tony Fredianelli
Tiek Bane	Time Out	Tipper Gore	TKO	Todd	Tomahawk	Tony Hernando
Tierra	Time Requiem	Tipsy Slut	Tleskac	Todesblei	Tomahawk	Tony Martin
Tierra de Nadie	Time Symmetry	Tir Nan Og	TME	Todesbonden	Tomb	Tony Tears
Tierra de Nadie	Timecode	Tiralinor	TNT	Todesfaust	Tomb	Tool
Tierra de Negro	TimeDust	Tirania	TNT	Todesgeist	Tomb	Tool Silence
Tierra del Dragon	Timefall	Tiranilor	TNT	Todeskampf	Tomb	Tools of the Trade
Tierra Santa	Timeghoul	Tirant Sin	To Arkham	Todeskult	Tomb Infusion	Tools of Torture
Tiger Cult	Timekeeper	Tishvaisings	To Be Eaten	Todesrune	Tomb of Gods	Toorn
Tiger Junkies	Timekey	Tisic Let Od Ráje	To Burn the Skies	Todesschwadron	Tomb of Time	Tootsie
Tightrope	Timekrush	Titan	To Conquer the Night	Todesstoss	Tomb Of...	Top Brown
Tiglath	Timeless	Titan	To Deeper Sorrow	Todestrieb	Tombcrusher	Top Dead Center
Tigres	Timeless Hall	Titan	To Elysium	Todesweihe	Tombe	Tophet
Tilarids	Timeless Miracle	Titan	To Our Grave	Todez	Tombstone	Tophet
Tilaris	Timeless Necrotears	Titan Force	To Plokami Tou	Todfeind	Tombstone	Tophet
Tile	Timelord	Titan Mountain	Karharia	Todgeweiht	Tombstone	Tor
Tiles	TimeMage	Titan Steele	To Resist Fatality	Todhelm	Tombthroat	Tor Marrock
Tilivan	Time's Forgotten	Titana	To Scale the Throne	Todtgelichter	Tomcat	Tora Tora
Till Die	Timesand	Titanesk	To Separate the Flesh	Together	To-Mera	Toranaga
Till the Dawn	Timescape	Titanic	from the Bones	Toil	Tomhet	Torax
Till Thy Dying Day	Timescape	Titanic	To Something	Toilet Tantalizer	Tomhet	Torben Enevoldsen
Tilt	Timestorm	Titanic	Beautiful	Toiletation	Tomhet	Torch
Tim Donahue	Timo Rautiainen	Titanium	To the Darker	Tokkata	Tommyknockers	Torch
Time	Timo Tolkki	Titanium	Grounds	Tokyo	Tommyknockerz	Torch of War
Time Collapse	Timor	Titanium	To the Eternal Sands	Tokyo Blade	Tomorrow Will	Torch of War
Time Curve	Timor et Tremor	Titanium	To the Seven	Tokyo Yankees	Be Worse	Torch the Day
Symmetry	Tin Omen	Titanium Black	To the Sky	Tolath	Tomorrow's Dream	Torchbearer
Time Eclipse	Tindra Stjärnöga	Titanum	To/Die/For	Tolerance	Tomorrow's Eve	Torche

Triarchy	Trigger Zone	Triplever	Triumphal Arch	Trollkiller	Troya	Tsubo
Triarchy	Triggered	Tripple Six	Triumphator	Trollmann	TRSX	Tsunami
Tribal	Triglav	Tripple Six	Triumphator	av Ildtoppberg	Truculence	TT Quick
Tribal Rage	Triglav	Tripwire	Triumphator	Trollrath	True Violence	TTMOX
Tribasativa	Triglav	Tripwire	Triumphus Mortis	Trollschwert	Truenemy	Tu Carne
Tribe Maelstrom	Trilogy	Triquinosis	Triumvirat Xul	Trollskog	Truffle	Tualatin
Tribe Of Judah	Trilogy	Triskèle	Triunfo e Vitória	Trollskogen	Trupny Yad	Tuatha de Danann
Tribes of Caïn	Trilogy	Triskell	a Satã	Trolltjern	Truppensturm	Tube
Tribes of Neurot	Trimegisto	Triskelon	Trivial Act	Trolltokt	Trust	Tublatanka
Tribulance	Trimonium	Trismus	Trivial Thorn	Trollzorn	Trust	Tuborg
Tribulation	Trimorphes	Trisomy	Trivium	Trom	Trust Rocks	Tucan St.
Tribulation	Zentrum Xul	Trist	Trizna	Trombe di Falloppio	Truth	Tudor
Tribulation	Trinakrius	Trist	Trogir	Tromsnar	Truth Corroded	Tuho
Tribunal	Trinity	Trist Vintry Vandre	Troglodyte	Tron	Truth In Ruin	Tuikkala
Tribus	Trinity	Tristan	Troglodyte Dawn	Tronador	Truth In Ruin	Tukkus
Tribuzy	Trinity	Tristana	Troglodytic	Tronn	Truth Kills	Tulus
Tricifix	Trinity	Tristania	Trogmorton	Trono	Try Again	Tummler
Trick of Light	Trinity Test	Triste	Trojan	Trono de Angel	Try Redemption	Tumor
Trick or Treat	Trinnity	Triste Sir	Trojan	Tronraner	Tryckvag	Tumour of Soul
Tricky Means	Trino	Tristessa	Tröjan	Tronus Abyss	Trymhbiu Ra	Tumult
T-Ride	Trionfale	Tristesse	Trokar	Troodon	Trymheim	Tumult
Trident	Triora	Tristesse	Trolderiget	Trooper	Trypanon	Tumulto
Trident	Triosphere	Tristisaltus	Troll	Troops of Brutality	Tryskellion	Tumulto
Tridium	Trioxia	Tristitia	Troll	Troops of Brutality	Tryskhell	Tumultuous
Tridus Elasticus	Trioxin	Tristwood	Troll	Troops of Death	Trytan	Tumulus
Triekonos	Trioxin	Triton	Troll Gnet El	Troops of Doom	TS & Outros Vicios	Tumulus
Triera	Tripalium	Triton	Trolldom	Trop Feross	TSA	Tumulus
Trifixion	Triphammer	Triton	Trollech	Tropa de Shock	Tsatthoggua	Tumulus
Trifixion	Triphammer	Tritón	Trollenwoud	Trophy Bride	Tsavo	Tumulus
Trifixion	Triphase 95	Tritone	Trollfest	Trörkrvisätänsrökrëh	Tsavo	Tumulus Anmatus
Trifixion	Triple 7	Tritonus	Trollhammer	Trotyl	Tscabeze	Tundra
Trifog	Triple Forte	Triumph	Trollhammer	Trotzreich	Tsidkenu	Tundra
Trigger 9	Triple X	Triumph Divine	Trollheimen	Trouble	Tsjuder	Tunes of Dawn
Trigger Point	Triple X	Triumph of Dawn	Trollheim's Grott	Trouble	Tsond	Tunes of Grey
Trigger Renegade	Triplesix	Triumph of Death	Trollhorn	Trouble Agency	TSPC	Tungstem
						Tungsten

⟨ Tunguska

TunnelVision	Tvangeste	Twilight Abyss	Twisted Into Form	Tyburnjig	Tyrant	Tystnaden
Tunrida	TVirus	Twilight Dreams	Twisted Minds	Tyccoma	Tyrant	Tytan
Tuolvok	Twat Appetizer	Twilight Falls	Twisted Minds	Tyfoon	Tyrant	Tyton
Tuonela	Twelfth Gate	Twilight Glimmer	Twisted Motivations	Tyga Myra	Tyrant	Tyvragen
Tuoni	Twelfth Hour	Twilight Guardians	Twisted Sacrifice	Tygers of Pan Tang	Tyrant	Tzaphkial
Tuonyca	Twelfth of Never	Twilight Illusion	Twisted Silence	Tykküs	Tyrant	Tzar
Turambar	12 Days of Anarchy	Twilight in Fire	Twisted Sister	Tym Morrison	Tyrant	Tzefa
Turbine	12 Eyes	Twilight Is Mine	Twisted System	Tymah	Tyrant	Tzelmoth
Turbines Drive	Twelve Gauge	Twilight Kingdom	Twisted Tower Dire	Tynator	Tyrant	Tzompantli
Turbo	12 Gauge Dead	Twilight Mask	Twisted Truth	Type O Negative	Tyrant	Tzun Tzu
Turbo	12:06 A.M.	Twilight Mist	Twister of Truth	Typhoid	Tyrant	
Turbo	12 Ton Sledge	Twilight Moon	Twitch	Typhon	Tyrant Disciple	
Turbo	Twelvexseven	Twilight Odyssey	Twitch of	Typhon	Tyrant Eyes	
Turbo	21st Century Killing	Twilight of Christ	the Death Nerve	Typhon	Tyrant Imperia	
Turboangel	Machine	Twilight Ophera	Two	Typhonic Blast	Tyrant Lord	
Turbostill	20 Grit	Twilight Opus	Two-Bit Thief	Typhoon	Tyrant of War	
Turbulance	TwentyInchBurial	Twilight Passion	Two Eagles Request	Typhus	Tyrant Throne	
Turdpedo	21 Lucifers	Twilight Project	2Excess	Typhus	Tyrant Town	
Turea	2112	Twilight Prophecies	Two Foot Candle	Týr	Tyrant Trooper	
Turisas	23 Roadkill	Twilight Symphony	Two Majesties	Tyr	Tyrants	
Turisas	24Give	Twilight Symphony	2 Minuta Dreka	Tyr	Tyrants	
Turmion Katilot	29Jaguar	Twilight Tales	2 Minute Hate	Tyrael	Tyrants	
Turning Black	Twenty Third	Twilight Tower	Two Mirrors	Tyran' Pace	Tyrants Blood	
Turning Crosses	Chapter	Twilight Zone	2nCuk	Tyranath	Tyrants of the Flesh	
Turning of the Gears	Twice as Mortal	Twilight Zone	206 and Thinkers	Tyranex	Tyrant's Reign	
Turning Point	Twilight	Twilight Zone	Two Ravens	Tyranis	Tyrax	
Turrigenous	Twilight	Twilight Zöne	2 Son Multitud	Tyrannium	Tyresia	
Turris Spectrum	Twilight	Twilightning	2000 A.D.	Tyrannum	Tyrmord	
Turul	Twilight	Twin Obscenity	2 Ton Predator	Tyranny	Tyrranicide	
Turulvér	Twilight	Twinspirits	Two Ton Wreck	Tyranny	Tyrrany	
Tush	Twilight	Twist of Fate	220 Volt	Tyranny in Ruin	Tyrrany	
Tusk	Twilight	Twisted Ace	Twyster	Tyran's Lie	Tyrus	
Tuska	Twilight	Twisted Autumn	TxExF	Tyrant	Tyrus	
Tusks of Blood	Twilight	Darkness	Tyburn	Tyrant	Tyskland	
Túzmadár	Twilight	Twisted Harmony	Tyburn	Tyrant	Tysondog	

	Ugly Wanda	Ulterior Decimation	Ulveheim	UN	Unchain
	Ugnélakis	Ulthrash	Ulver	Un Moment de	Unchained
	Ugra Karma	Ultima Candela	Ulvhedin	Silence	Unchained
	Uhrilehto	Ultima Forsam	Ulvhedinn	Unanimated	Unchained
	Uhygge	Ultima War	Ulvhedner	Unatur	Unchallenged Hate
	Uigg	Ultimate Massacre	Ulvnatt	Unatural Desaster	Unchaste
	Uirapuru	UltiMatium	Ulysses	Unaussprechlichen	Unchecked
	Ulan Bator	Ultimatum	Ulysses Siren	Kulten	Aggression
	Ulcer	Ultimatum	Umbah	Unauthorized	Unchosen
	Ulcer	Ultimatum	Umbakrail	Unauthorized	Unchrist
	Ulcer	Ultimatum	Umberhulk	Unawakened	Uncle Fester
	Ulcer	Ultimatum	Umbilical Cord	Unbeing	Uncle Slam
	Ulcer Uterus	Ultimatum	Umbilical Fetal	Unblessed	Unclean
	Ulcerate	Ultimatum	Strangulation	Unblessed	Uncomposing
	Ulcerate Fester	Ultimatum	Umbilical	Unblessed	Unconcern
	Ulcerate Liquor	Ultimo Mondo	Strangulation	Unborn	Unconquered
	Ulceration	Cannibale	Umbilicus Mundis	Unborn	Unconsecrated
	Ulcerous Phlegm	Ultimos de Cuba	Umbra	Unborn	Uncork
	Ulcifer	Ultor	Umbra Animae	Unborn Death	Uncover
U.D.O.	Ulcisia Castra	Ultra	Umbra Mortis	Unborn Suffer	Uncover
U.G.	Ulcus	Ultra Mayhem Org.	Umbra Nihil	Unborned	Uncovered Noise
U.G.B.	Ulcus Molle	Ultra Vomit	Umbra Noctis	UnbornGeneration	Uncreated
U.G.H.	Ulf Reich	Ultra Vomit	Umbra Within	Unbound	Uncreation
U.N.I.T.	Ulfang	Ultrahead	Umbra Within	Unbounded Terror	Uncreation
U.S.M.	Ulfbiorn	Ultralord	Umbraculum	Unbred	Uncreation
U.T.M.	Ulfengard	Ultramundane	Funebris	Unburied	Uncreation's Dawn
U4EA	Ulfhednar	Ultrapodre	Umbrae	Unburied	Uncrossed
U8	Ulfheðnir	Ultraspank	Umbral	Unburied	Uncut Despite
Uaral	Ulfhethnar	Ultrathrash	Umbral Presence	Unburied	Undamaged
Ubbo Sathla	Ulfhethnar	Ultratumba	Umbrtka	Unburn	Undead
Ubergehen	Ulfsdalir	Ultratumba	Umount	Uncanny	Undead
Ubermensch	Ulfur	Ultratumba	Umrattawill	Uncanny	Undead
Übermensch	Uller	Ultraviolence	Umtakati	Uncerta	Undead
Ubersoldat	Ulterior	Ultrawurscht	Umusibyan	Uncertain Future	Undead
Uberthrash	Ulterior	Ululate	Umwelt	Uncertainty Principle	Undead

Ubisumpt	
Uccultum	
UCK Grind	
Udainsakr	
Úden	
Uder Smrti	
UDK	
Udumbal	
Udun	
Ufir	
UFO	
Ufomammut	
Ufych Sormeer	
Uglstyk	
Ugluk	
Ugly Ogre	

Undead
Devourment

Undead Funeral
Undead Orchestra
Undefeated
Undefined
Undence
Under
Under
Under Age
Under Aspect
Under Black Clouds
Under Curse
Under Darkest Skies
Under Destruction
Under Eden
Under Fetid Corpses
Under Forge
Under Moonlight
   Sadness
Under Mountains
Under Of Hell
Under Prexion
Under Siege
Under Siege
Under the Drone
Under Threat
Underbred
Undercode
Under-Construction
Undercroft
Underdark
Underdark
Underdark
Underdark
Underdeath
Underdog

Underflow
Undergang
Undergång
Underground
   Groove Front
Underhand
Underhate
Underking
Underlord
Underneath
Underneath
Underneath the Gun
Undernoise
Underoath
Underoath
Under-Radio
Under-Radio
Undersave
Underskin
   Crawler
Undertaker
Undertaker
Undertaker
Undertaker
Undertaker
Undertaker
Undertaker
Undertaker
Undertaker
Undertaker of
   the Damned
Undertakers
Undertaking
Undertaking Risky
Undertow
UnderWater Moon
Underworld Giubileo

Undiscovered
   Moons of Saturn
Undish
Undivine
Undivine
Undone
Undone
Undone
Undor
Undun
Undying
Undying
Undying Inc.
Unearth
Unearth
Unearthed
Unearthed
Unearthed
Unearthed Corpse
Unearthly
Unearthly
Unearthly Trance
Uneasiness
Unerase
Unever
Unexpect
Unexpected
Unfaded
Unfeigned
Unfit Ass.
Unfleshed
Unfolding
Unforgiven
Unformed
Unforsaken

Unfragment
Unframed Mind
Ungern
Ungl'Unl'Rrlh'Chchch
Ungod
Ungodly
Ungodly
Ungodly Death
Ungoliant
Ungolianth
Ungoliantha
Ungraced
Ungraved
Unhallowed
Unhallowed
Unhallowed
Unhallowed
Unhallowed
Unhallowed
   Dissonance
Unhandled Exception
Unhealthy Dreams
Unhealty
Unheil
Unheilvoll
Unhola
Unholier
Unholy
Unholy
Unholy Archangel
Unholy Black Blood
   Baptism
Unholy Cross
Unholy Crucifix
Unholy Crusade

Unholy Death
Unholy Death
Unholy Deathren
Unholy Dominion
Unholy Flames
Unholy Ghost
Unholy Goat
Unholy Grace
Unholy Grave
Unholy Horde
Unholy Impaler
Unholy Inquisition
Unholy Land
Unholy Legion
Unholy Massacre
Unholy Massacre
Unholy Matrimony
Unholy Morgoth
Unholy Penetration
Unholy Plague
Unholy Pope
Unholy Procession
Unholy Ritual
Unholy Scripture
Unholy Storm
Unholy Temple
Unholy Trinity
Unholy Trinity
Unholy War
Unholy Wrath
Unhuman
União
Unicorn
Unicorn
Unicorn

Unicornia
Unicrons
Unicum States
Unida
Unified Theory
Uniilã
Union
Union Carbide
Unit 53
United
United Forces
United Forces
Unitheism
Unithia
Unity
Unius
Universal Mind
Universe
Universe
Universe Denied
Univerzum
Unjust
Unkind
Unknown
Unknown Death
Unknown
   Dimensions
Unkreated
Unlead
Unleash
Unleash Hell
Unleash Hell
Unleashed
Unleashed
Unleashed Anger

Unleashed Hell
Unleashed Power
Unleashed Soul
UnleasHer
Unlegacy
Unlife
Unlight
Unlight
Unlight
Unlight
Unlight Domain
Unlight Order
Unlighted
Unlike Those
Unlimited
Unliver
Unlord
Unlucky Buried
Unmaker
Unmemory
Unmerciful
Unmoored
Unnamed
Unnamed
Unnatural
Unnatural Shelter
Uno Actu
Unorthodox
Unorthodox
Unorthodox
Unowned
Unpain
Unpersons
Unprovoked
Unpunished

Unpure

V.A.C.K.
V.A.R.
V.E.I.L.S.
V.I.C. Royal
V.O.I.D.
V:28
V12
V12140
V13ault
V8
Vaakevandring
Vaande
Vacant Grave
Vacant Planet
Vacant Stare
Vacarme

Vacui Segno
Vacuum
Vacuum
Vacuum
Vade Retro
Vader
Vado Mori
Vae Solis
Vae Solis
Vae Victis
Vae Victis
Vae Victis
Vae Victis
Vae Victis
Vagabond
Vagabond

Vagabond
Vagerke
Vagézaryavtre
Vagh
Vaginal Carnage
Vaginal Chicken
Vaginal Discharge
Vaginal Incest
Vaginal Molestation
Vaginal Purulence
Vaginal Stabwound
Vaginel
Vagl-Eygr
Vago
Vagotomy
Vagrant Enemy
Vagrant the Noachian
Vague
Vague
Vague Empress
Vahalla
Vahladian
Vahrzaw
Vai
Vaikus
Vain Rachell
Vainglory
Vaira
Vais
Vaitikas
Vajrah
Vaka
Vakarm
Val Caim
Valafar

Valak
Valalorn
Valar
Valarauk
Valas
Valaskjalf
Valaskjalf
Valborg
Valcyrie
Vàld
Vàld
Valdes
Valdesgard
Valdkynd
Valdreg
Valdris
Valdur
Vale of Siddim
Vale of Tears
Vale of Tears
Valefar
Valefar
Valefor
Valenta
Valentine
Valerio Garavaglia
Valgaldar
Valgaldrar
Valgrind
Valgrind
Valhala
Valhall
Valhalla
Valhalla
Valhalla

Valhalla
Valhalla
Valhalla
Valhalla
Valhalla
Valhalla
Valhalla
Valhalla
Valhalla
Valhalla
Valhalla Saints
Valhallian
Valhalus
Valheron
Valheru
Valhom
Vàli
Valiance
Vàlinor
Valinor
Valinor
Valium
Valium
Valium
Valkija
Valkily
Valkiria
Valkiria
Valkylie
Valkyr
Valkyre
Valkyre
Valkyria
Valkyria
Valkyrian

Valkyrie
Valkyrie
Valkyrie
Valkyrie
Valkyrie
Valkyrie's Cry
Valkyrja
Vallachia
Vallansgardh
Valle Crucis
Valley's Eve
Valmer & Hook
Valonsurma
Valor
Valor
Valour
Val'Paraiso
Valpurga
Valpurgia
Valpurgisnight
Valraukar
ValSans
Valsblut
Valsgarde
Valth Beake
Valume Nob
Valuri Negre Dezlegate
Valvadrach
Valve 2.001
Valvet
Vama Marg
Vampira
Vampira
Vampire

Vampire Hall
Vampire Mooose
Vampire Vane
Vampiregaze
Vampiria
Vampiric Dominium
Vampiric Euphoria
Vampiric Motives
Vampiris
Vampyr
Vampyr
Vampyro
Van Camp
Van Canto
Van EE
Van Halen
Van Helsing's Curse
Van Scott
Van Stone
Vanadium
Vanadium
Vanadium
Vanadyum
Vanagloria
Vanaheim
Vanaheim
Vancool
Vancouver
Vancyria
Vandal
Vandal Killer
Vandale
Vandalis
Vandals
Vanden Plas

◄ Vandenberg

Vandöd	Vanvid	Vargthron	Vassago	Vedogon'	Veil of Sorrow	Velnias
Vandrar	Vanzor	Vargulf	Vassago	Vedonist	Veil of Winter	Veloce Hystoria
Vandroya	Vapid	Varhem	Vassilium	Vedova	Veil Torn	Velocet
Vaneast	Vapulah	Varhorn	Vast Forest	Vedtmist	Veiled Allusions	Velocidad Absurda
Vanessa	Varagor	Vari	Vastago	Vedymini	Veiled Moon	Velonnic Sin
Vanexa	Varanat	Väri Avaruudesta	Vastator	Veelzevul	Veilhalt	Veltha
Vanguard	Varathron	Variabel Parabel	Vastion	Vega	Veineliis	Velula
Vanguard	Vardager	Variant	Vastum Silentium	Vega	Veinen	Velvet Cacoon
Vanguard	Vardan	Varicose Vein	Vastus	Vegan Uprise	Veinen	Velvet Cut
Vanguard	Vardemis	Varix	Vat of Fat	Vegnah	Veinless	Velvet Masque
Vanguard	Varden Fall	Varjosielu	Vatican	Vegr	Veinsuck	Velvet Spider
Vanguard	Vardis	Varmgard	Vatican	Vehemence	Veivi	Velvet Thorns
Vanguard	Vardøger	Varnacht	Vatican Plague	Vehemence	Veksha	Velvet Vex
Vanguard	Varech	Varnas	Vaticide	Vehemence Discordia	Vektor	Velvet Viper
Vanguard	Varg	Varnish	Vatreni Poljubac	Vehemencia	Vekum	Velyal
Vanguardia	Varg	Varon	Vätteanda	Vehemens	Vekygach	Velzevul
Vanilla Rex	Varga	Varraghor	Vault	Vehemens	Velaad	Vemod
Vanish	VargAgraV	Varsam Daud	Vault	Vehement	Velatorio	Vemod
Vanished Time	Varganatt	Varso	Vault of Heaven	Vehement	Velattore	Vemoth
Vanishing Point	Vargariket	Vartagorh	Vault Vestige	Vehement	Velchans	Vena Cava
Vanishing Point	Vargas	Varthgulz	Vaultage	Vehement	Velcro Overdose	Vena Torquere
Vanishing System	Vargathrone	Vartroy	Vauxdvihl	Vehement	VELD	Vena Valley
Vanitas	Vargavinter	Varulv	Vavel	Vehement	Veldlokk	Venal Divinity
Vanitas	Vargavinter	Varuna	Vaveyla	Vehement	Veldraveth	Vendaval
Vanity	Vargavinter	Varuna	Vazal	Vehement Storm	Veles	Vendavall
Vanity 4	Varghkoghargasmal	Varvar	Ve	Vehement Thrower	Veles	Vendetta
Vanity Dies Hard	Vargleide	Varya	Vebrifuge	Vehementer	Velial	Vendetta
Vanity Fair	Vargnatt	Varyag	Vechnochern'	Vehementer Nos	Velimor	Vendetta
Vanize	Vargnatt	Vasalla	Vectom	Veil	Velinas	Vendetta
Vanmakt	Vargnatt	Vasaria	Vector	Veil	Velinas	Vendetta
Vannvidd	Vargnogk	Vasco da Gama	Vector Underfate	Veil	Vëlinës	Vendigeit
Vanquish	Vargoroth	Vasilisck	Ved Buens Ende	Veil of Anguish	Velkä Mandu	Venduzor
Vanquished	Vargsang	Vassafor	Vedervärdig	Veil of Darkness	Velle Witch	Venedae
Vantage Point	Vargshelske	Vassago	Vediog Svaor	Veil of Maya	Vellocet	Veneficium
Vanth	Vargsriket	Vassago	Vedmak	Veil of Maya	Vellozet	Veneficum
Vantro				Veil of Mystery		

Victory
Victory Flag
Victum
Vidar Vang
Vidder
Vide
Vide Éternel
Videre Mortem
Vidharr
Vidia
Vidneûtsâ D'irki
  V Noskah
Vidres a la Sang
Vidrighet
Vidsyn
Vielftava
Viento Norte
Vietnam
Vietus Mortuus
Vigdis
Viggen
Viggen
Vighun
Vigil
Vigilance
Vigilance
Vigilant
Vigilante
Vigilante
Vigilia Mortum
Vigilia Septima
Vigour Abruptness
Vigred
Vigrid
Vigrid Plains

Vigsoroth
  Moshamarahoth
Vihollisen Äänet
Vihr
VII Arcano
VII Gates
VII Profezia
VII Strada
Viikate
Viingrid
Vike Tare
Viken
Viking
Viking Crown
Viking Skull
Viking Throne
Vikingblood
Vikings
Vile
Vile
Vile
Vile Inside
Vile Intent
Vile Scar
Vilefuck
Vilexistence
YilgefortZ
Vilipêndio
Vilitas
Vilkates
Vilkduja
Village of Dead Roads
Villain
Villains
Villainthropy

Villan
Villieläin
Villon
Vim Patior
Vinagron
Vincebus Eruptum
Vincent
Vincent Van Gogh
Vinculum Terminatii
Vinden Av Krig
Vindensang
Vinder
Vindex
Vindicate
Vindicate
Vindicator
Vindicta
Vindikation
Vindsval
Vindsval
Vindsvale
Vinductus
Vingança Suprema
Vingdar
Vinland Warriors
Vinnie Moore
Vinnie Vincent
  Invasion
Vintage Horrors
Vintage Solemnity
Vintegaas
Vinter Nebulah
Vinterfrost
Vinterfrost
Vinterheim

Vinterkaos
Vinterland
Vinternatt
Vinterrike
Vinterriket
Vintersemestre
Vintersorg
Vintersphrøst
Vinterstorm
Vinterthrone
Vinum Sabbati
Vio System Divide
Viocosis
Viogression
Violación a Domicilio
Violador
Violador
Violate
Violate
Violate
Violated
Violated
Violation
Violation
Violation
Violator
Violator
Violator
Violator
Violator
Violator
Violator
Violator
Violator
Violemosh

Vio-lence
Violence
Violence
Violence Call
Violence Unleashed
Violencia
Violencia Coletiva
Violent
Violent Asylum
Violent Attack
Violent Changes
Violent Death
Violent Design
Violent Devoties
Violent Dirge
Violent Dissorder
Violent Dreams
Violent Force
Violent Fury
Violent Hammer
Violent Hate
Violent Homicide
Violent Impact
Violent Marv
Violent Mood Swing
Violent Night
Violent Obsession
Violent Playground
Violent Power
Violent Solution
Violent Souls
Violent Storm
Violent Vórtex
Violent Warpath
Violent Work of Art

Violet Halo
Violet Moon
Violet Moon Shining
Violet Vortex
Violletta Villazz
VIP
Viper
Viper
Viper Venom
Vipera
Vipera Aspis
Viperia
Viperine
Vir'
Vira
Viral Load
Viravoid
Virgem Atómica
Virgen
Virgin
Virgin Black
Virgin Forest
Virgin Killer
Virgin Killer
Virgin Killers
Virgin Sin
Virgin Snatch
Virgin Soldiers
Virgin Spy
Virgin Star
Virgin Steele
Virgin Witch
Virginia Wolf
Virgins
Virgin's Cunt

Virgo (Matos/Paeth)
Virgo Sacrum
Viriun
Viron
Virtual Insanity
Virtual Pain
Virtual Void
Virtual Voyage
Virtue
Virtuocity
Virulence
Virulence
Virulence
Virulence
Virulent
Virulent Blessing
Virulent Re-Shapes
Virulentos
Virulus
Virus
Virus
Virus
Virus
Virus
Virus
Virus
Virus
Virus 7
Virus IV
Viruzy
Vis Nox
Vis Vires
Viscera
Viscera
Viscera Infest

Vomitrocity	Voracious Hate	Vortex Syndrome	Vrak	VulneratA	Vytal
Vomitron	Voracious Souls	Vortexia	Vrani Volosa	Vulnus	Vyvoroten'
Vomiturition	Voracity	Vortice	Vrankenvorde	Vulpecula	Vzaeurvbtre
Vomoth	Vorago	Vortice	Vrata Snov	Vulpecula	VZwoA
Von	Vorak	Vortice	Vrata T'my	Vultos Vociferos	
Von Branden	Vorax	Vórtice	Vredgad	Vultur	
Von Dymon	Vordr	Vorticis	Vreid	Vulture	
Von Helsing	Vordven	Vostrogor	Vremja "NET"	Vulture	
Von Kempelin	Vore	Votan	Vril	Vulture	
Von Kull	Vorgasm	Votary	Vrolok	Vulture	
Von Sirius	Vörgus	Vothana	Vrolok	Vulture Industries	
Von Skeletor	Vorkreist	Votum	Vrolok D.	Vulture Lord	
Vonavemor	Vorkuta	Votum	Vrykolakas	Vulture of Corpse	
Vond	Vormit	Votum Mortis	Vrykolakas	Vultures	
Vondur	Vornagar	Votur	VS. the World	Vulturine	
Vondvort	Vörnagar	Vougan	VS777	Vulturul Carpatilor	
Vonn	Vornat	Vow	Vspoloch	Vultyr	
Voodoma	Vornicor	Vow Dreams	VTA	Vulv	
Voodoo	Vornoff	Vows in Ashes	Vual	Vulva Infernum	
VooDoo	Vorongrai	Vox Dei	Vucub Came	Vulva Intestines	
Voodoo	Vorpal	Vox Interium	Vuelo Nocturno	Vulvacroma	
Voodoo Child	Vorpal Bunny	Vox Mortem	Vuist	Vulvark	
Voodoo Hill	Vorphalack	Vox Tempus	Vukodlak	Vulvathrone	
Voodoo Lordz	Vortech	Voxhumana	Vulcain	Vulvectomy	
Voodoo Shock	Vortex	Voyage	Vulcan Tyrant	Vulvulator	
Voodoo Shyne	Vortex	Voyage	Vulcano	Vuohivasara	
Voodoo Temple	Vortex	Voyager	Vulcro	Vuotare	
Voodoocult	Vortex	Voyager	Vulga	Vurtula	
Voodooshock	Vortex	Voyager UK	Vulgar	Vuvr	
Voor	Vortex	Voyeur	Vulgar	VVI Gates	
Vopo's	Vortex	Vpaahsalbrox	Vulgar Degenerate	Vvrika	
Vorace	Vortex	Vrademargk	Vulgar Pigeons	VXN	
Voracious	Vortex Core	Vrael	Vulgarizer	Vyndykator	
Voracious Gangrene	Vortex of End	Vrag	Vulgata	Vyper	
Voracious God	Vortex of Insanity	Vrain	Vulkro	Vyrus Survivor	

W.A.B.S.O.T.O.W.H.
W.A.K.O.
W.A.S.P.
W.A.S.T.E.
W.C. Noise
W.E.B.
W.O.P.
W.O.U.N.D.
W.R.A.T.H.
W.S.H.C.
w00d5b17ch
Wa
Wackhanalija
Wackor
Waco Jesus
Wade Shöken

Wadge
Wadgelmir
Waffen SS
Waffen SS
Waffentreu
Waffenweihe
Wagchor
Wages of Sin
Wahn
Wahrer Krieg
Wahrheitstag
Wai Dee Zai
Waiting for Chaos
Wakboth
Wakboth
Wake

Wake Up On Fire
Waking Hour
Waking The Cadaver
Waking The Destroyer
Waking Theo
Waklevören
Walaskialf
Wald
Wald
Wald Geist Winter
Waldenburg
Waldgeflüster
Waldschabe
Waldtroll
Wale of Souls
Walhalla
Walhalla
Walhalla
Walknut
Walkyrya
Wall of Silents
Wall of Sleep
Wall Red Murder
Wallace
Wallachia
Wallcrawler
Wallop
Walls Of Jericho
Walpurgi
Walpurgis
Walpurgis
Walpurgis Nacht
Walpurgis Night
Walpurgisnacht

Walpurgisnacht
Walpurgisnacht
Walquiria
Waltari
Walter Giardino Temple
Wampyrinacht
Wanderer
Wanderer
Wanderer
Wanderlust
Wangelen
Wanhoop
Waning Moon
Wannsee
Wantdead
Wanted
Wanted Breed
Wanterkraaft
Wanterwollef
Wantit
Wanton
Wapenspraak & Drinkgelag
War
War
War
War & Peace
War 88
War Blade
War Blasphemy
War Command
War Corpse
War Crime
War Cross

War Cry
War Dance
War Empire
War for War
War Hammer Command
War Injun
War Kommand
War Machine
War Master
War of Ages
War of Feelings
War of the Putrid
War Plague
War Ripper
War Saw
War Swallowed
War Theory
War Torn
War Within
War Without Reason
War666
Warage
Warattah
Warbastard
Warbiff
Warblade
Warbled Arma
Warblood
Warborn
Warbreed
Warbride
Warbringer
Warbringer
Warburg

Warbutcher
Warchetype
Warchild
Warchild
Warchild
Warchild X
Warchitect
Warchylde
Warcollapse
Warcrusher
Warcry
Warcry
WarCry
Wardaemonic
Wardagger
Wardance
Wardeath
Wardeath
Warden
Wardog
Wardog
Warface
Warfair
Warfair
Warfare
Warfare
Warfare
Warfare
Warfare Incorporated
Warfarin
Warfaze
Warfield
Warfield Within
Warfire

Warfist
WarFred
Warfront
WARFX
Wargamark
Wargasm
Wargasm
Wargh
Warghoul
Wargod
Wargore
Wargrinder
Wargus
WarHag
Warhagan
Warhammer
Warhammer
Warhammer
Warhammer
Warhamster
Warhate
Warhate
Warhawk
War-head
Warhead
Warhead
Warhead
Warhead
Warhead
Warhead
Warhead
Warheart
Warholder
Warhorde

Werwolf
WerWolf Division
West Wall
Western Decay
Westfalen
Westhia
Wet Animal
Wetwork
Weverin
Wewelsburg
Weyland
Whaka Danger
What Weapons
  Bring War
Whats Killing You?
What's Up?
Whaw!Zaiks
Wheel of Doom
Wheel of Life
Whelm
When Day Descends
When Life
  Has Ceased
When Red Falls Silent
When the Angels Cry
When the
  eadbolt Breaks
When Tomorrow
  Doesn't Come
Where Angels Fall
Where Sadness
  Reigns
Where She Wept
Wherevictimslie
Whichheaven

While Heaven Wept
While Sad Spirits
  Around Me Stroll
Whine
Whip
Whiplash
Whiplash
Whiplash
Whiplash
Whirlwind
Whirlwind
Whisky
Whisper
Whisper
Whisper
Whisper
Whisper
Whisper
Whisper
Whispered
Whispering Forest
Whispering Gallery
Whispering Shades
Whispering Silence
Whispering Tears
Whispers
Whispers from a
  Dead World
Whispers of Fear
Whisper-X
White Ash
White Blade
White Crow
White Diamond
  Death

White Fear Chain
White Friday
White Frost
White Gallery
White Heat
White Hell
White Hott
White Hunter
White Lightning
White Lilith
White Lion
White Mania
White Mirror
White Night
White Pale Silence
White Raven
White Skull
White Spirit
White Tornado
White Zombie
Whitechapel
Whitecross
Whitefang
Whitefire
Whitehorse
Whiterose
Whites Load
Whitesnake
Whoracle
Whorde
Whore
Whore
Whore Mangler
Whore of Babylon
Whorecore

WhoreDom
WhoreGrind
Whorehouse
Whorelord
WhoreMastery
Whoremoan
Whores of Babylon
Whorgasm
Whorrid
Whorror
Whorrornight
Whroumm
Why Angels Fall
Why She Kills
Why?
Wiatr
Wiatyk
Wicca
Wiccan Rede
Wicher
Wicitra
Wicked Angel
Wicked Angel
Wicked Angel
Wicked Blight
Wicked Empire
Wicked Funeral
Wicked Garden
Wicked Gypsy
Wicked Innocence
Wicked Kemao
Wicked Kick
Wicked Lester
Wicked Maraya
Wicked Me

Wicked Mystic
Wicked Rich
Wicked Sensation
Wicked Ways
Wicked Witch
Wickedlott
Wickedness
Wickeds End
Widdershin
Wide Moor
Wide Open Cage
Wide Open Throttle
Widla
Widomar
Widow
Widow
Widow
Widowmaker
Widow's Grave
Wig Wam
Wigrid
Wij
Wijlen Wij
Wikingsholm
Wikka
Wikkyd Vikker
Wilczy Pajak
Wild
Wild Age
Wild Cat
Wild Dogs
Wild Fire
Wild Flag
Wild Forest
Wild Garden

Wild Karnivor
Wild Machine
Wild Pussy
Wild Scream
Wild Shark
Wild Spirit
Wild Steel
Wild Willy's Gang
Wildcard
Wilder
Wilderness
Wildesheer
Wildest Dreams
Wildfire
Wildness
Wildpath
Wilk
Wilkolak
Will O' Wisp
Will of the Ancients
Willard
William Cesar
Willow
Willow Wisp
Willow's Whisper
Wind
Wind
Wind
Wind Hearse
Wind of Hate
Wind of Pain
Wind of the Black
  Mountains
Wind Through
  the Trees

Wind Winter
Wind Wraith
Windesklagen
Windfall
Windfall
Windham Hell
Windigo
Windir
Windmills by
  the Ocean
Windrikje
Windrow
Winds
Winds
Winds
Winds Funera
Winds of Agony
Winds of Creation
Winds of Darkness
Winds of Eve
Winds of Funeral
Winds of Garden
Winds of Old
Winds of Plague
Winds of Sirius
Winds of Torment
Winds of War
Winds of Wrath
Windseeker
Windwalker
Windzor
Wine Spirit
Wineta
Wingdom
Winged

◀ Worthless

Worthless
Wortox
Worvhallag
Worwyk
Woslom
Wotan
Wotan
Wotan
Wotan Folk
Wotanic Commando
Wotanorden
Wotans Destiny
Wotanskrieger
Woudeherberg
Woudgeest
Woudgilde
Wounded Knee
Wounded Ways
Woundeep
Wounds
Wounds of Darkness
Wraith
Wraith
Wraith of Extinction
Wraith of the Ropes
Wraithen
Wraithriel
Wrath
Wrath
Wrath
Wrath
Wrath
Wrath
Wrath A.D.

Wrath From Below
Wrath Is Evergreen
Wrath Nature
Wrath of Azazel
Wrath of Gibryle
Wrath of Killenstein
Wrath of Man
Wrath of Ragnarok
Wrath of the Weak
Wrath Ritual
Wrath Tears
Wrathage
Wrathblade
Wrathchalice
Wrathchild America
Wrathful Plague
Wrathorned
Wreaking Havoc
Wreath of Decay
Wreck Creation
Wreck of the
    Hesperus
Wreck of the
    Hesperus
Wreckage
Wreckage
Wreckage
Wrecking Crew
Wrekking Crew
Wrekking Machine
Wrench
Wrest
Wrestling Isn't Fake
Wretch
Wretched

Wretched
Wretched
Wretched Asylum
Wretched Hive
Wretched Legacy
Wretched Spawn
Wretched Vixen
Wreterdess
Wrinkled Witch
Writhen
Writhing
Written in Torment
WRNLRD
Wrok
Wrong ID
Wrong Side
Wrought
WRTX
Wrust
Wschód
WSR
Wszystko Jedno
WTN
Wulcan
Wülf Gang
Wulfgar
Wulfgar
Wulfgravf
Wulfhere
Wunde
Wurdalak
Wurdulak
Wurm
Würm
Wurzburg

Würzel
Wurzelkraft
Wut
Wuthering Heights
Wuzor
WWII
WWIII
Wycked Synn
Wycliff
Wydfara's Prophecy
Wykked Wytch
Wynjara
Wynterborne
Wyrd
Wyrden
Wyrm
Wyrm
Wyruz
Wýtenka
Wytchcraft
Wytchfynde
Wytchkraft
Wyvern
Wyvern
Wyvern
Wyverna
Wyxmer
Wyzard

X	Xang	Xatarnite	Xeque Mate	Xiron	X-Tinxion
X Factor X	XAnimus	Xatitix	Xeranthenum	Xironix	Xtreme Obsession
X Japan	Xanthe	Xatran	Xerasia	Xiuhtecuhtli	X-tremity
X Project	Xanthoma	Xaztur	Xerasia	XIV Dark Centuries	Xtrunk
X Raptor	Xanthor	X-Caliber	Xerbeth	Xi-Void	Xtuumus
X.E.S.	Xanthos	X-Calibur	Xergath	X-Japan	Xudef Clas
X.Y.Z.->A	Xantossa	Xcel	Xerión	X-Kharon	Xul
Xaal	Xantotol	X-Cops	Xero	Xkizofrenia	Xulub Mitnal
Xadoom	Xaotiko Teloz	X-Creta	Xero	XL	Xur
Xainiax	Xapaharon	Xcursion	Xero	XIII Candles	X-Vandals
Xaiphodius	Xaphan	Xeah	Xerosis	XLR8R	X-Wild
Xalt	Xapharon	Xebgas	Xerpentor	X-Mantra	Xxaron
Xanadoo	Xaros	Xecutioner	Xeru	X-Mas Project	XXX
Xanatotanax	Xasthur	Xendra	Xerxes	Xordeal	XXX
Xandria	Xasthur	Xendra	XES	Xorth	XXX
Xandril	Xastur	Xenesthis	Xess	Xoteric	XXX Maniak
		Xenobia	XEX	XOTH	Xysma
		Xenofanes	Xexyz	XPDC	Xystenz
		Xenofex	Xezbeth	X-Piral	Xyster
		Xenofobia X	X-Factor	Xplore	Xystus
		Xenolith	Xharathorn	X-Rated	Xytras
		Xenolith Oger	X-Hells	X-Ray	Xyxyxma
		Xenomorph	X-Hero	X-Ray	Xzanthus
		Xenomorph	Xhzenat	X-Ray of a Graveyard	Xzoriath
		Xe-None	Xibalba	XSAD	
		Xenophilya	Xicrin	Xsavior	
		Xenophobe	Xihilisk	X-Seed	
		Xenophobia	XII	X-Sinner	
		Xenophobia	XIII	XT	
		Xenophobia	Ximielga	Xtaodecas	
		Xenotaph	Xipe	Xtazy	
		Xentrix	Xipe Totec	Xteria	
		Xeōhl	Xipe Totec	X-Terra	
		Xeper	Xiphoid	XthoughtstreamsX	
		Xepsüra	Xiquena	Xthtogg	

Y & T
Y Diawled
Y Draig Goch
Y.O.C.
Y3K
Yacöpsae
Yaguar
Yahatra
Yakamashii
Yakatarma
Yakuza
Yamaraja
Yamatu
Yana Raymi
Yanaconas
Yaotl Mictlan

Yaotzin
Yaotzin
Yaoyotl
Yargos
Yarmondiis
Yarvis
Yasha
Yatrogeny
Yattering
Yawgmoth
Yayeth Corpse
Yazzgoth
Ydalir
Ydin
Ydris Mortem
Yea and the Moon

Year of Confession
Year of Desolation
Year Zero
Year Zero
Yearning
Years of Fire
Years Spent Cold
Yeast Infection
Yellow Machine Gun
Yellow Machinegun
Yellra
Yersinia
Yersinia Pestis
Yesterday's Torment
Yeti
Yey
Yggdrasil
Yggdrasil
Yggdrasil
Yggdrasil
Yggtyrhyrkkh Hin
    Dystre
Ygy
Yhdarl
Yigga Digga
Ylian
Yllmangspach
Ymber Autumnus
Ymesh
Ymir
Ymir
Yngizarm
Yngwie J. Malmsteen
Ynis Vitrin
Ynnermost

Yob
Yocasta
Yog Sothots
Yogge Sothothe
Yog-Sothoth
Yog-Sothoth
Yog-Sothoth
Yogth Sothoth
Yokosuka Saver Tiger
Yom Kippur
Yorblind
Yortsed
Yosh
You Betray Me
You Should Have
    Slain Me
Young Blood
Your Anguish
Your Cell: Yourself
Your Days Are
    Counted
Your Envy
Your Own Decay
Your Shapeless
    Beauty
Your Third Eye
Youthanasia
Youthcorpse
Youthquake
Yperite
Ysigim
Ysorex
Ysyssy
Ytivarg
Yuggoth

Yuggoth
Yuhrott
Yukon
Yu-kotokikazu
Yuma
Yves Custeau
Ywolf
Yyrkoon

Zakata	Zbor	Zenithrash	Zero Vision	Zihard
Zakeus	Z'e Psy	Zenobia	ZeroCold	Zijl
Zakk Wylde	Zeal Camera	Zenolyth	ZeroCrowd	Zilch
Zaklon	Zealous	Zepherus	Zeroed	Zillah
Zalnik	Zealous Witness	Zephyrous	Zeroed	Zillion
Žalvarinis	Zeb Dragon	Zeramoth	Zerofour	Zimmer's Hole
Zamak	Zebra	Zerber	Zerogod	Zimowy Chmura
Zanarkand	Zebulon	Zerberus	Zerokarma	Zinc Alloy
Zandelle	Zebulon Pike	Zerg	Zerozonic	Zinc Organ
Zandrium	ZED	Zero	Zerstorer	Zion
Zangentod	Zed Yago	Zero Based	Zerstörer	Zion
Zangryus	Zedher	Perception	Zerzyan Loathe	Zions Abyss
Zanister	Zee Docta	Zero by None	Zess	Zircon
Zanthicus	Zeelion	Zero Cipher	Zetörhead	Zirconium
Zao	Zeenon	Zero Control	Zett	Z-Iron
Zar	Zeitgeist	Zero Degrees	Zettilmeyer	Ziryab
Zara	Zeitgeist	Freedom	Zeus	Zirze
Zarach 'Baal' Tharagh	Zeitgeist	Zero Enemies	Zeus	Zithma
Zaragone	ZeitGeist Co.	Zero G	Zeus	Z'Kazan
Zaraq	Zelda	Zero Gravity	Zeusas	Zlata Svarga
Zarathustra	Zeldar	Zero Hora	Z-Gen	Zlaya Korcha
Zarathustra	Zelyon	Zero Hour	Zgoda	Zlo
Zaratustra	Zembus	Zero Hour	Zgoda	Zlomrak
Zaraza	Zemial	Zero Hour	Zhalim	Z-LOT-Z
Zarg	Zemial	Zero Illusions	Zharmaq	Zmierzch
Zargof	Zen	Zero Kelvin	Zhatsaraeth	Zmijevik
Zarpa	Zen Venom	Zero Nine	Zhelezny Potok	Zmrochny Dol
Zástup jiných	Zendas	Zero Option	Zhgoryth	Zmrok
Zatmenie	Zendik	Zero Signal	Zhraja	Znich
Zatokrev	Zênite	Zero Signal	Zi Xul	Znöwhite
Zaum	Zenith	Zero Signal	Ziad	Zoberbia
Zauron	Zenith	Zero Silence	Ziege	Zobibor
Zavorash	Zenith	Zero Tolerance	Ziel	Zocabra
Zaxas	Zenith	Zero Tolerance	Ziff	Zodiac
Zazozora	Zenithal	Zero Tolerance	Ziggurat	Zodiac

Z	Zadok
Z	Zaebos
Z	Zaebros
Za Frûmi	Zafira
Zabb	Zagam
Zabiis	Zaghurim
Zabulos	Zagros
Zaburon	Zagros Atica
Zabytye Tverdyni L dov	Zahareth
Zacai	Zahgurim
Zadan	Zahgurim
Zadar	Zahgurim
Zadera	Zahrim
Zadkiel	Zahrim
Zadögoat	Zahrim
	Zaius

Zodiac

I   Forty million years ago, the gorillas that would eventually metamorphose into the earliest humanoids split off from the evolutionary line of African great apes. Thirty-nine million seven hundred thousand years ago, we see the first signs of a proto-human (*Australopithecus afarensis*) that can be traced directly, through a continuous set of fossils, to Homo erectus, the most common mammal that exists in the year of the creation of this book, the year two thousand eight of the Common Era.

There are those—the author of this book included—who believe that in that shadowy stretch of three hundred thousand years, the blink between great apes and humans, a distinct race much like ourselves came into existence, evolved, flourished, and ultimately destroyed itself by monstrous means, wiping clean the surface of the earth with horrific, fire-bearing tools of their own design, leaving but a thin layer of compacted ash to be dug through in the later search for thicker paleontogical meaning.

Perhaps they formed books like the one you now read, books that recorded the knotted, frayed, and powerful doings of the Ur-men, the very first of those whose faces leveled gazes against each other, and toward the horizon; who grasped the ape's tool—the stick—and sharpened it, or lashed to it a stone, or struck it against a hollow tree in concert with the beating in their chest. Perhaps they fashioned books of reeds or bark painted with dye or ink or blood or mud, scribed in wild tongues now dried and shriveled, jacketed in stone or skin or plant or such stuff as exists no more, in no way envisionable by our later minds.

It may be these early women and men did and made and acted in such lofty or lowly ways that would uncloak us as simple clods.

II   The names in this book are invisible tokens to be uttered aloud, each conjuring a group of humans formed to play rock in its extreme forms—with the greatest impact of sound, in which the floorboards shake and walls quiver, and ears split and leak blood; or of sight, with faces painted, hair preened bird-like, horse-like, arms and belts packed with stone and metal, skin stained life-long with arcane or vulgar signs; or of speech, wherein is screamed and growled what woman and man alike shun to speak of: death, abuse, horror, evil, hate, and the ever-yawning black maw.

Not only do these bards proclaim the fears that shadow human life as ghastly blood blots cobbled roads—in doing so, they also summon the vital forces that rise up in the face of these appalling dangers. Picture the whaleboat staved in twain by a great whale breaching beneath it, the oarsmen snarling, ready to make clubs of sweeps, harpooner turning to pierce the beast, even as he is tossed, to be swallowed in the foaming thing's wake.

III The names in this book were amassed as grains of sand in a bowl—the more that were piled, the more that evaded one's grasp. The grains of metal players and hearers are scattered in their vast multiplicity throughout society,

ubiquitous but concealed. Never has a music relegated to the underground of a civilization had so many devotees; no radio need transmit its power, for it is sought fiercely and freely by the doomed and the dispossessed, those whose ears are never touched by songs of love and weakness.

This volume contains just under fifty-one thousand bands. For each name that is used by more than one group, that name is listed once for each distinct group. Should one presume that each of these bands had an average of four members, and multiply that by the quantity of bands, one might calculate that at least a quarter of a million humans have undertaken this quest—to unearth, embody, aim, and deliver power itself—and have brought that quest into the harsh light of the public world.

IV The names were collected by the author, with no direct aid from other humans, gathered from the ether in relative secrecy, using the tools of this moment: a kind of book with a static but changing screen made of light, and an invisible web tying many such books together, wherein language and pictures are transmitted through a refined form of lightning. But when the light books sputter out and die, this brick of paper shall remain. This dusty volume, which you may have unearthed from a tomb, or a burned-out library, or from a metal box submerged in desiccated mud. If you can read our language, then read of these beings who once populated the earth, and who now are gone. Examine this stone and read in it a fallen civilization.

Read it—and weep. ❧

△ △ △ △ △ △ △ △ △ △ △ △ △ △

M<small>C</small>SWEENEY'S

SAN FRANCISCO

www.mcsweeneys.net

Copyright © 2008

*Design by Alvaro Villanueva, Dan Nelson,
Eli Horowitz, and Autumn Wharton*

*All rights reserved, including the right of
reproduction in whole or part in any form.*

ISBN: *978-1-932416-92-3*

♥ ♥ ♥ ♥ ♥ ♥ ♥ ♥ ♥ ♥ ♥ ♥ ♥ ♥